ISBN: 9791222035659
Author: Antonio Specchia
Published by:
Strategic Links London Ltd,
124, City Road, EC1V 2NX London, U

Published: December 2022

For more information:
https://managingsalespipelinewithpipedrive.online/

To whom it may concern ...the readers!

Once convinced by the easy-to-use concept, many users may get stuck and feel guilty for not being able to use it or, they may blame the tool for being inadequate or too complex...

For users that feel in need of help **this book wants to be the guide to go beyond** what can be easily found on Pipedrive knowledge Base.

One good news is that more often than not, it isn't the tool to be wrong, complex or little performant; on the contrary, the tool is great and offers more than many other CRM.
What is too often undervalued when a decision on a digital CRM is developed, is that any tool is ...just a tool.
If you know how to make the best use of a tool you will find it great. This book intends to enable anyone to become knowledgeable about the CRM, its strategic logic first, and then the technological possibilities.

The **CRM logic and strategy imply a specific know-how**. Now anyone can learn it with this guide.

We wrote for business people, managers or entrepreneurs who have chosen Pipedrive: they need operative support to get the best value of it.
People who haven't chosen Pipedrive yet, are probably seeking an understanding to decide.
To everyone, we also suggest taking a look at the more general book on CRM: **Customer Relationship Management for Medium and Small Enterprises -Routledge 2022-** which discusses the concept of CRM in a broader way.
Any developer or IT specialists person may also find this book useful under the business perspective about CRM.

To everyone who wants to achieve more with Pipedrive

About this book

A guide to the popular CRM, its use and its logic: to learn why Pipedrive is so popular, what works best and what is the value it creates for companies. Businesses of small size can find it useful to improve their use of what became an essential tool for sales process management in B to B.
CRM is still a growing topic in almost every industry. In the BtoC sector the needs are mainly for automated functions, events driven, capable of providing information to thousands of contacts points. Instead in the BtoB sector the role of the salesperson is still paramount for the sales process management. BtoB CRMs are tools that aim to smooth the sales process by supporting salespeople in their everyday roles.
in this book:

- 1st chapter includes a basic introduction to CRM
- 2nd chapter is an intro to Pipedrive its basic functions and description
- 3rd chapter is a case history
- 4th chapter begins to explain the CRM logic in Pipedrive
- 5th chapter discusses activities management
- 6th chapter is about deals management: the core of the sales CRM
- 7th chapter discusses the Sales pipelines management
- from the chapter 8th ahead we will discuss some logic approach, as leads generation, and several specific features, like Campaigns

The value of a book is not to repeat what any user can find in the system's guide-book and its tutorials. Books on digital tools should provide different perspectives, more operational, but at same time more logical than just descriptive of the tool's functions.

We focused on what really matters to the readers:
the CRM management highlighting what and how to achieve each one's business goals.
Many people made this book possible, among all of them James Tweddle and Mandy Smith who reviewed the writing, Kelly Goss who initially reviewed the tech aspects. More my team who really made the difference.

Even if many helped to make this book great, the mistakes are all mine.

Managing Sales Pipeline(s) with Pipedrive CRM

1 Understanding Pipedrive CRM

Introduction

In this chapter we will go through CRM from the point of view of business owners and managers who are aware of the function and benefits CRM creates in their organisations.

This chapter wants to be a preface to CRM in general and to Pipedrive logic in specific, helping to clarify some critical topics about CRM matter.

Then we will:

- analyse what possible solutions are available in general terms.
- review the logic of business and how a Pipedrive CRM can help on it, as CRM is a logic of management not just a tool
- discuss Databases as basic tools for managing information and how that evolved into CRM.
- discuss how Pipedrive was born and what makes it an interesting tool compared to other platforms in the market.
- review a bit of the history of CRM, just to see how it developed from the very early stage till today's solutions.
- introduce the concept of LowCode development, both to develop new solutions, or better, aiming to integrate different systems.

Right through this book, we will lead you through the secret of the CRM that changed the CRM, and we will help you in becoming an effective CRM expert. Please come with us into the secret of Pipedrive CRM!

Taking confidence with Pipedrive and CRM in general

You probably already know how Pipedrive looks like. Many of you probably have an account already in place. For those who haven't opened it yet, we suggest to do it now. You can use the free of charge trial that lasts for 14 days, browse around, and learn. You will also have lots of tutorials and the strongest asset: *the support team*. If you try to do something and you are stuck, then just ping the **Talk to us** chat and the lovely folks at the customer care team will be ready to help, always understanding and supportive. The wonder is: will it be enough to learn how to make the best out of a CRM, namely Pipedrive? Even the ones who already have imported data in it and are actively using it, may feel the need to improve the efficiency on how to use their method of CRM.

That's why we write this book: offering a toolkit to anyone who aims to improve the use of Pipedrive to make it easier. In this book we will talk also about CRM in general: we strongly believe that understanding the CRM, in its less known logic, may effectively help to improve the comprehension of Pipedrive too.

> Pipedrive was the first to introduce the **Visual Pipeline**, and has been a game changer: the Kanban model wasn't in use in CRM until Timo Rein, Ragnar Sass and friends adopted it into their approach of managing sales processes.

It must be said that CRM was previously mainly a tool used for customer care, and eventually in contact centres activity, hence its definition by Thomas Siebel. The move into a Sales Process Management tool, even if it was intended from the very beginning, has seen a slow adoption. Pipedrive has reinvented and led this shift by focusing the tool on the pipelines' management. The introduction of the visual stages using a Kanban style (Fig. 1.1) has made the CRM for sales processes easier to use, enabling a powerful overview of the whole sales process. In fact, the possibility of a vision d'ensemble of the deals crowd in the sales process is so important for sales forecasting processes giving the feeling that the whole process has a greater impact than any number for the perception of the subtle trends. It gives sales people the visual perception of the tendencies and possible scenarios.

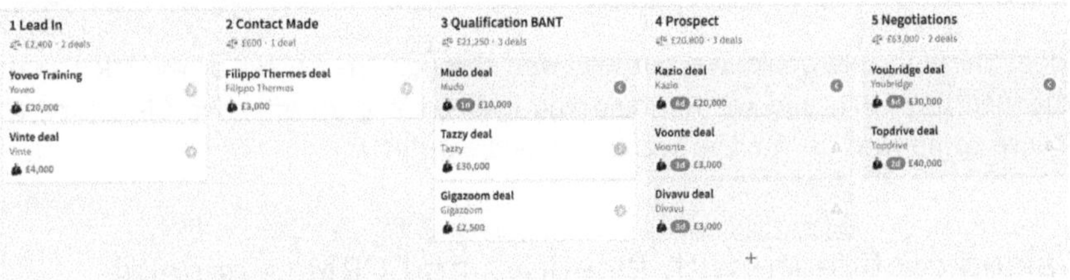

Fig. 1.1 - Visual Pipeline: the sales process made visual

In fact, if reading numbers gives a more precise view of what is going on,

visualising information using deal cards sitting in each stage of the sales process gives an immediate overview of the whole process.

> Pipedrive strongly focuses on the effort to enhance the user interface. The initial intention was to offer not only a new view that empowers sales managers to control the sales process, but also to make it enjoyable.

Nowadays that the User Experience topic has become more fashionable (even if there is still a lot to do to make the concept clear) Pipedrive is second to none in it. Pipedrive's very initial vision was strongly based on a radically different user experience, not only an improvement of it. Timo Rein wanted Pipedrive to be a game changer in many ways. Upon this logic, we will better understand the product that has actually changed the CRM industry.

The IT behind the tool

As you may probably know, a CRM is just an application over a database, in general terms everything works over databases (in IT only!). Theoretically, you can create any application over a database, even your own CRM just starting from scratch using a simple database. This is what many of us, in my generation, did in the late of the last millennium, developing in the '80s over the good-old DBIII a series of functions for different purposes. And that was probably when Thomas Siebel also started, just making it a bit better than everyone else.

But what exactly makes a database usable for CRM purposes? A database is a data container. You can differentiate them mainly per type of Data Definition Languages, speed, and data security. In fact what creates the usable functions for a specific purpose is predominantly the piece of software that lies between the human interface and the database.

If you would like to develop a CRM using a database, you should be able to define all functions that you need to perform, and develop a proper software to run them in the way they are required. This is the reason why using a spreadsheet as a CRM is not efficient: a spreadsheet only has a user interface that naked databases miss.

Pipedrive has a database with 6 (visible) tables, each table runs under specific parameters and behaviours. You can consider those tables like separate groups of data stored and managed for specific purposes. The software connects those data via specific relationships, enabling functions that should be easy to activate and capable of performing specific actions.

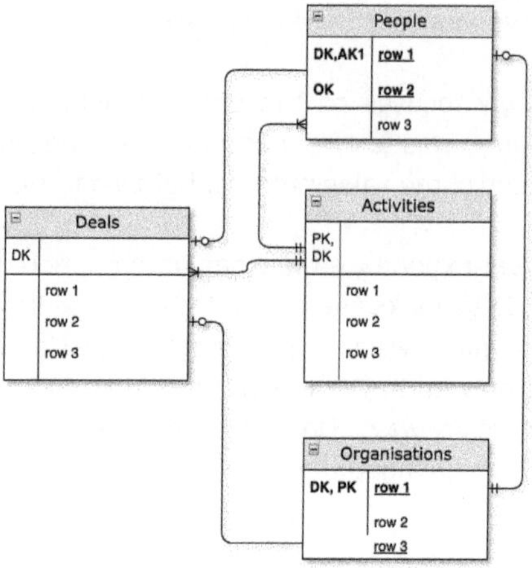

Figure 1.2 - Tables relationships: People, Organisations and Activities. (where DealKey [DK], PeopleKey [PK], ActivityKey [AK] and OrganisationKey [OK] are the connection links)

Let's analyse just the simple flow on how the DEALS table is working in relationship with other tables: PEOPLE, ACTIVITIES and ORGANISATIONS (Fig. 1.2). These tables are all directly related: each organisation (company) may have many persons in it (people), while activities are related to people. Many deals can be opened against each organisation and they can be related to different people to whom you can relate many activities that have to be performed by CRM users (that last relationship introduces another data table, that we are not going to discuss).

On one hand, the CRM should be able to capture every action easily; on the other hand, the users should be able to find out any relevant information in the whole history of the relationship with that person/organisation at any time, related to any present or past deal that ever arose with them.

> What really makes the CRM useful, especially in sales, is the ability to track each action, task, communication done and received, with any contact in relation to DEALS and ORGANISATION.

You can now see how the complexity can become huge when you try to explain the way in which functions should work. Imagine what happens when you have many users, with thousands of records and dozens of functions to design and run them smoothly. Now, let us state this: design and efficient CRM is not something that happens overnight.

When did digital CRM become popular

It is not prosaic to affirm that humans can reach the same result just using paper and pencil; this is what has been done for centuries before the IT revolution took place. The invention of the Rolodex boosted productivity in the first part of the last century, enabling people to manage client's data faster. At that time letters were the way to manage information.

> There are no, or very few, organisations that today affirm CRM is not relevant to them. Because velocity is the most relevant parameter in a company's journey towards growth, enabling speed and productivity should be the ultimate goal of any management.

Wondering what tool can boost productivity better, a pure database, may be in the shape of spreadsheets, is also a tool -definitely better than the Rolodex-, but probably not fully up to date in terms of possibilities that information technology has opened to us (if you are not a hard code developer...).

During the fading of the last century digital CRM was mainly adopted by big corporations, the only ones capable of investing huge resources seeking for productivity enhancement. It was then that a new player entered the market with a strong unique selling proposition. In Fig. 1.3 you can see the USP of that (later) famous company and its journey to become the most prominent world CRM software provider:

HEAVEN	= Where Business operation and Infrastructure are Efficient and Effective
HELL	= Where operations stuck, infrastructure are slow or broken and the effort to achieve anything is excessive
SIN	= Buying software from companies like Oracle or Siebel: very expensive and inefficient
CORRECT SHIFT	= Use software as a service, and letting services by a provider that manage it efficiently for you
NAMELY	= End of Software development / ownership (CapEX reduction)

Figure 1.3 - The Unique Selling Proposition of a big CRM vendor

At that time the message was disruptive:

Corporations are living in **HELL**, when they would instead thrive in **HEAVEN**, the reason is because their bad choices (**SIN**) in buying the wrong software. Luckily they can now amend that error (**CORRECT SHIFT**) by renting a much better software developed and managed more efficiently on behalf of them. This will also give them great financial benefits (**NAMELY**): reducing investments -CapEX- with an impact on their risk management.

Even if the statements can appear a bit twisted reading them from today's view, what is relevant is the new approach, the USP, that created a huge value for the time:

> One of the hardest pains of companies was the complexity of CRM software. At that time huge investments were required to put in place custom functions in the software. The proposed change was to develop most of the usual functions a business would need in a centralised software, then letting companies use the same software over a dedicated database.

Later on the very same concept took the definition of Software as a Service (SaaS). Thanks to cloud technology vendors are now enabled to distribute the same software through hundreds of thousands of organisations. The benefits of it are clear: continuous improvement is one of them, while development only once for everybody is the other relevant one. This technology shift has enabled companies like Pipedrive to develop solutions that were not possible and not even imagined before. This is also the most important, modern, option when it comes to a CRM tool: to get a pre-built framework in SaaS instead of developing it from scratch.

Knowing the CRM roots enables everyone to understand its role in business and its strategic value. Let's see what are the possible options to consider before embracing any CRM tool.

Selecting the right technology for your business

It would be beneficial to recall that there is never one unique best solution for everybody. Let's analyse the pros and cons of two ways of technological choices, but let us be clear: only the real, specific needs and the unique personal attitude of the business management are in charge for the final decision making.

> A flexible solution is developing it over an open database: let's imagine starting from a white paper and decide what we want to achieve. Everything will be possible, the white paper is there to be filled! Theoretically it is only a matter of knowing what to do and doing it.

Honestly, coding a CRM from scratch has little or no sense in today's world, if nothing for the scarcity of programmers. Let's consider that choosing to build upon a "green field" option or starting using a pre-built framework are two opposite decisions and, between them, you can choose many intermediate solutions. In that space there are platforms that enable everyone in building software solutions over a database even in lack of a proper coding know-how. They are called LowCode (or NoCode) platforms. They enable 'theoretically' everybody in building anything, even a CRM solution. The final output will probably be better than a spreadsheet, but quite far from an efficient solution developed by knowledgeable experts to be sold and used by highly knowledgeable people. And it is not about performance, but is about the internal logic, its security and ultimately the "ease to use" of the interface. But if entrepreneurs are keen to develop one in search of a bespoke solution, they can try the LowCode technology. We warn them to take account the cost-opportunity of their own time: they should be sure that their time is cheaper than a pre-built solution, fully featured and ready to use.

Most common LowCode platforms propose to build solutions over databases in a relatively easy manner.

On the frontend, there are several possibilities on the market, even WordPress, is one of them, with its limitations, but widely used. ***Builder.io*** on the other hand appears as a powerful tool for LowCode development and it can have the possibility to join flexibility in building frontend web pages, easily connected to a backend. ***Bubble*** got a huge investment recently in order to develop the most powerful LowCode application in the market capable to support frontend app creation as well as backend strong solutions. Will they win that challenge?

Access, ***FileMaker*** and lately also ***Salesforce*** can be considered offering LowCode database management solutions, even if the first is no longer in fashion and Filemaker is mainly used by a niche of true lovers. In some way, those two tools were precursors of the idea to enable developing solutions without coding. Salesforce is a different story. It is now both a customizable CRM solution and a platform to support development of almost any APP.

The good thing is that the new generation of tools are generally more flexible, powerful, and less expensive than them. The idea of a complete no-code technology is probably not yet fully operational, but with time and patience probably we will be there. Meanwhile it is already possible to develop something that works without having knowledge of programming languages.

Three limitations of what has been called "LowCode movement" are

1. the effective effort required
2. the know-how / know-why needed

3. the lock-in risk

Without that know-why in the first place, and the know-how just to start, it is strongly recommended to avoid embarking yourself in such a challenge.

On the other extreme, the market proposes quite rigid pre-built frameworks, but they are often low cost, allowing little or no alterations. Those alternatives offer such a limited flexibility to become extremely distressing when organisations try to adapt them to their needs. They are generally overall quite cheap since their implementation is relatively simple, or at least requires little effort. Flexibility is not only about user interface setting, but also about structure and functions. Typical clients/users of those solutions are digital newbies who have limited knowledge and even less requirements to fulfil.

> Between the two extremes we probably list something like 1000+ CRM solutions available at any price -some of them also for free- and they show degrees of flexibility. It is impossible to name even a portion of them, but what is important to clarify is that each solution, wherever it sits, is a compromise between full flexibility and readiness to use.

Let's think this way, full flexibility is when you develop over the green field, while ready to use is what you can get using a pre-built framework. Those last solutions, often defined as off-the-shelf packages, can be developed with an industry in mind and they work pretty well for that specific business. Meanwhile, bespoke solutions are developed from scratch and they cover specific requirements of each single business—one company, this wouldn't be as easy using a pre-built framework.

> On the other hand, creating a CRM from scratch, even if it is possible, is still a big challenge and extremely time consuming, the main effort is not the development itself, but the definition of the logic to make a CRM effective. This part is almost always undervalued.

Creating a real, effective value with a CRM tool is the final outcome that every organisation expects. Let's analyse it.

Creating value using CRM

It is relevant to focus on the basic features of a database and its capabilities in order to extend them to CRM, understanding what a database is, enables us to describe how a well developed CRM may create value:

Rod Stephens describes a database as a tool that: *"...stores data, and lets you create, read, update, and delete the data in some manner"*.

A definition of CRM might be:

CRM is an organisational commitment of understanding customers, feeding their expectations and meeting their needs, allowing us to hit organisational goals.

Then CRM is not just a (digital) tool but much more than that: it is an approach, a strategic asset of business. It can eventually be done by different tools (paper and pencil are still valid). Thus, we will discuss the tools used to ignite efficiency in the development of knowledge about markets and individuals, defined as potential or active customers or even stakeholders.

Then we may consider:
1) **CRM as a logic**, as the strategic organisational method to look after the relationships with stakeholders
2) **CRM as a digital tool** that enables efficiency in this function.

A CRM software provides a digital environment that enables organisations in running their own way to build, nurture and maintain relationships in the market. To achieve that the CRM tool provides data storage to process, maintain, and retrieve transactional, behavioural, personal, and social data in the most efficient way in order to create effective, meaningful information sets available in real time to any data-consumer. It may enable an effective support to the company's mission achievement.

CRM is then much more than the software itself, among its features we can list that it:

- Provides information to support marketing activities such as campaigns, events, and communication to specific audiences
- Enables the organisation to preside over multiple contacts (leads), understand individuals and organisations, as well as qualify potential customers at the right time
- Enables understanding of the market by comprehension of tendencies through individuals and organisations' feedbacks
- Facilitates execution of sales processes, especially when they are long and composite
- Enable management of sales process, by reporting over sales processes efforts and results, support forecast management and

permitting sales process planning

Specific purposes of a CRM platform are:

- To ignite efficiency in the organisational duties of collecting data to forge reliable information over individuals and organisations to hit marketing goals
- To ignite efficiency in sales process management to enhance sales
- Providing data to the organisational digital infrastructure in order to meet business objectives
- Enabling sales forecasting

Let's check now why Pipedrive can be a good choice: avoiding overcomplication, enabling a certain flexibility in a pre-built framework, Pipedrive may boost organisational effectiveness and igniting efficiency; both outcomes that will pay off the investment pretty soon.

Why Pipedrive

Pipedrive reached an interesting balanced point between a ready-to-use framework and good flexibility. The secret is not just about the technology which can be easily replicated (but nobody did it), its real secret relies on the strong know-how of the needs of the function it aims to: provide a solution to salespeople needs.

To tell that with Simon Sinek: *when you know your own why, the rest is easy*. Probably Timo Rein and Co. knew the reason why they had to develop a CRM that wasn't built yet.

In fact, each product has (or should have) a "*reason why*" before its conception. Any successful product/service has a remarkable and powerful *reason why* that drives success, and more important, who created them are people with a clear picture of that "*why*", which is like a lighthouse beam: wherever they are, they have a solid route, even in the deep storm.

> Knowing how sales people work, their complexity, their problems, their preferences and focusing on creating a valuable tool for them has been the competitive advantage of Timo Rein and partners.

What we must acknowledge about Timo Rein, is that he has always kept the direction clear: "this is what we are going to do". Visionary people can see something that other people don't. That's the motivation to stick to the mission.

Pipedrive thus has been designed keeping in mind what a sales process requires and what salespeople need in order to improve efficiency in their job. This made Pipedrive a killer application for sales process management, related to B2B, where people in sales have a prominent role among all the marketing policies. In Pipedrive, each sales person manages contacts and activities on a personal level. This is what is expected when interactions with prospects/customers are paramount for success. With this perspective, we can better understand why Pipedrive has been built focusing on enabling sales people to have the best control of deals, activities, pipeline milestones and sales process timing. Something that also empowers teams in collecting the right data to support information management upon sales processes and set the operations to succeed.

> Pipedrive has been developed as a laser application in a pre-built framework, which makes the solution practically an off-the-shelf, ready to adopt.

This approach is still valid: users do not need to make great efforts to start with Pipedrive, setting up an environment is easy and anyone can start working on it from the very first day.

Pipedrive's mission is to ease the job of its users. That's why it also allows a degree of flexibility, not much in terms of User's Interface, but in data and processes management. On top of that, the Pipedrive product team has a strong, effective focus on continuous development; this is among the reasons why in the 2021 Pipedrive Inc hit 900 employees: a big challenge to keep the enhancement the priority beside the growth. One special mention goes to users' feedback management: Pipedrive team has always used feedback to improve. This is why the customer care team has been so responsive to any users' enquiry, because of its importance in the continuous improvement strategy.

What you can do (better) with Pipedrive

Pipedrive is a tool designed to effectively support the salespeople's job when they are called to run long, complex sales processes with relevant transaction values.

This mission clarification helps to establish clear boundaries over expectations on Pipedrive. We can also make it clear how, in its first 10 years, the company has done a lot to add new features and focused functions in order to enlarge the product scope well beyond its initial specific unique purpose of the pipeline management. But Pipedrive performs the best when applied to certain businesses:

> A long, complex sales process with relevant transactional value, run by salespeople, that typically implies B2B business models -but not solely-.

Today Pipedrive is still developing the tool with a mission in mind: to conquer the leadership in the SME market. In doing that Pipedrive is launching new features aimed to satisfy small businesses needs of more efficient tools. We can add that Pipedrive was developed with fully open APIs, this is a benefit that enables any company to develop solutions around the CRM.

Let's discuss Pipedrive by a parameter: fully comprehensive tool Vs focused solution.

While many vendors tend to be fully comprehensive, Pipedrive is more laser focused on its kernel function: the sales process management.

In Pipedrive's environment the CRM is the central hub where integrations with specialised solutions are a huge added value to help clients in better shaping their own digital infrastructure.

> The strong advantage of a born as integrable system is that users have more choices, more possibilities to select the features they like, shaping the system around their preferences rather than taking what fully comprehensive systems developed.

A system created for integrations relies on other vendors capable of providing more specialised functions. The marketplace makes it possible for users to find many different options about each function with different prices, features and capabilities. Users can choose what best fits their needs, but also change it along the way: it enables competition between different solutions, making the system virtually unlimited while boosting for better performance.

In the last year Pipedrive started to develop ancillary features to support the value of the solution. This seems to go against the previous approach of relying on integrations of other vendors. Probably something that Pipedrive had to do in order to support its growth as a company, as a business (prices) by leveraging the proposed value.

Let's check what organisational needs Pipedrive really helps in handling:

- Sales process overview and management
    - ◇ To grasp the whole sales process at a glance is provided by visual pipeline, highlighting trends and forecasts in a glimpse.

    - ◇ Sales process management complexity can be clarified with the kanban tool, staging tasks and actions.
- Effectiveness in sales
    - ◇ Task management is critical in the sales process, sometimes complex for salespeople. The embedded Activities Based Selling is a real game-changer.
    - ◇ When productivity is uncertain in sales, we use a simple approach to focus on what really matters, then stick with the job to be done. A UI with a clean data view (less is more) nourishes efficiency.
- Data management
    - ◇ Availability of valuable information based upon reliable data is the basis for success. Applying a correct data architecture for it is the way to go that Pipedrive enables.
    - ◇ Data ownership is a problem that more companies are starting to understand. Too many systems make it hard to reuse data.
- Digital infrastructure
    - ◇ The development of an effective digital infrastructure can be a real headache for small businesses, the required knowledge and investment make it complex even to plan it. With Pipedrive you may start just with one core function: the sales management. Then add other functionalities by easily integrating other solutions.

These four points matter when choosing a CRM, let's list some parameters useful for decision making:

- Type of business model: B2B or B2C
- Type of Sales Process(es)
- Value per transaction (deal)

If your business serves other businesses with valuable services or products, and has long, complex sales processes managed by a team of salespeople, then Pipedrive is definitely a go-to solution.

> It is important to frame the conditions for using a CRM before deciding the tool, then figure out which software may work better in specific conditions.

Too often companies first start with the implementation of a software solution, then they stretch it in order to fill in all possible functions. We believe in a different approach: focusing on the original purpose, limiting the scope to what really matters the most, then Pipedrive can create great value providing efficiency boost.

When (if) you need more

Companies in B2B also need new, fresh leads on a daily basis. They need to nurture the market to get other businesses in search for the solution they offer.

When setting up a business it's often imperative to keep costs under control, then select a Leads Generation platform which may be less fully comprehensive, but more cost efficient. In that stage a complex tool won't be effective, no matter how many options it may include.

Pipedrive marketplace enables users to select the solution that fits their requirements according to the stage of their business, use it for the time they need it, then change it when their needs may change.

It is true that the CRM tool can also be substituted, but in general the CRM is a more sensitive tool. Changing it may have a bigger impact on the organisation and it may be difficult to plan it properly in advance. The CRM should support the sales processes enabling performance enhancement of salespeople by the best working environment. It is always useful to test CRM tools before adopting one in search for the perfect fit, knowing that a change of this tool is painful: CRM is the kernel of the digital infrastructure, where many different software may converge, it should be ready to exchange data in real time, so that companies may choose any ancillary solution, from most convenient marketing automation, to the most effective project management tool.

When the business grows it may trigger the idea that the pattern of tools in use are not good enough to support the next business stage. Sometimes it may be true, but we suggest properly scrutinising the matter to improve decision making: problems and limitations are often due to compromises taken at the stage of implementation. Reviewing it to investigate if the tools may achieve the new requirements is the first thing to do. Then plan a substitution of the tool that shows the limitations, according to the new needs it may be useful to change only one tool at a time and keep others in place. Changing everything is a big leap that involves many risks.

The good news is that Pipedrive is among the few solutions in the market that enable clients to retrieve their data in a format easy to transfer. Maybe you won't need it, but it is good to be aware of it from the beginning.

Summary

In this chapter we introduced the general logic of the CRM as a business strategy and an operational execution, then the tool. The purpose was to clarify the basics of CRM and Pipedrive at once, then introduce some specific benefits.

2 Setting Pipedrive, Using it, Learning It

Introduction

When you start using Pipedrive the account can be opened in seconds and you can start adding your contacts and managing your sales process with simplicity. Simplicity is great even if: *"things should be made simple, then even more simple. But not too simple..."* [1].

It means that users can expect to find Pipedrive simple, but need to be aware that there is a complexity behind CRM. For this reason approaching it with the proper method and a clear roadmap is paramount to implement it successfully and reach your goals. Everyone may go beyond just a shallow use when they know what they want to achieve and what has to be done to achieve it. If solopreneurs tend to develop the tool directly, organisations can benefit from the support of CRM architects and solution providers: investing in professional advice will change the learning curve about the system, and can also smooth the organisational complexity. In business, velocity in reaching targets is paramount.

Simplicity can lead users to not fully appreciate more complex functions; then many users risk just sticking to its more shallow usage without even wondering if Pipedrive can create more value to them. When it happens, we notice users complaining about it, (but it happens to any CRM tool), then they start evaluating to move away in search of something better.

> Frequently, people are unaware that it is not the tool itself that is problematic, but its implementation: the concept of simplicity was used in the design and implementation of the tool, which resulted in an ineffective setting.

Before deciding that a match is not in place, and that other CRM tools can be better, we strongly suggest a restart from the design: clarifying the purposes and defining the scope of the tool. In general, this is the main missing analysis that results in the perception of an inadequate tool.

> It is good news that, if you decide to change, Pipedrive does not impose any barriers since exporting data is simple and effective. Something that is not always so straightforward with other digital CRMs.

[1] A. Einstein, credited

In this chapter, we will go through some tricks of the account setting, users' setting, and initial start of use. They are small parts of the process that can be unclear when dealing with settings. Users will learn how to set Pipedrive properly and speed up the process instead of getting stuck on unclear issues.

We will go through the following topics:

- Default settings at starting an account
- User's settings
- Tables use and settings
- Task Manager
- Fields manager

By the end of this chapter we will be able to understand the foundation of Pipedrive, and how to start using it.

Default settings at starting an account

As you can appreciate, opening an account and setting the first user is extremely simple. Once subscribed to Pipedrive, an environment will be created in your company's name: **www.yourcompanyname.pipedrive.com**. The initial set up is automated and an empty account is ready for your upload of contacts: People and companies (organisations). As a standard trial, you can use it for free with no card required for 14 days.

Essentially the Pipedrive environment has 7 operational areas, plus 2 add-on: Projects and Campaigns. They are all listed in the vertical black belt on the left of the screen. The main one is the pipeline, here is where it opens at start. We will see them one by one from Leads wich sit on the top of the list.

Users Settings

Once started, you will have to invite all your colleagues. Each user must be created by an administrator and given one permission set each. Then each colleague has to set up preferences and settings such as emails and calendar sync, and most of the time each adds an app link and setting.

After the user has joined that seat, you can upgrade that seat to admin, if you need it. Please keep in mind that in Pipedrive the licensing is per person/ user. One account is the company account and to it belong a number of seats (users). Pipedrive charges per person/user, if you remove a colleague from the organisation's account, you must delete the seat to stop being charged if you do not want to use it for a new colleague.

Note

Pipedrive is focused on a single user setting. Everything is based on the single user view. In every View, setting, filter, workflow automations, each user is independent.

Small companies, where each user has to set autonomously views and settings that fit the needs will find it easy. In the case of many users, this method may show limits: each seat will have to be set one by one for every user.

If you want to connect the account with a marketplace app, most of the time each user has to run the installation procedure of the integration within their seat.

This setting is how Pipedrive was born: "single user centric" at its very beginning. We expect Pipedrive will move beyond this logic as it is likely to become more interesting for medium-sized organisations. We expect they will create a Super-Admin account where Certified Solution Providers may be able to manage everything on behalf of their clients.

Users Permission

In the area of permission setting, Pipedrive has recently released a quite important update (autumn 2022).

This brand new functionality finally enables full control over each user permissions set and availability of features. We won't discuss much about how to set up permissions as the video tutorial linked in the permission page is totally clear and fully explicating.

Here we only refer to the usability of permission setting to control what users may or may not do. For instance operators (Regular Users) shouldn't be enabled in creating and deleting data fields or deleting entities like Leads, Deals, Contacts or Organisations. Managers may have some more control over settings. While Admin users should be very few people in the company.

The new setting enables the exclusion of users of any kind from the billing page that remain for Admins only.

Fig 2.11 Users Setting and Permissions control page. Each user may be authorised for each application

Be aware

Functions and features are enabled individually for each user, while the permissions in settings are grouped in Regular Users, Managers and Admins. The only great missing here is still a SuperAdmin role. The account is still user-single-setting: each user needs to set his own environment and settings. It is missing the possibility to centralise some settings of view. (Unfortunately when the privacy rule is misunderstood this are the effects.)

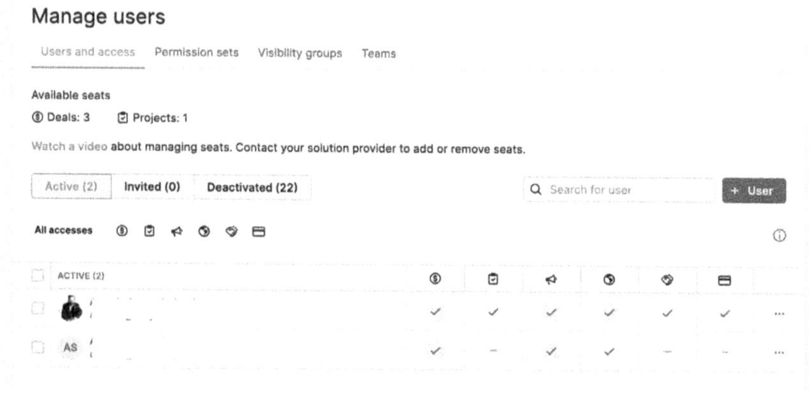

Fig. 2.12 The features of the enabling panel for each user

We are glad to confirm that, with this release, Pipedrive definitely reached a fully comprehensive control over users settings and features control.

Leads

This is a relatively new feature: it was developed less than two years ago as part of the Pipedrive continuous improvement programme that strives to move as fast as possible. This has been placed at the top of the black belt in the left side of your screen view because, ideally, it would be run before the sales process, but we actually left it at the very end of this dissertation just to simplify the analysis.

In the LEADS area you will find the table of contents that are completely unknown to you, either because they are contacts entered from any contact point as they have been collected through a campaign or they arrived in lists of market operators. Pipedrive recently rolled into this feature some tools such as **Live chat**, **Chatbot**, **Webforms**, and **Prospector** which is one of their latest developments. Then you can find the ADD ONS of **Web Visitors** and now **MESSAGING** the now in beta-test feature that enables users in using Whatsapp and Messenger.

> In this approach, leads management is separated from sales, allowing a dedicated team to qualify leads and move them into the sales process once they become MQLs (Marketing Qualified Leads).

When a marketing activity is in place for a relatively high volume of leads, it can be helpful to have some people focusing on this stage: qualify the leads before investing salespeople time on them.

This may contribute to keeping salespeople focused on the sales process at all times. Dedicated resources who do not have a sales agenda and probably neither the sales commitment may focus on qualifying marketing leads even better.

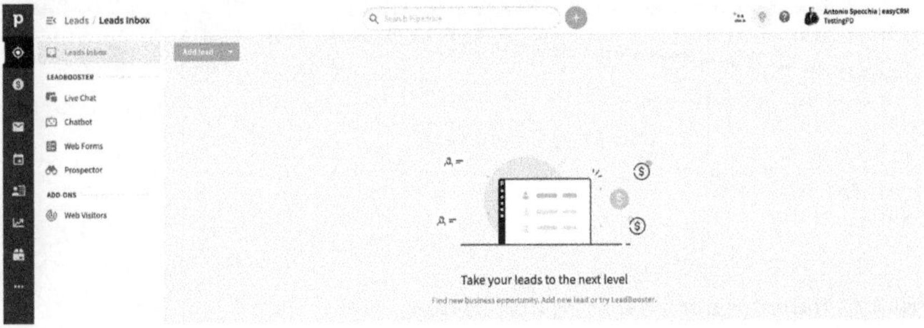

Fig. 2.7 - The leads' management section.

For micro businesses where leads generation is not performed as a structured activity, this area may result less critical. Leads are simply new contacts with whom someone in need to discuss their needs. When this case recurs, small business and solopreneurs may tend to use only the pipeline, by setting a stage New Leads or Leads In and move from there.

Deals

Pipedrive is very direct and operational, it starts from the pipeline overview instead of opening a dashboard. The logic is that the tool should be directly operative, that's why it always starts from its most operative area: the visual pipeline. Here is where the sales process takes place, and where salespeople's daily job is run. (Fig. 2.1)

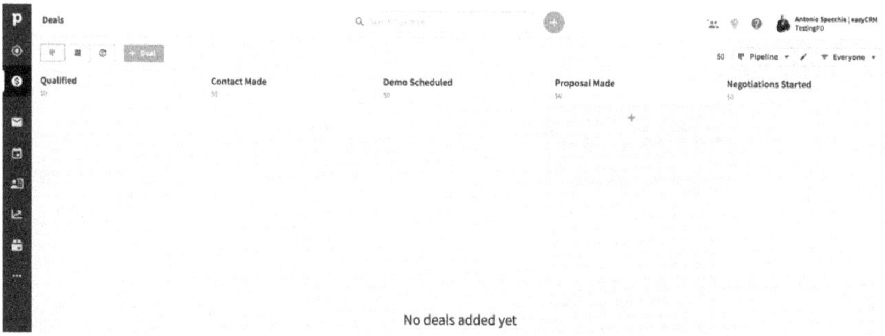

Fig. 2.1 - The visual pipeline in a default account.

Once deals are in place, this view will be useful. However, at the very beginning it can be a bit confusing: "What should I do?" may be the question newbies ask. Let's skip this step and not add deals at this stage: adding deals also requires adding contacts and companies. Our suggestion is to logically start from that point to avoid cluttering of data. In addition, we will discuss how to upload data.

Projects

A brand new add-on feature introduced in June 2022. The purpose of this section is clear: when the services provided are more complex to require a delivery phase, the implementation of the service at the "client's house". The logic is to visualise each project likewise a deal in the sales pipeline, where the pipeline here is formed by the different stages each project should pass through.

Likewise the sales process pipelines the project stages' pipeline makes sense when each project goes through the same stages. And like for sales process pipelines when the process includes different stages then you better create a new pipeline.

The project task management is integrated within Pipedrive's task manager, if your team runs both sales and project delivery that will simplify the task tracking and management.

A more detailed analysis of the feature Projects is developed in chapter 13.

Campaigns

From spring 2022 this is an add-on feature available as a fully integrated mailing tool natively connected to the CRM database and because of that, capable to perform campaign management but also to store campaign data directly in the contact record.

Selection of audiences is now extremely simple and dynamic: filters (database queries) are directly included from Campaigns. Later we will see its features in detail.

More details about Campaign will be developed in chapter 12.

Mail

The functionality of Pipedrive here is likewise an email client: from this page you can manage your mailbox almost like you can do in Outlook, GoogleMail or Apple Mail. The inbox is the first view and it has interesting features like one click to acquire new contacts, connecting them to existing deals or creating new deals straight away. But to do so you first have to set the mailbox sync.

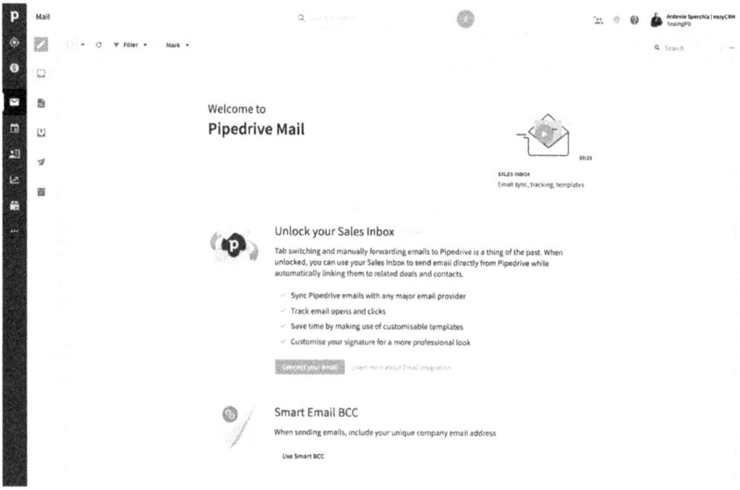

Fig. 2.2 - Mail manager before sync the mailbox

To sync your mailbox you will proceed by hitting the green button on the screen (Fig 2.2) and this will lead you to the setting area. The setting is simple: authorise your email server and define the main rules.

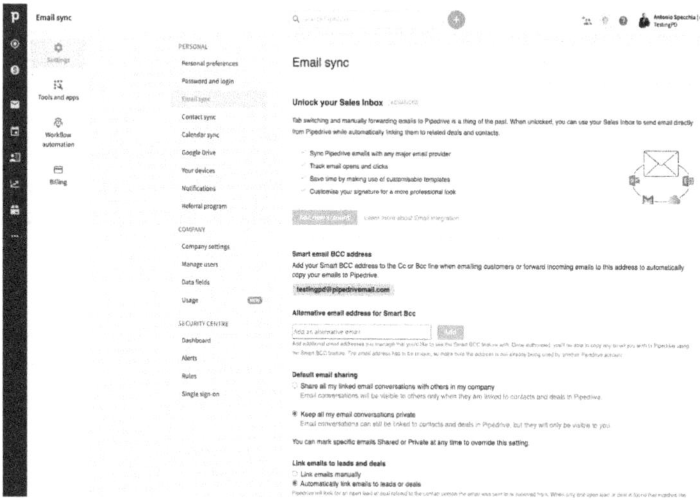

Fig. 2.2.1 - Mail manager synching area

Going through each setting (Fig 2.2.1) is a matter to each user's preferences, here we found a concern from clients at implementation time: "Would then everyone be able to read everyone's emails?"

Email content sharing: some organisations, oddly, shown concern in the possibility that email exchanged between their people and contacts would be shared within their own organisation. We believe that is an organisational culture's topic, that may deserve a better understanding, but to be straight, if your organisation believes that someone's communication shouldn't be shared with other organisation's member, then Pipedrive allows to set for each user' seat individually "Keep all my email conversations private" even if, in the more standard setting, the default option is: "Email conversations will be visible to others only when they are linked to contacts and deals in Pipedrive". (see Fig. 2.2.2)

Fig. 2.2.2 - Mail manager, email sharing setting.

The Smart BCC address is another interesting feature: when you add the BCC email address to messages from other mailboxes that are not synced with Pipedrive, they are automatically received in Pipedrive and connected to deals and contacts (Fig. 2.2.3).

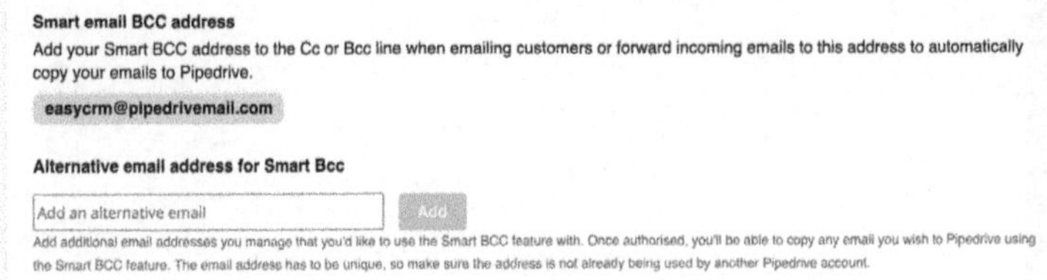

Fig. 2.2.3 - Mail manager, Smart BCC address.

Then it boosts your productivity allowing users to create new contacts and deals directly from messages in their inbox (Fig 2.2.4).

Fig. 2.2.4 - Receiving emails, users can upload contacts data in seconds

Users have the option of creating contacts and deals whenever a message lands in their Pipedrive inbox. Pipedrive connects them automatically when the sender's email address is already collected in Pipedrive.

> The importance of email management for businesses becomes more relevant when it comes to CRM. Though many claim that emails are dead, in fact they are still one of the most important tools for business's communication in B2B.

For that reason, Pipedrive set a tool that enables companies to run everything, also email communication, within their CRM environment, tracking everything and connecting everything.

Activities

The next area is the activity manager (fig. 2.3). Here will take place all the daily tasks that each salesperson should perform. The logic of Pipedrive lies on the activities management, as we will see later on.

> The Activity Based Selling methodology has inspired the Pipedrive's founders since the beginning and this section is the place where the best of the ABS methodology becomes real.

Note, users can create activities directly within the deal's page, then they will see all of them in this section, selected by parameters: per type of activity, per period of due date, or even selected under filters (queries) that just show a portion of them, per user... This section aims to manage daily planned activities in a row, without jumping to each deal's page.

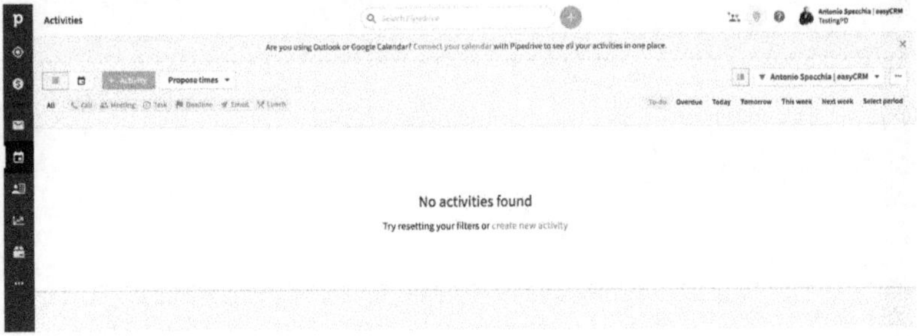

Fig. 2.3 - Activities manager section at first setting.

ABS and activities tracking may be unfamiliar to your company if you haven't already used it. We will see more about Activity Based Selling later in the Task Management chapter, and you will find something good that may replace all of your to do lists if you are used to creating to do lists on sales activities.

Be aware: Creating activities on this page is truly unnecessary since your counterpart (person in the client's company) and the related deal are automatically connected when creating tasks within the deal's page. Creating tasks within deals also impacts the activity tracking in real time: how many deals do you manage? How many activities per deal do you perform? What is the most successful activities rate per won deals? These are just a few of the possible reporting queries that Pipedrive enables.

Another important point is that activities are automatically synchronised with your calendar. They will be easily visible by any calendar, inside as well as outside Pipedrive.

> For this reason it is recommended to set the time when you create activities: it will imply to occupy only a time slot and not the whole day in your calendar as it happens if you do not place a time into your newly created activities.

Let's leave a deeper discussion about 'activities management' until later in the chapter 'Task Management' in this book, let us proceed with the overview now.

Contacts

They are the main tables of the CRM database, they are the tables that contain all the client's data. Even more relevant, for CRM purposes, is the Deals Table. But let's see the contacts' table section.

Clicking the fifth icon from the top of the black belt you will find the two tables: People and Organisations. This section will start from where users have left it when closed. Does it make sense? Yes, as using queries (filters) users would come back here on that same view without starting it again.

In Fig. 2.4 you can see a mock data, just to fill in the tables, but its organisation is the one used by default. Tables here are very much like a spreadsheet, and they also have very similar functions: fields are columns you can adjust, re-organise, move, hide or show according to your more useful view. While hide and show is governed by the small gear on the extreme right of the columns' titles, where you can select what to see (even from other tables!); the sequence and the dimension of columns can be altered like any spreadsheet: just clicking on their borders (at title level) to redimension it or click on the title itself to drag and drop it elsewhere. Just be careful as this functionality is not perfect (you may need to drop it temporarily and drag it again) and can clash a bit with the sorting function (a small arrow ^ appears next to the title). Sorting function works fast in A-Z or (double click) to Z-A. Sometimes that fast action can go unnoticed by users.

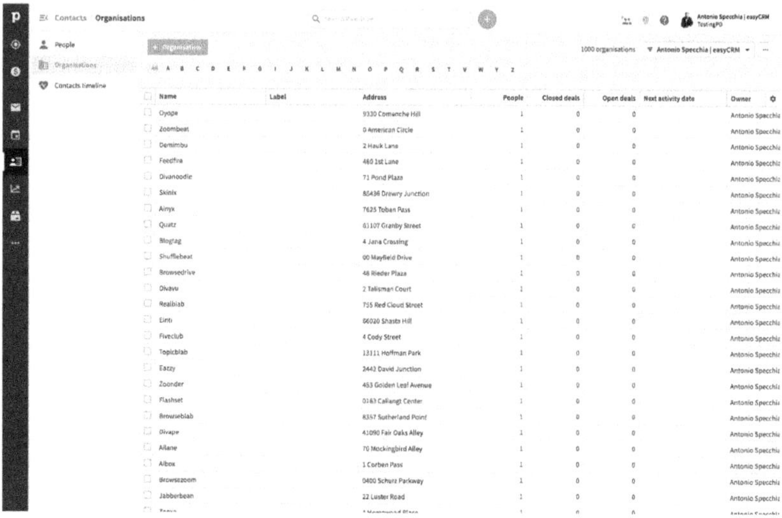

Fig 2.4 - The contacts' tables section.

The most important point of this section is the view of selected AUDIENCES.

> Using the "Filters" feature (see next chapter), users can define selection from the whole population in audiences of homogeneous people for contacting or manage data in bulk.

These tables (People and Organisations both work likewise) are the ones each company should start developing at the very beginning by these suggestions:

- Define the data architecture
- Define the dataset of each field
- Upload data in bulk matching the designed data architecture

Before you start using the CRM, you must fine-tune the database content. Later we will enter in details of how to set each table.

Insights

The importance of reporting and forecasting for CRM tools cannot be overstated. The standard use of ERPs system may be limiting for reporting and totally useless in forecasting no matter how the business performs. With the capability to perform a reporting function within the CRM, salespeople can use their everyday tool even more effectively. Then you can transfer information into the ERP to store it in direct connection with all the other business functions controlled by the ERP. Using the ERP system in substitution of CRM has been done for a long time. And it also convinced ERP vendors to create CRMs beside their tool. But an ERP should run the economics (and finances) upon business' resources, while the CRM has a different purpose. This implies that reporting could be run on ERP, but forecasting probably lies better on the CRM data.

Pipedrive introduced INSIGHTS in 2020 the name gives the idea that here you may find "insights" about your own business. (Fig. 2.5)

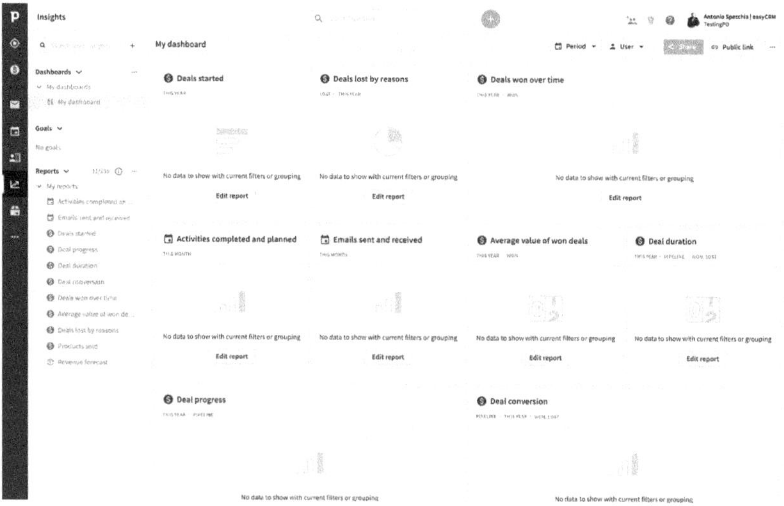

Fig 2.5 - INSIGHTS section: Reporting and forecasting via dashboards.

During account setting you will see some examples of charts within an example of a dashboard. When you start using the CRM you will be able to see data in real time here, then you may start developing your own reports and dashboards.

> The insight is: here is where data will be shown in the form of aggregated information. This section provides information for decision-makers. Consider that a good preparation and design of the information your business requires, helps in defining the data architecture.

Reporting and forecasting are two sides of the same coin, collecting data then aggregate them producing information over trends, in the past, as well as hypotheses, about the future. Relying on a well developed database and some good tools may make a great difference in developing a better picture of what your company is going through.

Products

There is a bit of a challenge here as generally speaking products are already listed in the company's ERP, while duplication means siloing information.

In Pipedrive, you can create a products/services catalogue with the purpose of support proposals development, using stored data, then track deals and clients/

product relationships: know to whom certain products are offered/sold.

> Pipedrive can be synchronised with ERP via API and it may enable updating Pipedrive Products database from the ERP.

In the lack of an ERP system in place, businesses can track products and services here, then using integrated invoicing solutions, directly invoice with the same products/services.

This feature may be beneficial for small companies that can use this feature for services description and prices, or connect it with a products inventory management tool. This feature has been announced for a revamp in 2023. It may be a good move.

Mobile

We will spend very few words about the mobile app. Let's clarify that has been awarded as the best mobile app for CRM. And we tend to agree with that, using the app you feel you are not missing out any functionality compared to the web-app. More, the mobile app enables you to perform unique features specific for mobile use. Some of them are:

- Voice recording for tasks and notes, being travelling may be better to dictate or record a voice note instead of typing it all.
- Focus view, which enables you to look after activities, view a calendar sequence (next day's list), alerts for new emails, check for deals and locate nearby deals by map!

Anyone who needs to look after CRM information on the move, will find it absolutely intuitive and simple. We won't discuss much about it, as it is part of the system in use.

Summary

Thus, we have only figured out the basic CRM features of Pipedrive as they appear by default.

If it is true that any digital CRM tool should facilitate a smooth implementation of all the previous functions, the business workflow design and the setting, by easy and intuitive methods, it is also true that the majority of out-of-the-self digital CRM miss this capability. Not for Pipedrive that remains easy and intuitive for no-tech people too.

In this section we propose each operational section's purpose, developing an overview of the environment in Pipedrive and its features. The book will also help you in understanding how Pipedrive can boost your business processes.

3 Setting a team of 50+ salespeople in Pipedrive CRM

My role is to manage and optimise operations and processes, especially for startup activities, taking the best of implemented digital solutions.

When we decided to implement a CRM we chose Pipedrive. We believe that Pipedrive is a balanced solution that enables medium businesses in developing even complex infrastructures very quickly at a fraction of the cost usually required by big vendors.

I had to set an environment for a team of over 50 people, including a sales force of freelancers. What I found really useful is the ability to define as many fields as you need, that allowed us to create a sort of survey tool within the CRM itself, it enabled the sales force to complete the survey directly in the mobile application.

Pipedrive allowed us to build a CRM that meets most of our needs, this has been done in just a few weeks, then we could scale up very, very quickly since. It would be relevant to say that we are using Pipedrive well beyond the classic use of a CRM, our set up includes implementing the operations management after the contract has been won.

A sort of limitation I encountered is that Pipedrive may be a bit too open to modifications. In fact, by definition, the first users of a CRM are the salespeople, who are rarely the most rigorous profiles in a team! Moreover, as we work with independent salespeople, they feel not as bound by the instructions as employees do. So we would need to have read-only fields for regular users. However, defining fields as mandatory at certain stages was fundamental to remind them what is expected to do, and I really hope Pipedrive will make this key feature available also on the mobile application.

At the moment, we correct users' non-compliance by workflow automation, which would be eventually substituted when that control will be in place also in the app.
The automation possibilities offered by Pipedrive have improved significantly in recent months, but sometimes we find the need to go beyond its possibilities. In this case we use the no-code platform Integromat.

This solution helps us to go further automating repetitive operations without human touch. It dramatically improves the system's possibilities, helping us in achieving more: for instance we set a process to retrieve all the files of a Deal separately on the cloud, automatically rename them, then re-route them according to the type of file and the actions to be carried out subsequently by the different teams.

Pipedrive easily enables creating complex systems when combined with tools like

Integromat, well beyond the CRM, up to a complete business process management. The system we set this way will help us meet our growth target next year.

Véronique Brun, Paris, France

4 Pipedrive's CRM Logic

Introduction

The ultimate test of any tool is its use in real life. It may be even more critical when it comes to information technology: it is too simple to show off features, performances, and capabilities of a software solution, just on a website: they all sound great. And it is also probably complex to test a complex solution in just 14 days. What happens with critical application software? It would be useful to test many different CRM solutions: finding a really user-friendly, will be noticed.

In chapter 6, we will discuss Deals table setting and use, since Deals and Sales Pipeline are considered the two primary tools for managing sales processes. Before that, in this chapter we will go through the setting and use of the main tables:

- Leads
- Organisations
- People

Pipedrive's tables are very similar to spreadsheets. There is a list of rows that contains elements such as sales leads, people, organisations, products, activities, and deals. Many common spreadsheet functions can be performed with this view, including arranging data by column in A-Z order (or Z-A order), moving columns, and hiding them.

> However, that setting goes far beyond a spreadsheet. Fig. 4.7 shows how users can open up each record in a page to view all fields in detail, where users can examine each field of a single record.

By using the table-view, users can choose what fields they want to see, and they can combine fields from different tables with just a few clicks, improved compared to spreadsheets.

As a view of a database, table-view has the search and selection function improved compared to spreadsheets. This feature will be discussed in more detail when with audience creation (later in this chapter) for both, people and organisation tables.

Every table has the capability of exporting data accessible directly in table view, or by "import data" or "export data" at the bottom of the black belt on the left of the screen. All data can be exported using the export function available from the whole database by selecting which table and what format to export. To make future reference easier, logs will display who, when, and what has been imported or exported.

A hidden function is activated by three small dots on top right see Fig. 4.0: [Export filter result] download a file with the content of the table as you can see it, with segregated records if a filter is active.

Other options are shortcuts linking to each specific function page.

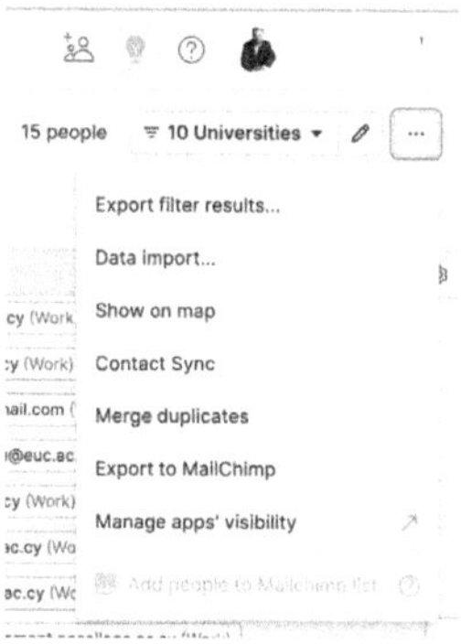

Fig. 4.0 - Hidden control for some funcionalites

Additionally, Pipedrive enables several ways to add contact, even manually one by one. Companies with a limited number of contacts are likely to find this function the simplest for them.

If you are used to meeting people in person, maybe at shows, then you will enjoy the mobile app. When newly met people will give you their business cards, you will recall the great app you will have purchased in the marketplace: ***Business Card Reader for Pipedrive****. This app will dramatically improve your efficiency with business cards management.*

No more business cards storing, one shot and the data will be imported in Pipedrive, creating a new contact and storing the business card image in its record for further needs.

How to segregate new contacts when they are in Pipedrive?

This is simple: later in this chapter we see the Audience creation process, by which you may segregate contacts under specific parameters, like uploaded in a specific day or period: for instance selecting 22-26 May 2022, while you were attending at the *World Economic Forum in Davos...*

If you prefer adding people one by one this is also simple in the mobile app, or on a desk. In doing so, you have shortcuts available to adding (anything) function, available in any view using the key "period" (just hit the [.]) on your keyboard.

Period opens the dialogue window add-anything (Fig. 4.1). If you are a keyboard wizards you will like it:
Use [fn]+(*) where [fn] is the function button and (*) is the key:

» **L**(lead)
» **D**(deal)
» **A**(activity)
» **P**(people)
» **O**(organisation)
» **R**(product)
» **N**(note)

A dialogue window follows and you can enter the data in the designated fields.

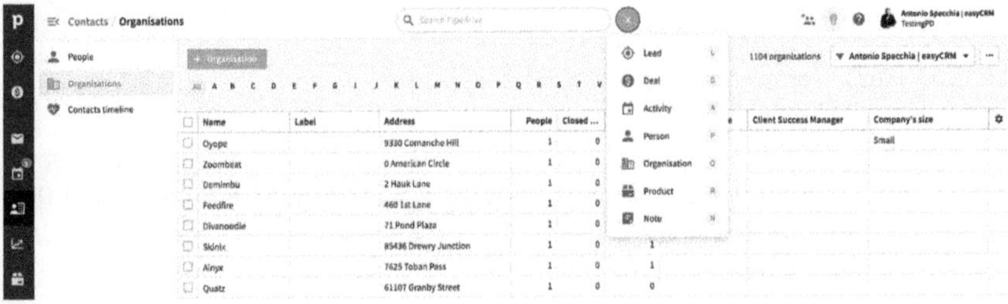

Fig 4.1 - Add "anything" dialogue window

Be aware:
When adding a new entity, such as an organisation or a person, Pipedrive checks the name if it is already stored in the database. A clock icon will appear in the data entry field, followed by a dialogue box with existing options (see Fig. 4.1.2).

> When users rush ahead without fully understanding this feature, they may end up creating lots of duplicates.

A CRM manager is aware that duplicate entities can result in data loss and information mismatches, which makes managing contacts more difficult. Pipedrive helps to avoid -or limit- the duplication at data entry.

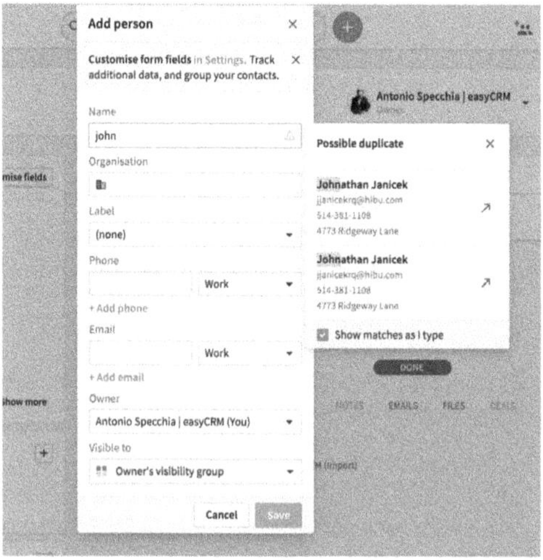

Fig. 4.1.2 - During adding names, users may give Pipedrive time to find out existing entities that match the entering name.

Generally, all tables operate in the same manner, but some tables have specific functionalities that enhance their information effectiveness. Let's take a closer look at each table.

Leads

Its function offers several very specific features making it easy to manage the entire process of leads. A process of leads qualification that, if positively ended, moves them into the sales process.

Starting from the input: leads are added by any possible tool, from Leadbooster or a manual input, or even by API integration with other software.

Be aware

Pipedrive just announced the development of a Round Robin feature in 2023, this is important because assigning leads manually is not always so easy. Today a Round Robin functionality can be added from the marketplace, by Social Oxygen, a company based in Utah even if it is not clearly shown who they are.

This table is extremely operational: it includes all functions to run the leads qualification process. Even if it doesn't use the Pipeline's Kanban structure, the table is a complete leads process management tool. Here leads are not unknown people, instead it operates in the stage of post-engagement and qualification. Leads are already unveiled, at least as for their existence if not yet by contact data.

We will clarify later, in the leads generation chapter, the role of content and how leads engagement take place. Pipedrive Leads management, using Leadbooster features, enables lead capture by contact forms or, simpler, pursuing people who visited a website.

Essentially this special function of a CRM is intended to look after leads before they may be mature to enter in the sales process.

The benefit of this feature is to empower the leads management team in the company in performing every action needed to qualify leads, directly working into this section.

On the logic of process management the MQL stage doesn't belong to the sales process as, instead, the SQL stage does.

> *Unqualified leads (non-MQL) are people and companies that are not in the conditions to use the solution. They cannot become prospects.*

The setting of the marketing qualification stage in the leads management tool not only enables a more focused and dedicated work on leads, possibly performed by dedicated resources, but it enables to track and measure the leads generation efficiency before entering the sales process.

It is paramount for any organisation to compare the results of the leads generation process against the effort for it, while the results of the sales process are related to the resources allocated for sales.

A mistake organisations may incur is to not track the effectiveness of leads generation, losing the possibility to highlight the quality of this process. When leads are pushed into the sales process before being adequately qualified, the CRO [2] manager will be unable to point out the quality of the two processes.

- Is the leads generation effectively capable of "producing", engaging, the right type of people from the market?
- Is the sales process really capable of converting good prospects into paying clients?

---

[2] About CRO role check: https://en.wikipedia.org/wiki/Chief_revenue_officer

When leads are not selected before entering the sales process, the qualification stage expunges a relevant rate of leads, with the effect of a big gap between leads added and sales.

If leads are not managed separately by deals (opportunities in the sales process), your organisation may face several effects:

- An excessive volume of leads entering the sales process
- Allocating sales resources in qualifying leads
- Low rate of qualified leads become sales opportunities
- Sales people can't rely on leads quality
- Sales people may reduce effort on contacts entering the sales process
- Poor sales process results
- Sales people and marketing team blame each other

More about leads management functions included in Leadbooster feature are available in chapter 9, Leads Generation.

Leads manager

In Fig 4.2 there are a bunch of leads: the process will start in table-view, where new leads in bold are ready to be worked.

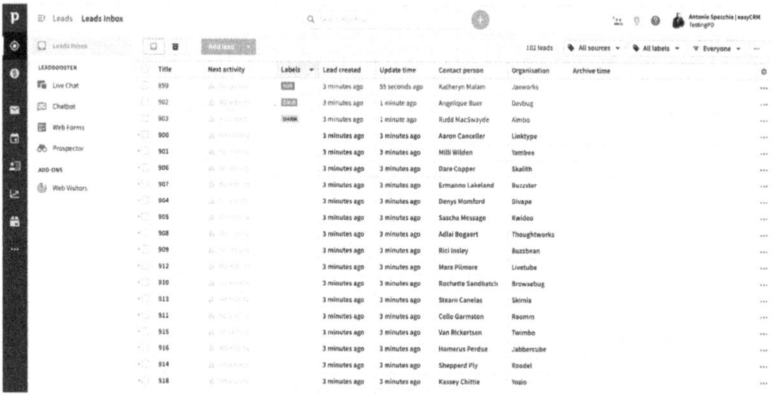

Figure 4.2 - The leads in table-view (mocked data)

The keys of the **leads management process** are:

- **Title** -that defines the lead- which generally is the business name
- **Activity** -that shows activities planned- next activity is relevant
- **The time logs**: -created/updated- showing the work in progress

Operators can open the record page when working on it: verify data on the person (maybe searching on Linkedin); set activities to progress with contacting. The contacting procedure is better if carefully planned to exploit the best from it. It must be more than just talking to someone to verify its existence. Is a time frame, a stage, that may include something relevant to achieve. Like providing the person with useful content capable of nurturing their interest, engage them in some dialogue that highlights their real situation... It is really something that each organisation must plan accordingly with the style of their business and with their need of information.

Marketing Qualification and Sales Qualification

A process that should enable the salesperson in developing a comprehensive view of the contact's (lead) circumstances: business status, position, as well as the possible match with the buyer persona, and based on this, if the lead is qualified according to the marketing parameters to be a client - **MQL** -.

> **Marketing Qualified Lead** is a person who belongs to the target group. Someone who may have the problem that our company offers to solve

When qualified, the process implies to set an opportunity with that person by entering his name in the pipeline. It means to create the digital entity of the opportunity, the "deal", in the Pipedrive's pipeline: a DEAL is an opportunity that has to be pursued.

The sales process includes a qualification of the deal as an effective "opportunity". It means to verify if that person/company is actively looking for a solution or at least in need of it (called an SQL - Sales Qualified Lead).

Let's clarify it with an example:

We enter into a (professional) "relationship" with a company's manager (lead) who looks after the company's fleet.

*Is this information relevant to us if we sell **vehicles**?*

*Many sales oriented people would answer "yes". In fact it may depend on other factors: let's say we sell **refrigerated vehicles** to couriers, in this case a qualified lead should be a manager of a company whose business is in temperature-controlled logistics.*

- *In fact a MQL is a person whose company is in the right business, a company that (may) require the solution.*

- *Furthermore, an SQL is a buyer with an active purchasing process in place.*

This example shows how to start with the vendor factors, what we do, in order to design qualification parameters.

In more general terms: vendors determine their positioning and, by this, their audience. The MQL process checks if a person belongs to the right audience, while the SQL process verifies they are actively looking for the solution (offered).

Qualified Leads

These persons are transferred in the sales process by the button [Convert to Deal] (Fig. 4.3). And from this point on they proceed in the pipeline. The deal creation process activates the creation of Person and Organisation, both related to the deal and including all the available data.

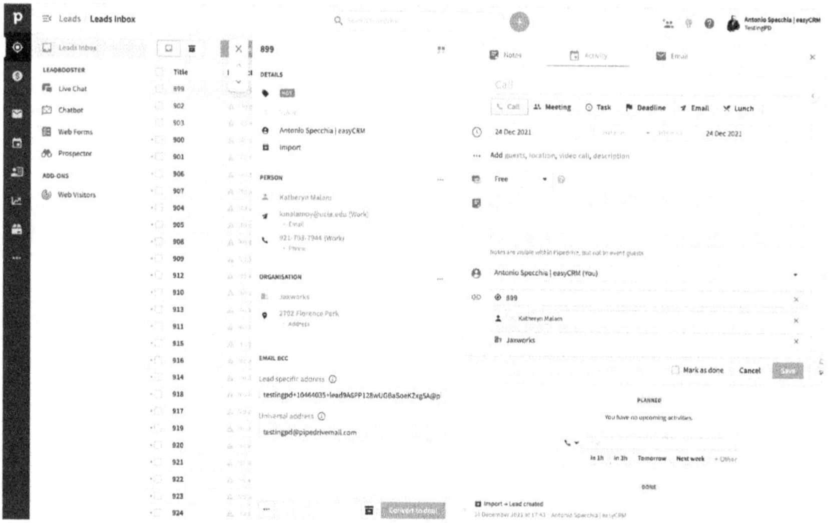

Fig. 4.3 - Lead page-view and its control of conversion to deal

Un-qualified Leads

Leads that have nothing to do with your business may be archived straight away. It means they will be stored in the archive deleted by the lead process.

In case of manually adding those leads again, a match will be suggested with the previous one. In case of importing lists, the automated merging feature of the importing procedure will avoid finding them in the leads process again.

The logic is: once the missing qualification takes place, the system keeps account of this and selects those who really are new leads for importing into the leads process.

To benefit from this Pipedrive capability, users who look after the leads qualification process may archive instead of deleting leads, and add all the possible, useful information for any future reference.

Managing information correctly

Collecting useful data may help in shaping the traits of the lead. At the time of contact having this knowledge may enable the leads manager to choose the ONE single question that matters.

The workflow enables shaping the person's circumstances using data:

- Using the Label = quickly shows a single piece of relevant information
- Setting activity = operatively working on each lead

"Labels" are, like "tags", shortcuts to define a person/contact situation or attribute and show it visually.

> Label is a very simple tool, too often abused: adding labels (or tags) manually to each contact helps in creating homogeneous groups. Then it leads to work on labels or tags maintenance manually.

The situation of each contact changes so, tags should. In lack of automated update the data will soon become unreliable. Why is that an issue? Because when leads data are reliable and people trust them, it increases usability and decision making.

Working on leads

Users work on a table, single view at glance, opening each record in page-view, work over the data view, decide or set another activity in the future, move to the next record.

Next, efficiently run the leads management process, qualifying them or archive in seconds, to feed the sales process with a few clicks. (Fig 4.3)

People who are familiar with Excel will probably need time to get accustomed to the improved features. One feature people are not always accustomed to is the activities management, planning them, taking care of them and leveraging activities to work consistently. Activities in Excel do not exist, at least in the form of an automated task management that feeds users on a daily basis.

Lead's page-view enables users to take notes of the dialogue in real time, create an activity for later and communicate via email. It eases the workflow enabling a fast and straightforward approach.

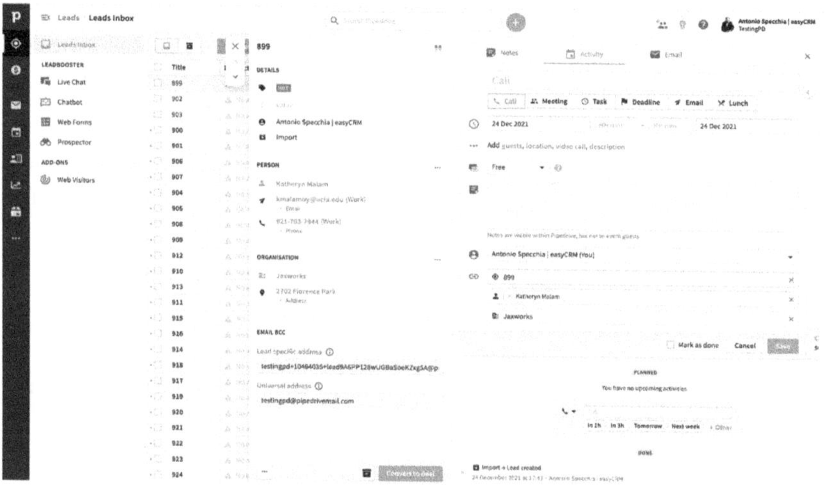

Fig. 4.3 - Leads table view with record's page view "over". Moving up and down between records.

Each company defines the qualification parameters and data useful for deal's management.

> In a process where a human contacts another human should take account of the human factor, leads qualification likewise sales process, in B2B, is a game for humans: machines support, but it is the human interaction that matters.

Understanding each other and getting an open door is a people's job.

Collecting the right information by data

Consider the previous example: we contact a company that runs a business as logistics of refrigerated products and is keen to update a portion of its fleet within a certain period. We want to collect this information in the CRM. How to translate qualitative information into a quantitative set of data?

Shaping information by essential data, enables us to recompose the data and build multiple information according to different purposes. That is why databases, especially CRM are so valuable.

Collecting data that humans may easily collect, often just estimate, empowers people in shaping information effectively:

> *"Mappas own a total of **50** vans, **40** are refrigerated vans. **20** of them are **2** years old, **25** are around **6** years old, **10** are about **10** years old. They consider a van's lifetime to be **12** years."*

By this example of data set, readers may shape a more informative report about the client company's circumstances. This data is very dynamic and can enable multiple types of reports.

---

1 Interactive challenge - Data architecture

Verifying how to transfer this information into structured condensed data is the challenge. If readers would like to exercise by creating a dataset to store the data of the previous example, you are welcome to submit it on this book's website. It can be a simple google sheet with the name of fields in the first column and data in the second column.

The expected output should at least be able to:

- Clarify the prospect's circumstances
- Identify business opportunities (now and later)
- Be searchable
- Capable of creating alerts or reminders for later opportunities

Readers are entitled to submit one result for the interactive challenges of this book. Anyone who would like to verify all the interactive challenges for solutions and explanations on what can be improved, may be requested to subscribe to the service.

Organisations

In Pipedrive deals are considered to be set primarily against one person then, they are related to one organisation: One person, one organisation. After that, users may add more followers and people to it, but the main person is always the reference.

Consider the fact that an "Organisations" table is not always available in CRM tools. The power of a dedicated set of tools at the organisations' table level is important in the logic of the B2B business model - focusing on managing relationships between organisations is the primary purpose of the relationship between provider and clients.

> Pipedrive, developed for B2B purposes, enables users to use a companies' database since they are the effective counterpart of business.

Each company's purchasing process may involve more than one person, the connection of them with the same legal entity, the "organisation", is paramount for the vendor. Furthermore, people are important, but organisations may change them: it is the company that prevails as the business ultimate counterpart.

Among the organisations' table functionalities, selecting visible columns or reordering/hiding them is less intuitive than a spreadsheet. To perform that, users can click on the gear-function on the right of the table(Fig 4.4), which opens the dialogue window where fields may be selected: view/hidden. Meanwhile, reordering them is a simple matter of drag and drop columns.

The logic of this table is to show fields that belong to the company record: the record that stores company's data, which is the main entity related to Deals and People. Each entity (company) may list many related people (employees, consultants or whatever). While, on the other hand, one person always belongs to one organisation only.

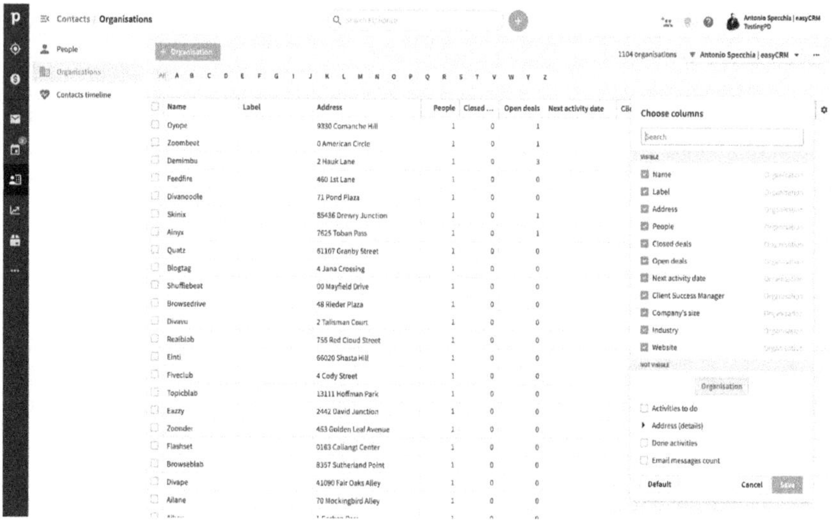

Fig. 4.4 - Organisations table with fields' view selection

Note

This may be felt as a limitation if users want to include a person-role (a consultant?) who works for more companies; that may be the case of architects who are connected to several building companies or landlords as clients. If you need to track interactions with people who are connected to more companies, we suggest you create a company for each person mentioned (who actually may be self-employed) then connect this company to each company they are related to.

Page-View

Pipedrive is a CRM not just a spreadsheet, it means many more possibilities beyond table-view. Drilling into each record, also in this organisations table -just clicking the name- will open the page-view where all the data fields will be visible in a more organised way. On the left side, users will find the column with data. On the right side, the operational area with history of contacts exchanges and activities. The result? A clean setting of each area of interest and operations-control.

You can't change the layout of this page, but you can adjust the data view: clicking the 3 dots icon on the top right will enable you to change the data boxes order on the left column. This may be useful to highlight some information on which your business operates.

Inside the "details" box which contains all the company's datafields, you can organise fields order by clicking the "Customise fields" option - while the icon on its left reduces the space hiding unused fields.

The last icon on the left enables you to fill in the fields: if for instance you need to add more data manually instead to save each field you may decide to input all data then save them in bulk.

That box also contains the **Smart Contact Data Info** that enables users in finding contact data effectively available by scraping the web, mainly Linkedin. Later we will go into further details of it.

The Page-view presents an overview of all the information available on the company (Fig. 4.10). The email messages, notes, phone calls, documents, proposals, contracts... whatever has been exchanged with them.

Data fields have a paramount role in the CRM setting. Later in chapter 16, we will go into details of the data architecture: the logic behind setting up the data fields in quantity, quality, admissible dataset, and relationship to each other.

Fields manager

It may be worth mentioning how creating fields for organisations tables is something easy and quick in Pipedrive -maybe even too easy and fast-. If this is done without a plan, just as it comes to the user's mind, it may result in the creation of excessive data fields, sometimes even wrong types of fields, and it results in cluttering the database and reducing its informative power.

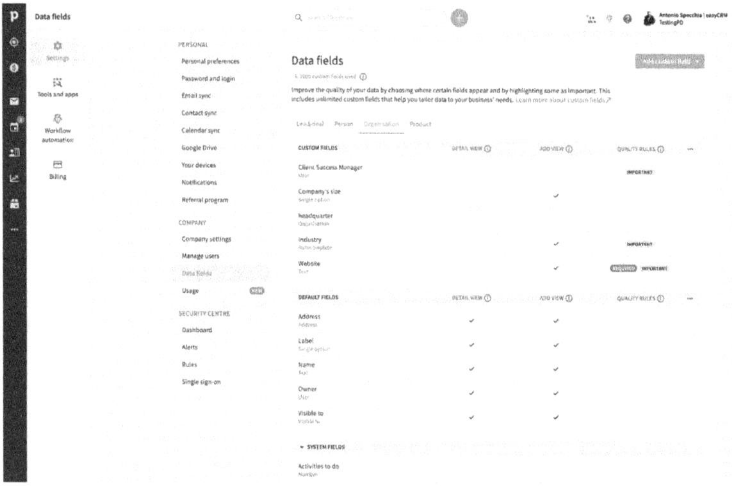

Fig. 4.10.1 - Data fields manager, by the Company Settings area.

In Fig. 4.10.1, we can see the data fields manager, where users may set the data field rules. Custom fields, up to 1000, can be created, edited and deleted, while default fields (set by the system) can only be set in terms of visibility. System fields are untouchable. They all may be used via API, each field token is collectible from this page. The data fields manager works for every table.

Organisations have an important role in B2B and the relationship with those entities may be relevant, according to each business model, as Pipedrive enables their complete management. If your business doesn't include companies as elements of the CRM logic, that may not be useful to you, and a Pipedrive-centred approach may seem out of scope. The good news is that recently Pipedrive overcame the strict requirement of a company as counterpart of a deal. Of course, if you only include a person as your only deal's counterpart, you may need some adjustments, like adding the Address field into the People's database if you need to collect their addresses. But those are just small things.

Changelog

Playing around too much with organisations' data and the merging function may lead users to lose track of changes they have made. In Pipedrive the "changelog" feature is paramount to keep users informed about record's alterations -each entity's data fields that may have been altered- over time. Any action performed is well tracked: fields affected, at what time, from who, what data was there and what the new data are (Fig. 4.10). For some reason, changelog doesn't track merging performed, and any API-run alterations are only mentioned as made from an API call. Users should assume a merge checking the sequence of logs that show merging of data.

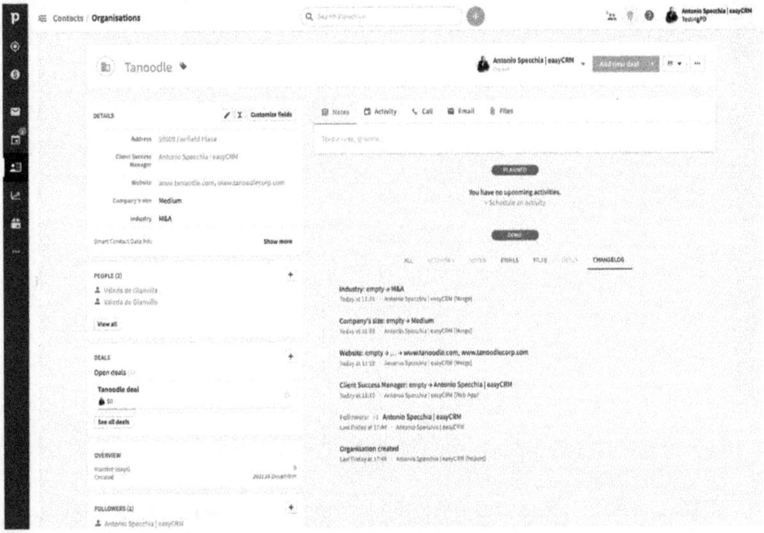

Fig 4.10 - CHANGELOG: the direct way to track any change occurred in the record's data

Be aware, merge can't be undone. If errors happen users may rely on Pipedrive backup, an automated service that can be really helpful when relevant mistakes happen. The recovery is available only through the Customer Care team by the [Talk To Us] function and may help when a user accidentally deletes data. Be aware: recovery is a good thing, but can be tricky: all data changed, updated, imported after the last available back-up -daily-, will be lost. Hence, it's best to use this feature when you know what data you are going to lose!

Duplicates control

This is a relevant feature for CRM purposes [Merge duplicates], it enables managing data more effectively. Everyone who uses CRM knows how easy it is to create duplicate data. Contacts that are entered twice or more, from different sources or by human mistake are extremely common. Even if Pipedrive has a control on the manual procedure of data input, people keep making mistakes.

We are mentioning this function here as basic knowledge enables us to grasp users' attention and be aware of how to use it both in the Organisations table (Fig 4.5) and in the People table.

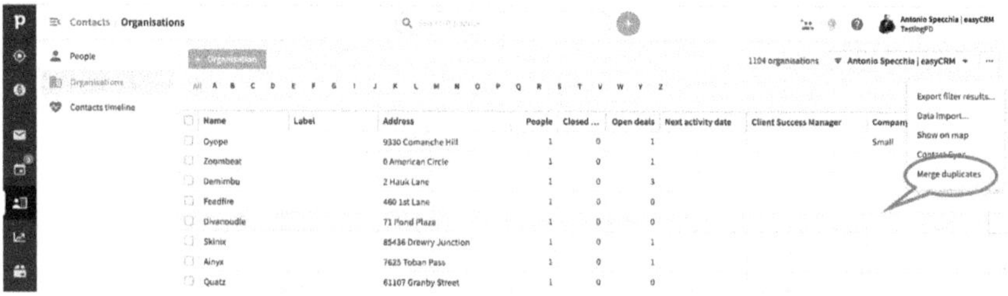

Fig. 4.5 - Table features: Merge duplicates. Accessible from top right 3 dots selection.

In that view Pipedrive shows all entities -here organisations- where name and address match. In the following Fig. 4.6, we may see the mock data of 98 duplicates of organisations and 102 duplicated people.

The duplicates' list-view (Fig. 4.6) sets together the entities that match the parameters enabling operators to decide whether to keep them as different entities or merge them. The following dialogue window shows data from both entities and offers the option to decide what is the more relevant.

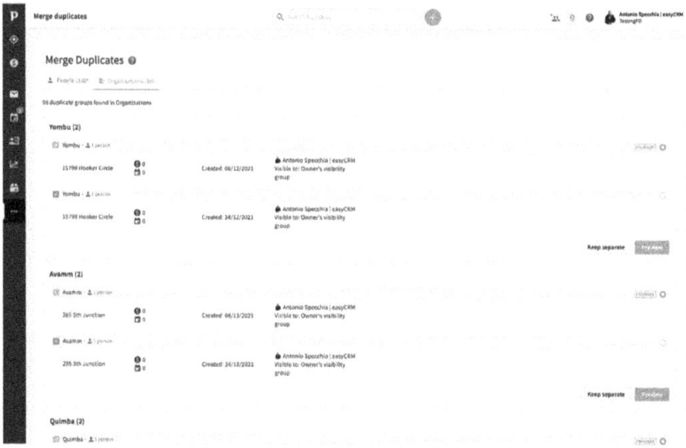

Fig. 4.6 - Merging process among organisations: by selecting the "Primary" entity, Pipedrive automatically defines how to carry on data in the merged entity.

In the page-view Pipedrive warns users if duplicates of the entity have been found (Fig. 4.6.1). If the entity is duplicated (based on name and email for contact and name and address for companies) it will show a box on the left titled "Duplicates" from which users may get access to the same procedure.

Fig. 4.6.1 - Warning box for duplicates found on the top left in page-view.

Be aware

When merging two entities, Pipedrive joins data using an intelligent approach. This means the user may select the primary contact, the relevant one, their data will be set as key, the data from the duplicate entity will be added by the following methods:

- A field is not a single-option field = data will be added, first the primary data then the duplicated data.
- Field is a single-option field = only primary data will be carried on
- Field is empty in the primary entity = if data exist in duplicate entity it will be added
- In companies People will be added - if duplicated they will be shown more times in the People box -
- Notes will all be added in sequence by date
- Deals, emails and files will all be carried on
- Changelog will show history (but not the merging operation)

In fact Pipedrive protects against data loss by keeping the data from all the original entities - it will delete the single option fields and the entity's name, of the non primary entity - (Fig. 4.7).

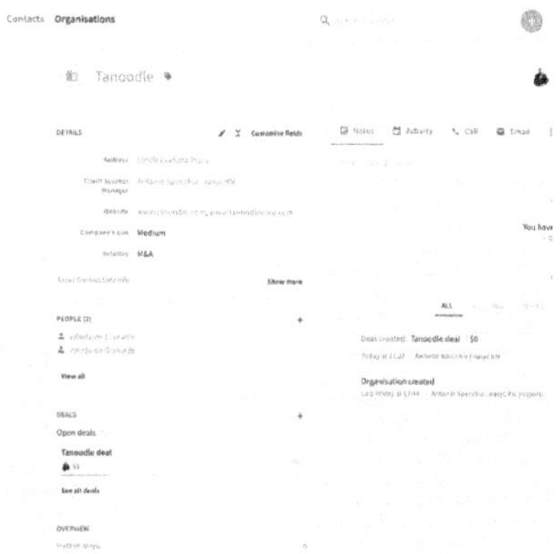

Fig. 4.7 - Merging process results: The company Tanoodle had data added (website) while some data from more relevant identity have been carried on (company's size and Industry) losing the data of the non relevant entity. Last, People (duplicate person) and Deals result added.

Merging feature works with two parameters:

- Name and Address for Orgs.
- Name and email-address for People.

When they match, they are considered duplicated.

The logic: adding more parameters makes it difficult to catch possible duplicates. By focusing on one parameter only, it may find same-name entities that are not duplicates. When you are unsure about it you can perform some simple search in the table to see how many times an entity name occurs.

> *As tables are like spreadsheets, one very simple method to find the element you are searching for is to perform an alphabetical ordination of a field (column) and scroll down to find the data you search.*

Another method would be to create a query (filter) to select all the records that have that string (name, word) in the field of searching. The two methods both have benefits. Which one would be more beneficial in a specific case depends on certain criteria: Creating a query may be the most efficient way to perform several searches for different names in a database with a great amount of records. By investing a bit of initial effort in creating the query, it will pay off by just changing the "searching" parameter for each search - the query will segregate all the records that match that criteria.

In the following figure 4.9 you can see a search performed by alphabetically ordering the NAME column. Moving down to find the "Y", you can immediately see that companies **Yumbu** may appear as duplicated only for the records that show "**15799 Hooker Circle**", while that name also exists in another 4 entries with different addresses.

The logic is that humans may identify similar companies or people with the same name but different addresses, and perform the merge - keeping companies separate if they come from different sources or different inputs by people who mistakenly used 5 different addresses. We need to understand if they are just branches or if they are effectively 5 different companies, maybe in different countries (this is a performance that recently also AI based tools are capable of a deep lists comparison).

> If they are branches of the same company then a good tip to keep them related to each other is to add them in a special field "Related Organisations" in the organisations dataset. That may relate all of them to the main one [the headquarter] (fig 4.8).

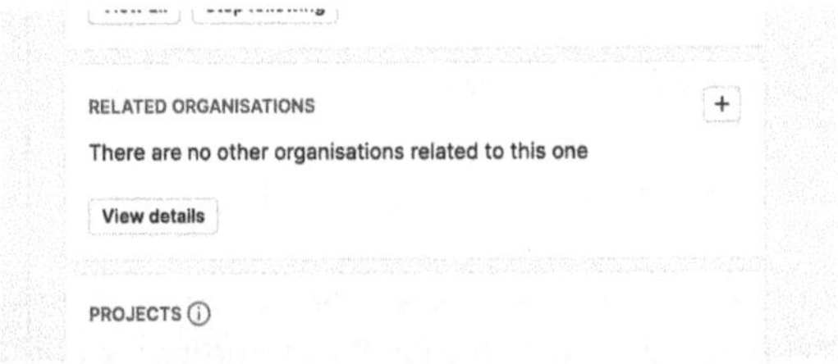

Fig 4.8 - Organisation tag field add procedure: it creates a relation between the company in the record and the company selected in the field.

If this is the case, you just need to be sure to select the right name from the list. If you input a name and give the system time to show the names already existing in the database, you can select the right one. If you run ahead without checking the existing names, then you may end up creating a new entity. (see paragraph Introduction Page 2)

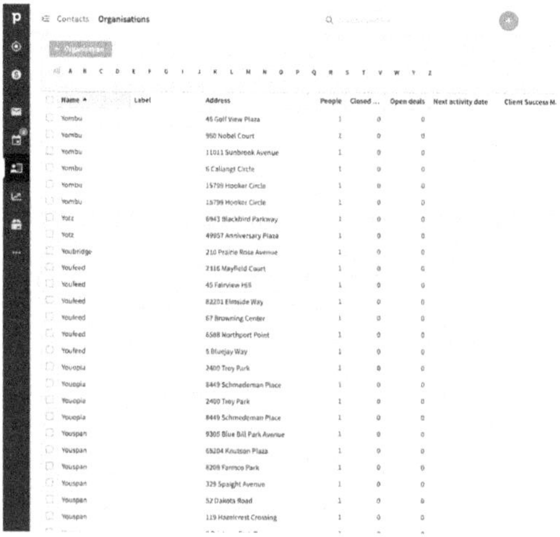

Fig 4.9 - Duplicates investigation by manual search: Yumbu, 6 entries 2 have the same address (possibly duplicates)

---

2 Interactive challenge - Companies Data set

Verifying how to create a set of fields to provide a good overview of a company in your business is the challenge. It can be a simple exercise using a google sheet placing the name of fields in the first column and type of expected data in the second column.

The expected output should be able to:

- Clarify each company's circumstances
- Include MQL data

Readers are entitled to submit one result for the interactive challenges of this book. Anyone who would like to verify all the interactive challenges for solutions and explanations on what can be improved, may be requested to subscribe to the service.

People

The People's table is very much like the Organisations' table. If many functions are the same, the main difference is that Pipedrive enables communication with people, (historically we called offices to request to speak to a particular person, but now we use a personal mobile contact). In Pipedrive it is the same: it is not expected to collect organisation's contact data, or perform communication to companies, only people are the direct contact points.

> Maybe this is also right nowadays: it always makes me laugh when I call a company's office and someone ingeniously replies: "You are speaking with: [company's name]..." Companies don't talk, people do!

For this reason the People table has features that imply the possibility to communicate with them, namely using the email address, -a field that is only considered for people while this contact management feature wouldn't work on the Organisations table even if you add a custom email field.

Group email

In Fig 4.11 we can see the "Send group email" feature available for Professional accounts even without the "Campaigns" add on. It enables you to create one email message to be sent to up to 100 contacts at once. This tool will be explained even better later in the Campaigns paragraph, but we recommend reading the paragraphs Audiences and Contacts Nurturing, where we will clarify how to create homogenous selections of contacts with whom to communicate by group messaging.

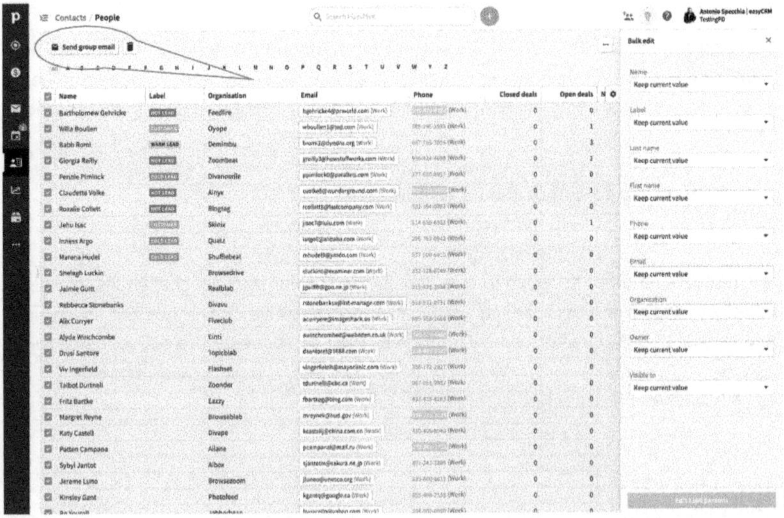

Fig. 4.11 - Bulk alteration view also proposes the "Send group email" option.

Users might notice that the person name, either at table-view as well as person-view input, is just one unique field. This is because the system is capable of splitting the name automatically between name and surname -isn't that smart?-.

The reason for that is simple: User's Experience. Rather than switching between two fields, how quickly and smoothly is it to enter name and surname in a single field? Maybe a small thing, but all great things are all made by many small, good things.

Then in page-view Pipedrive made it visible also in two fields, just to make it clear that users can utilise one or the other for automated field filling for email templates.

Using multiple devices

The table has its data sync with other tools, keeping the relevant people updated in all your devices and tools: Google, Icloud, Outlook, when and if you need it.

It is not always great to mix accounts like Google or Icloud or Outlook with the business CRM, but this is something everyone should carefully decide how to manage.

Show on map

A feature that can be nice-to-have is the "**show on map**": you can have fun seeing all the contact flags around the world. But, joking aside, the usefulness of this feature is its integration with Google maps that may give you the navigation control when you are going to meet clients. Finally we all restarted doing it...

Users can locate their contacts on a world map, as long as addresses are entered correctly, but most importantly, companies can locate contacts per area, understanding what are the most relevant business regions.

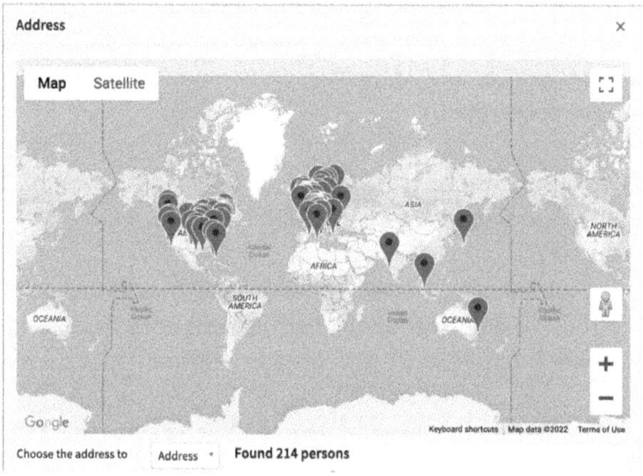

Fig. 4.12.1 Contacts located via direct integration with Google maps.

Viewing fields from multiple tables

Organisations table fields may be shown intertwined in the People table when in table-view. This is a feature that Pipedrive supports over several tables, and is possible for the People and Organisations table because they are related in a many-to-one relation. This means that one person belongs to one organisation, but one organisation owns many persons.

> One person's record will only include data of one Organisation. Hence the Organisation data can be listed aside person's data.

It may help in developing different views of your prospects.

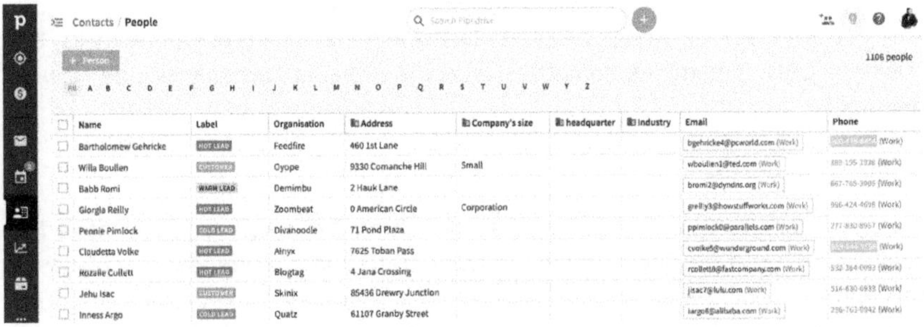

Fig. 4.12 - People table-view that includes company data.

Export dataset

Users can also export data from this table in spreadsheet form or using integration platforms such as Make or Zapier into any emailing tools. Mailchimp was the go-to mailing tool for many years and Pipedrive was used to connect it directly since the beginning. Lately, after the launch of Campaign, the direct connection to Mailchimp has been obliterated.

But this gives us the opportunity to talk about audiences' creation that should precede any mailing -see Audiences paragraph for more-.

The great point is that users may select the fields they need to export by creating a table-view with all the fields required: both people data fields and company's data fields can create a data export with greater informational power.

> If you think about a Rolodex, the people table is something like that, just a thousand times more efficient.

3 Interactive challenge - People table setting

The challenge is to develop a table that includes a set of fields capable of providing a good overview of the person and the company to which they belongs. The result should be a table with fields of both entities, person and company. The result may be exported and sent to us using the website of the book portal.

The expected output should be able to:

- Clarify each person situation regarding their circumstances
- Include company's data relevant for the business.

Readers are entitled to submit one result for the interactive challenges of this book. Anyone who would like to verify all the interactive challenges for solutions and explanations on what can be improved, may be requested to subscribe to the service.

Contacts timeline

Both People and Organisations tables offer another interesting feature: the timeline view. With Professional subscription, users may check the content and information for selected contacts using the timeline. When it comes to nurturing contacts or tracking the sales process effort, this feature can be meaningful. Prospects may need a type of nurturing: especially in slow decision-making processes where it is likely to take weeks or months to sort it out. It may benefit from regular contacts, even just to say "Hello" or "Merry Christmas" or, even better, to inform them of the just-released article about a specific use of your product or a market analysis sponsored by your company...

When it comes to the effort of tracking the sales process, users may check progress and continuity which may contribute to better results. We can see in Fig. 4.13 the people's names are coloured in red, it is a warning that for the period under consideration those contacts haven't been worked. If they would have been contacted, we should see along each row what activities were performed and when.

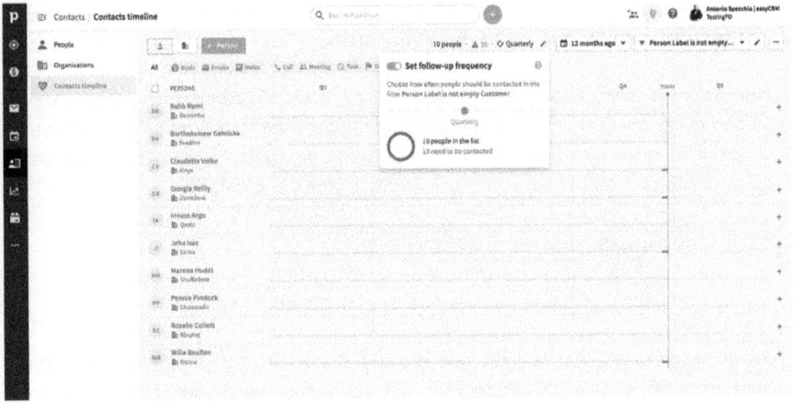

Fig. 4.13 - Contacts' timeline view. Follow-up setting on a quarterly basis shows the audience of contact hasn't been managed. (Professional and Enterprise Subscription)

This view is fully adjustable: filters may be set to check specific audiences: selecting the time frame and the "follow-up frequency". This view works for both people and organisations and may be focused on just some specific activities: calls, meetings, mails. As a result, everything is under control.

Be aware

Digital tools may introduce lots of features -generally superior to a Rolodex-, it doesn't mean that we may really use all of them. We should keep in mind the strategy first: What does CRM mean for us? Do these activities add value in our relationships? If we get in touch with prospects regularly, the question is whether this would cause them to feel pressured. A good mantra to remember is "*One mail a day takes the lead away*"

What kind of interaction frequency is right for our business/market/positioning? These questions and self-analysis are what improves the relationship with stakeholders, something that comes well before any digital tool possibility.

When the possibilities offered by a software are way too many, it may be difficult to have clarity on what to use and how, the learning curve becomes steep and priorities of business are always somewhere else. There should always be a WHY before doing something, let's find your why in nurturing relationships.

Bulk update

This is a logical function often overlooked by vendors: when users need to change some content across a number of contacts, they may find themselves having to export the group of records into Excel where they can perform the required changes in bulk.

Pipedrive's table-views are very similar to spreadsheets, so the ability to modify, add or delete content by multiple fields in bulk has been enabled.

This functionality can be activated by simply selecting the contacts, either just a few of them or the whole selection, then clicking on the checkbox on the left of each record, to select one by one, or clicking the checkbox on the top of the column to select all.

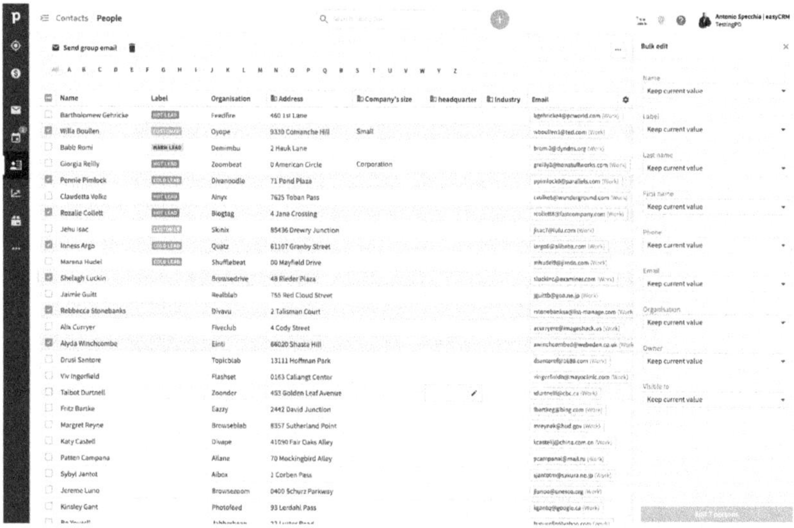

Fig. 4.14 - Bulk edit, to alter content of a number of records

As we can see in Fig. 4.14 the fields that users may alter appear in the dialogue window (column on the right), sometimes in a random order. Only fields related to the table can be modified, the organisation fields cannot.

Audiences

Pipedrive enables smooth and easy segregation of records based on specific selections, database queries do it using SQL programming. Pipedrive "filters" perform queries on the table content by parameters that can be set with simplicity.

Selecting audiences (groups) by complex parameters enables dynamic selections using existing live data.

Users may create as many filters they need and store and retrieve them. In Fig 4.15 you can locate the filters' creation.

Fig. 4.15 - How to start creating filters for table content.

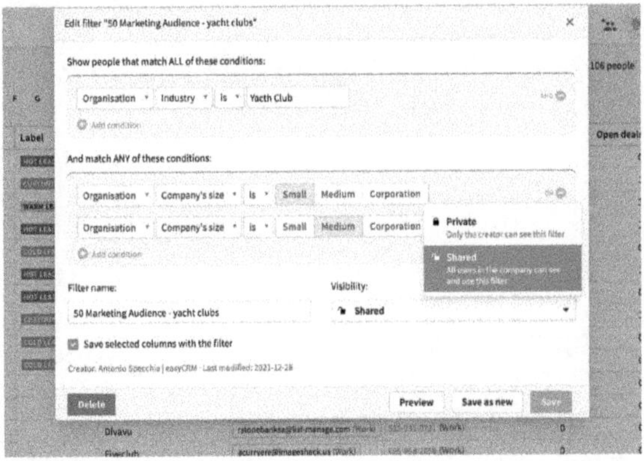

Fig. 4.16 - The Filter composer. Above the conditions that have to be true (all of them), below the condition that can be true (any of them: at least one)

Grouping them by a code according to purpose, and use the name to remind the audience selected. To avoid confusion when dozens of filters will be in place.

Creating an audience by Filter function (query)

Starting defining a simple audience (homogeneous group) on a table deciding what field to use and what parameter creates the segregation. Give it a category number and a name. You may define a specific set of fields included and you can save it as a template.

Pipedrive unfortunately always creates filters on Private basis, it means that they won't be available by other users -a non sense for a team's tool-, but it is enough for you to just remember to set each new filter to shared option. (Fig. 4.16)

It also enables you to select users as entities' owners too. If you do that, the output will be a list of all the entities belonging to that user.

Pipedrive shows some basic filters as examples. Testing how they are developed can help (or confuse) users on how to develop their own audiences.

The most relevant point users have to get when creating audiences is the difference between the two conditions:

- **Conditions that HAVE to be true**, they are listed in the upper side of the filter creator tool
- **Conditions that CAN be true**, they go in the lower side of the filter creator.

Let's explain the condition:

> In fig. 4.16 we set three conditions: this filter is going to select organisations in that industry -business is [yacht club]- and any of them which are either a small or a medium sized business.

We are using a very basic example here, made on some data that are not even automated, but you can provide dozens of conditions over fields populated by third party tools where the variables may vary along the time. The possibility here is to enable users to shape groups in a very fine way without operating manual selections one by one.

The formal explaining of the functionality is:

A condition that ***has to be true*** is a parameter to be found in the used field to match.

The Output will be: any record that contains that value in the defined field.

A condition that **can be true** are two or more values that can be found in the field to match.

Output will be all the records that match at least one of values (true), it is also said condition "OR".

Be aware

Each filter may show a different set of fields: columns. Unfortunately this simple function, which may be confusing, can be clarified: by keeping it flagged you can then change columns(see fig. 4.16.1). The problem arises when it is left as flagged and, by mistake, someone alters the view. Users may end up with a table that is completely different from the initial plan. If you unflag it, the setting will be changed all the time using the fields of your last seen view.

This is probably an illogical behaviour that may frustrate users.

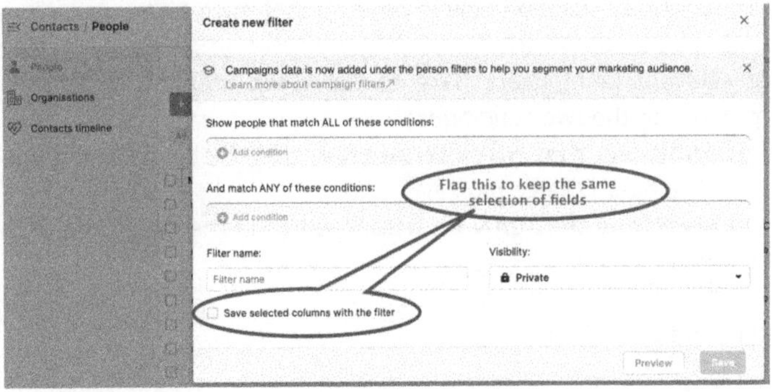

Fig. 4.16.1 Filtering tables: Here we can see the control for field view settings.

Alternative methods to segregate groups

A different method, much simpler but much less effective, is to use TAGS, let's take the example of the field LABEL. It may be simpler to place the labels [yacht-club-small, yacht-club-medium] to all the small and medium sized yacht clubs in your database, isn't it?

Consideration should be made to the time taken to maintain each TAG assigned to a record. If the database has 50 entities, updating all the TAGS used in them manually, will take some time but is still doable. However 500, 5000 or more entities to manage would be absolutely impossible to achieve.

Dynamic selection

We think readers can immediately see the difference between TAGS usage and a dynamic system of filtering over more variables: the tag use is static, it may make it easier to set once as filter parameter, but the output is less reliable: so what happens when circumstances change?

Technically speaking, we selected for simplicity of demonstration, another static field: [Business size] to which we only attributed a dimension using a tag: small, medium... Let's imagine that the [Business size] field would be periodically updated by the turnover value (a datum available in many public databases).

You can now see that we could set a min/max range of value to attribute a business dimension as small, medium or large business.

> The effect of a setting like this is to dynamically change the filter output according to the annual result of each company listed.

There are parameters that change with different frequency, for instance rooms in a hotel. It's a number that may change, but not that often. But what if the parameter is the number of franchisees of a newly established franchise company?

Readers may now find it better to get the real value of a dynamic audience setting.

> Audiences are paramount in CRM strategy, it means the capability to care to contact your counterparts choosing them within homogeneous groups in a more tailored manner.

Pipedrive eases this procedure of creating segregated groups using an intuitive and effective technique.

Data Import, databases, spreadsheets or other CRMs

To upload existing data in Pipedrive users have an effective tool, easy to use, but not too simplistic... Understanding how the Data IMPORT tool works requires a bit of focus and a clear knowledge of the data architecture that you have to set. For this topic readers can check the chapter 16 Data Architecture later in this book.

First solution, other CRMs:

Pipedrive can sync the databases of many other CRMs, Salesforce included. The data uploading may take place directly - which is a great option, but has to be applied carefully.

In fact, each CRM uses a different data architecture, optimised for the different functionalities. They also use different methods to relate tables like people-organisations or people-tasks.

However, the automated import is not capable of translating the data architecture of the old CRM into the logic of Pipedrive. As you can better understand in chapter 16, data architecture is not only a list of fields to fill in, there is a logic on how those fields are related to each other and how they work into a specific CRM engine.

> It may be useful to recall that the digital CRM is just an engine, a piece of software, that uses databases as containers in order to store, retrieve and handle data in the most appropriate way according to the tools' purposes.

Unfortunately, nobody has developed an AI that can grasp the two logics and translate data architecture from one logic to another. Yet. Like using languages to create meaning, you can't just translate word by word using a vocabulary. Likewise for languages, creating an AI engine capable of understanding the logic of each CRM and translating it into another CRM's logic is possible, but not yet business viable.

For this reason human understanding remains superior to any digital tool, the understanding of the business case, of the processes under management and the purpose of the tool is actually much more related to a strategic view of the CRM than its technical functionalities.

CRMs are in no way the same and there is not a way to switch from one to another without a human touch (luckily!).

We tested the Import2 service in Pipedrive and we couldn't achieve a useful outcome. Even if lately they have improved it, we really can't see how they can overcome the differences in logic, but never mind, users are invited to test it. Anyone who gets a useful result is invited to communicate it with us.

Import from databases and spreadsheets

When users decide to import a database in Pipedrive the best way is to export data into a csv file. We personally do not encourage using Excel as data transfer files, csv format is definitely lighter and faster.

On the contrary of what users may think, the procedure to import data is simple if you know what you want to achieve. It is not complex to transfer data into Pipedrive, the real complexity starts when you have to define the data architecture in it in order to efficiently replicate the right functions.

Uploading data without a clear picture of what a company needs to achieve and how Pipedrive enables specific functions may end up in a cluttered database. For this reason we suggest users that are keen to embrace Pipedrive as a team improvement tool by migrating from another CRM, clarify some vital points beforehand:

1. How data is used in their existing CRM to create information either aggregated or specific around the opportunity
2. Define which information is mandatory to run the sales process successfully
3. Clarify what information has to be shown in reporting and forecasting
4. Clarify processes and features supported by the existing CRM in logical

terms, not operational

What exactly does this mean?

Let's clarify that no two businesses run the same processes, not even in the same way. The procedures set in a CRM may also differ substantially within the same industry. The challenge is to declare the input and output of the processes without considering the how.

It is not what you do with a tool that matters, but what data you have, and what the outcome of the procedure is.

Examples

Using other CRM, users may get in the habit of using TAGS. Many tags with different meanings enable simple searching and segregation of data.

Similarly, in other CRM, the name of the contact entity may be one field and can't be altered for any purposes. (name and surname)

Of course, the purpose decided by some vendors is to enable users in creating groups, audiences to whom communicate or create homogeneous analysis. But, if with the migration project, the team expects to keep an identical tags segregation system, that will not only frustrate some much more advanced function available in Pipedrive, but Pipedrive is not even designed to manage tags in that same way. What's more, the "Labels" available for all entities are more a visual facilitation than an effective way to segregate groups.

If the existing CRM uses one unique field as a pivot, and it is the field for the entities' name, users may not be able to split the name and surname of people just using the import functionality.

Let's see in detail how to perform import data by a csv file.

Learning how to shape the data architecture for your specific purpose is the first step (see chapter 16), then we suggest to create a different file for each entity:

1. Companies
2. People
3. Deals
4. Tasks
5. Leads
6. Products

Theoretically, you can upload many items from the same sheet: leads, deals, people, companies... But that will create a lot of complications. Splitting the database into files with the same kind of entities will make it easier.

> The companies' file must always have the correct name of the company and its address in place. Other data may be missing.
> This will create a UNIQUE reference for the relationship between people and companies.

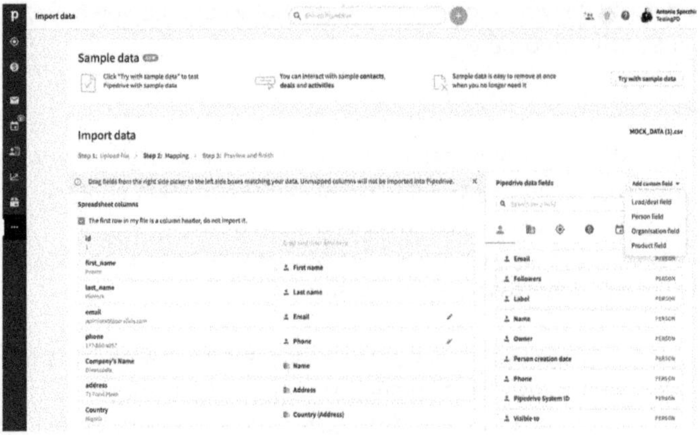

Fig. 4.18 - The data mapping view of import procedure

Once all companies in your database are in Pipedrive and you are sure that specific database includes only clean and correct data, then you can export it in only 3 fields:

- ID of Pipedrive
- Company name
- Company address

Same method is required to bond relationships between records of

- People-Organisations
- People-Organisation-Deals
- People-Tasks

The transient files exported by Pipedrive will be used to link People with the right organisations using Vlookup formula.

> For this purpose Google Sheets offers a pretty good set of tools, including an effective Vlookup formula management that enables you to effectively take control of the outcome.

This may also be done in Excel, if you are more familiar with it. The output should be a file where people are linked to a company including its Pipedrive ID (address may be passed this time).

The sequence of data import batches

There is a logical sequence of data to import following which, everything (should) go in place easily.

The sequence in which the main tables should be imported is:

- Organisations
- People
- Deals
- Tasks

The logic that explain the sequence is:

1. TASKS are related to DEALS, PEOPLE and ORGANISATIONS
2. DEALS are related to PEOPLE and ORGANISATIONS
3. PEOPLE are related to ORGANISATIONS

The difficulties of migration

When an existing CRM is going to be substituted, it rarely has the most efficient data architecture in place. On the contrary, you may find a cluttered database has inconsistent datasets and lacks clarity. A recipe that would kill any CRM. No CRM tool can solve the bad data collection problems (yet), humans are still in charge of looking after the data.

But, data can be cleaned, redefined, and reshaped by machines based on parameters set by humans. The data cleaning and redefining can be set up with a software program, a possibility more convenient when there is a large amount of valuable data involved, even better if data-scientists are involved. A process that requires a significant budget.

In medium-sized businesses, this very case is not so common, and it is rare in small businesses. Creating a proper data analysis and redefining the dataset with limited resources may be challenging.

To those using Excel® as CRM

When companies move into digital CRM for the first time, they often bring the tables in Excel file(s) used for the contact management.

When spreadsheets are used as a CRM, it can be challenging to translate them into a CRM. The lack of any defined dataset or minimal data architecture makes it impossible to upload data directly.

This is because in the rows, used as records, and cells, used as fields, users can enter whatever they like. In this situation we strongly suggest conducting a data analysis, cutting and dicing data to create multiple homogeneous sets that may be imported in Pipedrive.

Pipedrive mapping

Pipedrive's mapping tool works very well when users have a clear picture of what they want to accomplish: the architecture of data they can/should develop. Depicting it in advance avoids mess in the creation of new fields.

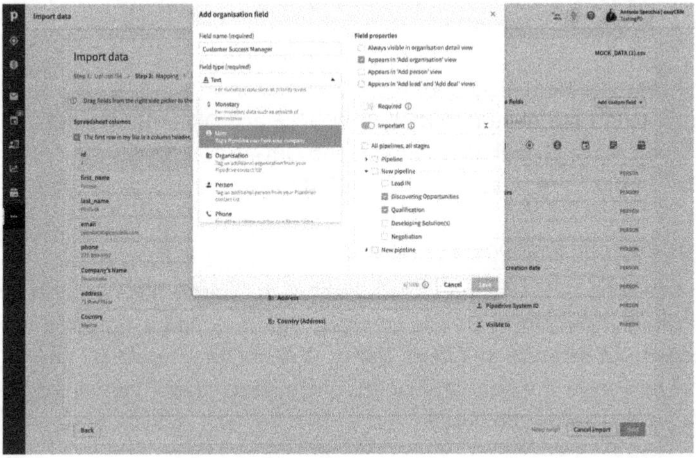

Fig. 4.19 - Creation of a new field. The IMPORTANT data, starting from a specific pipeline stage.

The import tool allows users to map each data-field from the spreadsheet to Pipedrive's database. It also suggests possible matching when names of fields are close to each other: FirstName and Surname (or LastName) will automatically match, while Name (of the company) could go wrongly into Name (of person) which is a special field in Pipedrive.

> The process of mapping data needs focus: the tool proposes fields from all the seven tables, it can be easy to mismatch one of them. If a datum is uploaded into the wrong field the whole database may be useless.

The great thing is that the import process can be reverted easily: mistakes can be recovered in seconds - avoiding starting over again.

For this reason we suggest not to make any alteration or adjustment to data in Pipedrive once uploaded. But, instead run a series of tests to verify the consistency of data. And you can revert imports every time when something is not as expected.

Import, mapping and data architecture. Take the opportunity to exert it!

All the alteration and adjustment of data are better performed in a transient spreadsheet, until data consistency is good enough to run properly in Pipedrive.

Are you ok with the data as they appear in Pipedrive? Then you can start adjusting and altering using some Pipedrive tools as intertwined tables.

If the data architecture has been properly defined in advance, then mapping the fields and their content for instance, in case of SingleOption or MultipleOption fields, will be extremely easy. To make it happen, a data analysis on the spreadsheet, using table queries to isolate patterns of data or recurring data is the way to go.

In the real world very few companies invest time in designing the data architecture before proceeding with importing data in a new CRM. Most of the time data architecture comes with experience and practice of the data manager. Importing data then has a strong component of design data architecture know-how.

For this reason Pipedrive allows creating fields while mapping (Fig. 4.19).

The other side of the coin is that, users who have limited or no understanding of data architecture may end up with cluttered databases and dirty data, while this stage should be an opportunity to invest in a deep data revamping.

The risk of creating too many fields without a strategy would just replicate an already cluttered, old database of the previous CRM you are dumping.

Missing data architecture is one of the most common reasons for complaints about their digital CRM for companies. Take the opportunity to design your data before starting with Pipedrive. It will be much easier to run it for the best outcome once your data are under control!

Smart Contact Data

Using Pipedrive, users may find themselves in need of some data of newly imported people, maybe leads. Maybe people just referred to them by word of mouth. Pipedrive offers a very functional feature: enriching your data through web collection - very smart! (Fig. 4.20)

> In one click, it will search the web, looking for social profiles that contain relevant information about the entity (person or company) you are investigating. This function only requires a couple of parameters: name and email address.

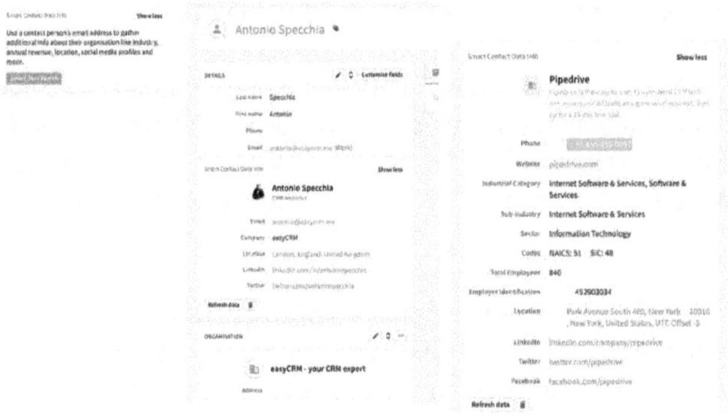

Fig. 4.20 - Smart Contact Data activated for a couple of quite well known entities

Salespeople can now find out more details about the counterpart they are going to contact in one click.

Dataset, default and custom fields

In this chapter we have seen the importance of the dataset, which will be explained in more detail later in Data Architecture (chapter 16). What is relevant to know here is that in Pipedrive, there are some fields that are part of the system and some fields that are in place for default. Then users can create fields for custom purposes.

Almost any CRM enables custom fields (not all the products do), Pipedrive is quite generous in terms of the number of custom fields. In fig. 4.20.1 we can see the availability of custom fields, generally speaking 100 custom fields are already too many, but it really depends on the functionalities and processes the tool will be integrated with. For the Sales Process Management it is quite rare to add dozens of fields. If they are not automatically filled, they require someone's manual effort to fill (usually the salespeople) who will soon get tired of adding data to a system instead of performing their mission of selling.

Feature usage limits	Essential	Advanced	Professional	Enterprise
Open deal limit (per company)	3,000	10,000	100,000	Unlimited
Custom field limit (per company)	30	100	1000	Unlimited
Reports limit (per user)	15	30	150	Unlimited

Fig. 4.20.1 the limitations of the different plans of Pipedrive: 10.000 deals open are generally speaking more than enough for a medium sized company, 100 custom fields are very rarely used and 30 reports are generally way too many.

There are system fields used to store logs. It is helpful to know that they exist and record what and when anything is done, so that you can check the ChangeLog list if you need.

The default fields are minimal, always-present fields that can serve to collect data about an entity, and they can't be changed or deleted. But, for instance, users may need to not have them shown in some views. The example below in Fig. 4.20.2 shows the Deal Value that will always be visible in the Deal Add window (good), in the feature Projects.

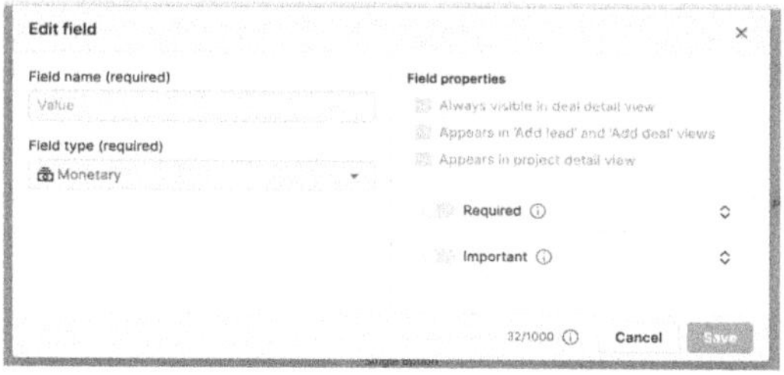

Fig. 4.20.2 Deal Value visibility can't be changed.

The set of default fields includes People, Organisations, Deals, and Products. Each company needs a unique set of fields to shape its own data architecture, the default fields are the basic, essential data required by the system (even this is debatable: personally I would have set even less), but a minimal set of default fields opens the opportunity to shape the data architecture accordingly with the truly effective needs of the business model.

The lack of "website" or "email address" fields in the organisations table may seem odd, but it is not important to have it by default since the logic enables each company to define the effective dataset required to run their own sales process.

Designing the correct custom fields enables shaping information, which is the basis of a tailored data architecture that meets the requirements of each business.

In the default data, there are two worth mentioning: label and note.

Label Field

Its value relies on its immediate visual power - with coloured labels helping to get information at a glance. Red, Green or Blue labels can streamline information about the sales process situation.

Labels may be even more useful when controlled by automation workflows, in this case the labels change according to events:

- Deal won: then the company is a customer, as shown by the Label
- Deal open: there is an opportunity with the person
- The Deal gets qualified: A label shows the contact as a prospect

Just keep in mind that it is like using a tag: a mono dimensional parameter. The real benefit is when they are used within other parameters and they are automatically updated. It is not beneficial to set them manually. Pipedrive announced for 2023 the possibility to use more labels at same time. It may be useful, as long as users do not rely only on labels, as tags, to select audiences and groups without automated control of the field's content.

Notes Field

Pipedrive includes two fields called Notes, one is in the dataset as default field. Another one is visible on page-view (all tables deals, organisations and people). While the first one may be of little benefit or even lead to loss of information, the second one is powerful and enables several features.

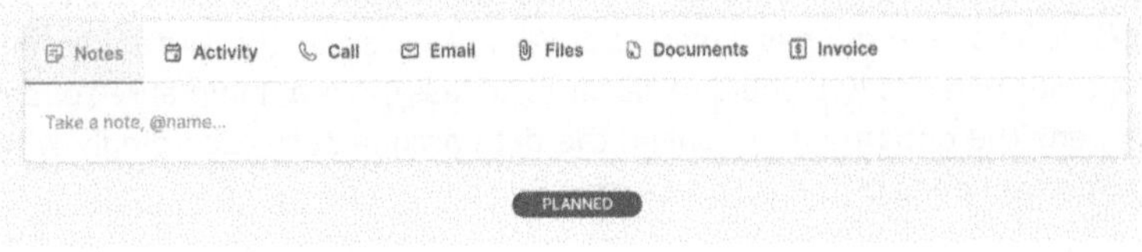

Fig 4.20.3 the field Notes in page-view

NOTES field allows field creation for longer text (above 256 characters) including hyperlinks. They may be useful to store a narrative of story, qualitative information that can't be grasped with just data. One-word datum enables queries to detect if the datum is true or not: "customer" may be true or not as well as deal "won". Qualitative information is more complex, it can be something like:

> *"During the last service (date), a problem (what) arose and the client (@ name) became worried. Our engineer (@person) resolved it and the client (@Name) appreciated it. I offered compensation but the client refused."*

Such events or information about the relationship with the client are helpful to keep in mind. These are transitional pieces of information that Pipedrive can efficiently store in a specific field.

Notes fields always appear along the timeline, they are searchable and may be specific to date, event and person. They enable hyperlinks to external objects or mention people or add images.

It enables salespeople in using a Notepad directly related to the deal/person and always visible on their timeline. On top of that, colleagues can add comments to a note and easily exchange opinions around a single topic. This may be a highly appreciated collaborative function. When Pipedrive is able to add features for teamwork, overcoming the single-user centred approach, sales teams will be able to share contact information and work together on deals management better than today.

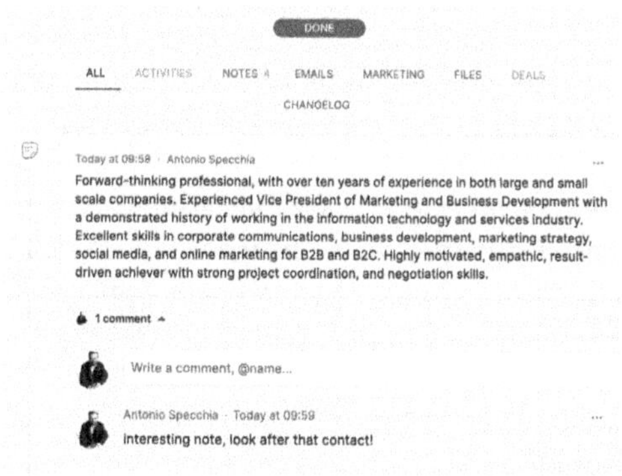

Fig. 4.20.3 Notes in the timeline. A Note accepts comments from anyone in the company. This may be really interesting: instead of adding content by creating new notes, teammates can just add comments in the very same note like a conversation.

Marketing Status

Mailing lists (and, generally, any contacts list) need to record the option of receivers: GDPR rules on privacy introduced this as a mandatory requirement. It implies the need to collect recipients' consensus to receive messages, hence adding this information into CRM is paramount. Some authors consider the rule strictly, some others not so much, but for companies it is better to track the process of consent collection: when and how recipients gave consent.

When Pipedrive introduced Campaigns, it needed the field Marketing Status as a default field.

Be Aware

Marketing Status is set on [No Consent] as a default, users may alter it manually or by automation if they received the consensus elsewhere. Users may be aware that the Double opt-In field strictly controls the marketing status. If a contact is marked UNSUBSCRIBED it is required to be updated by a new request using the Double Opt-in feature. Users have no control on the type of message sent as a request, a standard message which may reduce conversion. This may improve if using custom messages.

Currencies

Pipedrive manages currencies automatically, each deal can have its specific currency. It is great that the conversion rate is set in real time:

> *"Currency conversion in Progress is calculated from the World Bank exchange rate, through our partner Open Exchange Rates. Pipedrive automatically converts the value of deals won in different currencies to your default currency, excluding custom currencies."*
>
> *"Please note that these exchange rate values are for statistical purposes only. The conversion rate shown by Pipedrive may differ from that of you or your customer's banks, so the numbers demonstrated in the Progress tab may not reflect the amount received in your bank account."* [3]

In fact, it helps to figure out, even if not precisely, the value of foreign currencies' deals in your home currency.

---

[3] Pipedrive documentation

Summary

The focus of this chapter is on the logic of CRM in Pipedrive:

What users may find useful to know, what users need to do, and what users are required to do to thrive with positive relationships with prospects:

- How to use tables of data: Leads, Organisation and People.
- How tables work, focusing on subtle features.
- Table-view as well as page-view and related functions.
- Procedures like bulk edit, filter management, import and export data.
- Dataset, default and custom fields

It may be important to recall how Pipedrive is a B2B solution aimed to support human's driven sales processes where the relevance of salespeople matters. The process is not about "*automated data collection*" or "*automated processes*", instead it is about the personal touch and human sensibility of understanding.

The people's capability to figure out real circumstances is crucial in human driven processes. Relying on conduct of processes led by the person's understanding, is the ultimate sense. The CRM supports human work, doesn't substitute it. When processes are machine-driven, we are in the e-commerce domain.

This should be clear even against some author's opinion who credited Pipedrive as 1st CRM for e-commerce businesses. Articles like this point out how little people still know about CRM.
(https://www.yieldify.com/blog/ecommerce-crm-software-tools/)

5 Activities

Tasks Management

Introduction

Activities management, which is at the core of personal productivity, goes beyond the classical time management approach that David Allen depicted in his book: "*There is an inverse relationship between things on your mind and those things getting done*" [4]. In sales, activities to be done take an even greater significance: the relationship between salesperson and customer is fostered by the actions completed with the customer, which often is about decision making. Not only what is completed enables one to meet client's expectations, but also, and less obviously, it shapes the customer expectations. If it happens through a positive experience then it nurtures the relationship with the counterpart, the client.

Here you have one of Pipedrive's best features: enabling users to efficiently take care of customers by making activities easier to perform, more organised and easy to remember. It enables tracking consistency, commitment and results.

In this chapter we will go through:

- A basic overview of the Activity Based Selling methodology
- Tasks manager in Pipedrive
- Create, manage and report activities
- Calendar synchronisation

Let's move into one of the most important features of any CRM, the capability to support customers with more care to provide them with the best possible experience.

Activity-Based Selling methodology

At the very beginning we can clarify what ABS is:

> *Activity-based sales approach implies turning attention from results to actions. Rather than focusing on deals' closure, salespeople may focus on performing the actions that make the sale possible.*

[4] Allen, D., Getting Things Done, Penguin Books

Changing this mindset is the way to improve sales: what's the first idea that comes to our minds connected to the word "sell"?

It may be: "*closing deals*". Though it makes sense, we should shift to consider ***what*** makes it possible.

> Deals closure is often the outcome of a long, complex and graceful process. It rarely happens by shortcutting the process, rushing to the end and assuming clients are solely focused on negotiation - often considered as: persuasion[5]-.

By adopting the activity-based selling methodology and tracking activities performed during time, companies become aware of the real effort each deal may require and, on average, the effective productivity limit of sales teams. Developing this mindset properly enables building of a better workstyle while improving the closure rate at the same time.

Here we have some key points to set the activity-based selling methodology:

- **Mind your goals**. You need to know your goals from the beginning in order to set a specific plan for achieving them, regardless of how counterintuitive it may seem.
- **Focus on your real motivation**. There is something deeper than earning money to pay bills. People who focus on it have a stronger motivation.
- **Record your success**. Look at your actions over time and note when you succeeded. Search for commonalities between your successful schemes and strategies. Your own workflow may provide a lot of insight.
- **Look for references**. It can be beneficial to research some of the most successful sales management techniques, since they can provide excellent references to experiment. Being aware of how other people's techniques may not work for you. In pursuit of improvement, it is important to continue nurturing the actions that proved they already worked for you.
- **Find out your metrics**. You should identify your *Key Performance* Indicators based on your own goals. Track and analyse results. Make your comparisons and analyses easy to use.
- **Set daily tasks**. In order to ensure your goals are realistic, you must

[5] Cialdini, R., The psychology of Persuasion, 1984 (Book removed by its author). To verify a good discussion about the topic, check HBR: https://hbr.org/2013/07/the-uses-and-abuses-of-influence

know if your ambitions are too big and whether you can carry the daily load of steps necessary to achieve them.

- **Visualise the whole frame**. Review those metrics periodically (weekly?). Celebrate each success, then accept the lessons learned, analyse what has been done and work hard to make up for your missed opportunities.
- **Focus on continuous improvement**. Depending on your attitude, you will eventually notice a change in your results: a sign that things are going better than before.

When creating an environment capable of attracting more sales may require time, but a shift will happen. Sometimes entrepreneurs may be a little bit impatient to see the outcome of changes, but being confident with the decision made and persisting with the implementation will bring you to success.

What happens when teams start adopting ABS?

Over time, people become more comfortable in setting tasks in the calendar and sticking to them. At the beginning it may seem odd allocating time for admin, non productive stuff as well as meeting clients. But people will learn about their own habits, methods, use of time and how they nurture productivity.

In order to achieve that stage it is important to plan a proper Kick-Off and training. When a great amount of tasks are set in the calendar, people will understand the benefit of establishing task patterns and follow ups.

Calendar activities management is more effective when it is used for all activities, when shared with the team they become the bigger stones in the pot!

Automating daily tasks enables new tasks, like appointments, to be automatically uploaded in the calendar. Set procedures for creating, updating, and marking activities as done; keep updated calendar availability also shows the use of time.

With Activities Based Selling methodology, people can just proceed task after task, looking after the calendar, hitting milestones and moving to next tasks. This smooths the sales workflow, setting daily amounts of tasks and measuring results related to them.

By tracking activities, salespeople can improve productivity creating greater impact on the bottom line. Measuring performance boosts awareness of their value created by the sales process.

Task Manager

Pipedrive offers a task manager developed with an ABS approach: tasks management is central for sales; Pipedrive smooths the process and makes tasks effective by an intuitive and easy to use tool.

It impacts on productivity: the more effectively people work the more they can achieve, the happier they are. Further offering full control over tasks, easily relating tasks to people, deals and companies enables direct tracking against opportunities along the sales process.

Type of activities

Initial settings your own activities type will help to select different activities and report on them accurately. The default list is pretty fine, each company should set different activities to better match what the sales team really does. In Fig. 5.1 we can see the dialogue window to set tasks type in Company Settings.

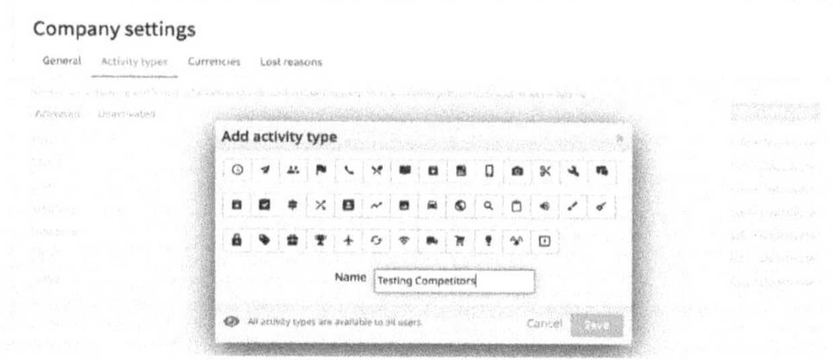

Fig. 5.1 - Creating a new type of tasks

Creating activities

Creating activities automatically strongly helps working smarter. In chapter 8 we will see the Workflow Automation for tasks setting by trigger on event. First, let's proceed in managing tasks manually, which helps in clarifying the logic. In Fig. 5.2 a deal's page-view and its dialogue window to set an activity.

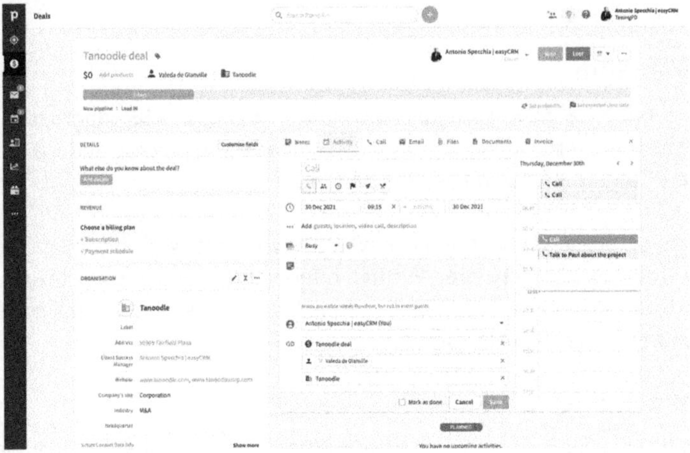

Figure 5.2 - Creating a task from the deal's page

When created inside the deal page-view tasks are automatically related to the person, the organisation and the deal. Each activity's title should be clear: if the title is set automatically, it will be the activity type: "*Call*" will appear on the calendar but nobody will know who or why.

> Better time management suggests titles like: "*Call Paul Tweddle about his boss' preference*".

Pipedrive may appear a bit too simple, enabling users to create tasks with little or no information. Developing a habit of showing essential information about tasks in the calendar will improve time management. Defining tasks required and sticking with them improves performance and tasks reporting.

> Often users incur this very mistake: creating activities to manage them in isolation: when created outside the deal page-view, activities don't relate automatically and they don't bother to relate them to the right counterpart.

Someone used to add too much information in the title like company, name, phone number... Missing the advanced features of CRM that Pipedrive well supports, creates a messy and dull tasks management, and frustrates the reporting.

In the sales process, activities are always done against a deal, a person and their organisation (B2B). If the activity is not related to them, it is not an activity that belongs to the sales process. If so, it probably shouldn't be listed in Pipedrive activities.

For instance, in project management the activities are also related to the deal/ person/organisation, but they are not included in the sales process, they are part of the service creation process.

In micro-business the solopreneurs are involved both in the sales process and in the service creation process. In that case it would be beneficial to run sales process activities in one tool, while the other tool serves to run the project management.

> It is more than just a separation of tasks: keep separate each process improves focusing. When you run sales, just do that, when you are developing the service for a client, just focus on it.

Setting activities in the right way from their creation is a good way to learn how to benefit from the Pipedrive's Tasks manager. Users may find it beneficial to change their habits for the better. Pipedrive offers the opportunity to improve the procedures, enhancing efficiency.

Tasks manager table-view

The tasks manager in table-view offers many features as described in chapter 4 about tables, and some new ones: first, it shows fields from all the three main tables: People, Organisations and Deals. Hence activities may be listed and selected by more parameters included on the other tables.

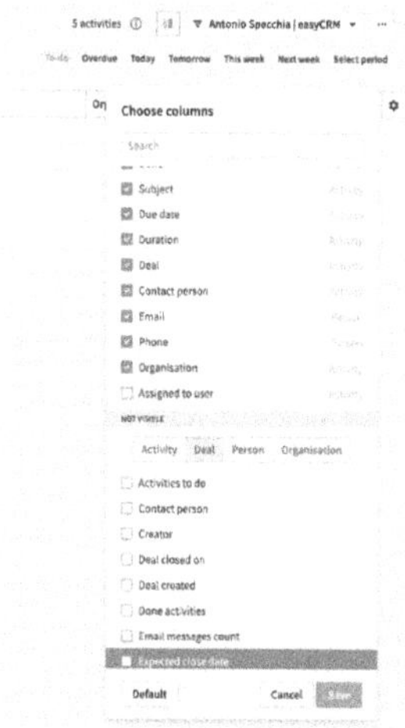

Fig. 5.3 - Activities tables may include all fields from other tables

Some filters are predefined for an immediate selection: In Fig. 5.3 we can see flags with selection activated. The names without a blue background are not active.

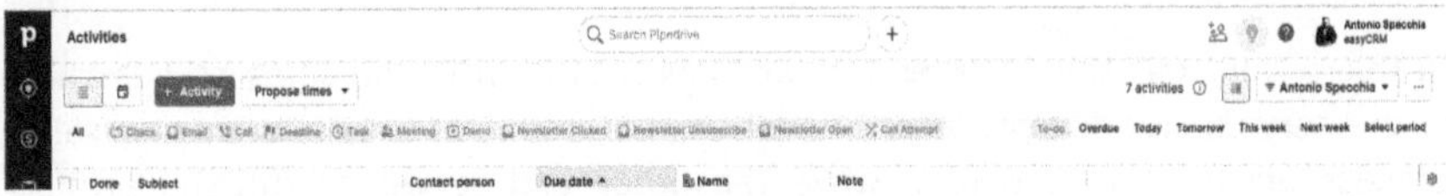

Fig. 5.4 Some filters for selecting activities on the top of the page.

Selecting activities may enable the features to send group emails. (Fig. 5.4) - the purpose of this function is not completely clear. An example may be the urgent need to inform all the counterparts to whom you have to see in meetings in the next 2 weeks that you have got Covid and you won't be available for meetings. Or maybe some users may find it useful for their own specific purposes.

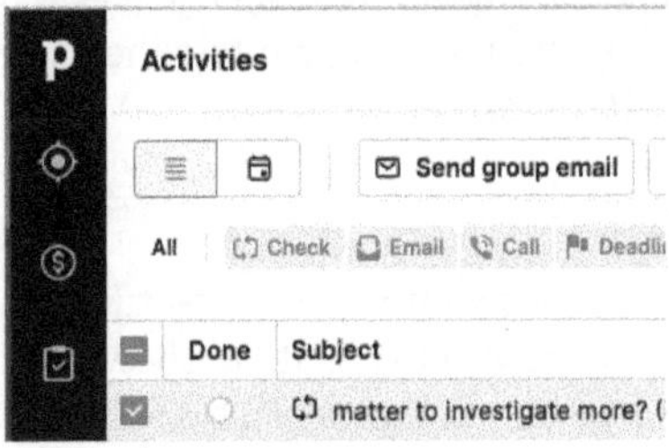

Fig 5.5 Send group email: to activities counterparts.

Table-view with ....window!

An interesting feature Pipedrive introduced in 2022 is the view of tasks by window over table-view. (Fig. 5.6)

This operational view enables salespeople to stay in table-view and open each task in a window and perform it. Once done, passing to the next task is intuitive. In the circle the control to move between activities or close the window [X].

The table with window is great to run activities management on the fly: start from the first and perform each one of the list from the top to the bottom. Better to stick with just today's list! This is why filtering with the **Today** filter (fig. 5.4) segregates today's activities and lists them in one view.

Note

Pipedrive could fix the [Mark it as done] flag. The intention is clear: user flag (clicking it), then save the activity (by clicking on the [green button]), this marks this activity as DONE and closes it. -It may be debatable whether it is intuitive to request clicking twice-. One single button to perform DONE is available in table view (see column Done), then add one in the page-view or in window-view would make it clearer.

In the "Table with window" view, users can take control of a long list of activities.

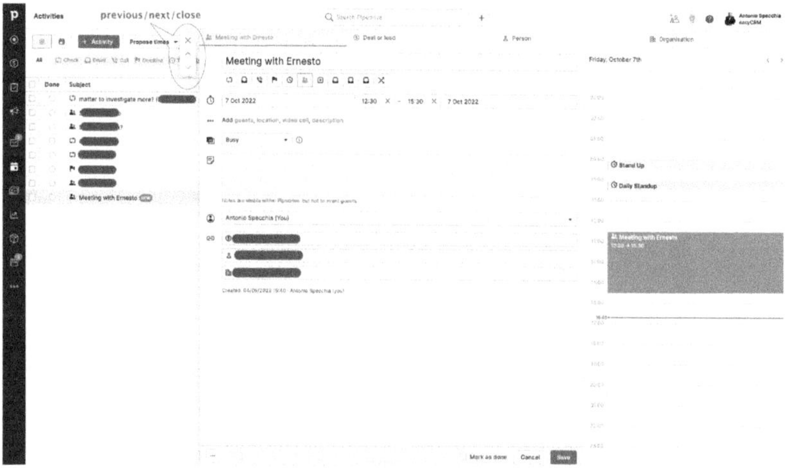

Fig. 5.6 Table-view with window.

Control of the Table with window view is set on the top right of the screen, nearby user' name.

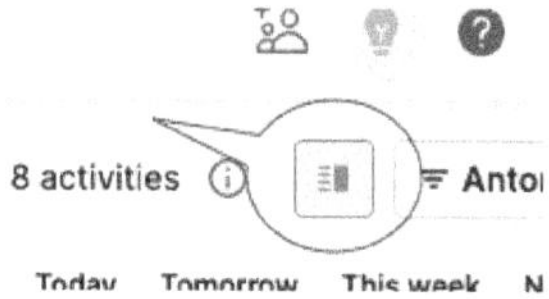

Fig 5.7 the icon for set the table-view with window

Calendars management

The task management system, natively synced with calendars, is the tool to perform Activity Based Selling.

Calendars that users can sync are Google and Outlook. Using a calendar in all devices, enables to keep at hand all tasks and meetings info. Users may even rely only on the Pipedrive calendar. Creating a calendar account with Google would make it more efficient when exchanging meeting invitations. Be aware that setting a calendar with your own email address in Google may be a good solution enabling two ways sync. Pipedrive calendar limits the ability to sync only one calendar, while taking control of more calendars enables users to dedicate each calendar for a purpose they may need.

> Managing more calendars is recommended: users can keep separated different businesses, as well as private and work life activities.

Pipedrive creates a task from a calendar input: creating an event in the calendar will add it as a task in Pipedrive (two way sync). Be aware that in this case you may miss the relationship with counterpart, organisation and deal. Something that may impact the reporting quality.

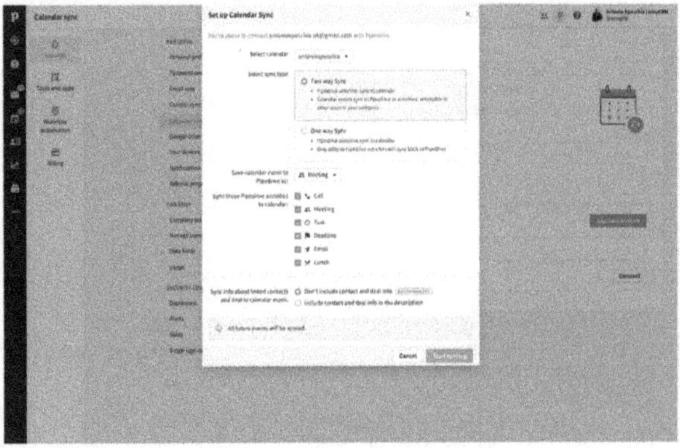

Fig. 5.8 - Set Up Calendar sync in Personal Preferences

Pipedrive's calendar works fine and one of its most beautiful features is called **Propose Times**.

This feature has two interesting functions:

- General Availability
- Specific Times

Setting the **General availability** users may create their own available time for the standard week, day by day and store it in Propose Time for different purposes.

Sharing one of the different types or availability in an email message enables the recipient to autonomously book a meeting by selecting a slot among any available hours. Slot already allocated won't be visible and recipients won't be able to book any slots that may include the time already assigned.

The **Pick times** is a different function, even more interesting: users may select manually a number of time slots among their own available slots then share a link that only shows those selected time slots. Recipients can only pick up one of them.

While the first feature is very much similar to Calendly, the "Pick Times" one is quite improved: it requires a bit of manual work every time we would like to communicate with someone, having to create the correct selection manually every time.

As a great benefit it enables users to take account also of other calendars not sync, or slots allocated as possibilities but not yet in the calendar.

Two suggestions about tasks:

- **Always set the start/end time for each activity**. General Availability relies on the real time data on your calendar, allocating more precise slots improves productivity.
- **Always mark as done every activity**. Managing workload by tracking accomplishments enables reporting about time allocation correctly, leaving tasks not done shows lack of management.

In Fig 5.8.1 and 5.8.2 show the Propose times function in the activities manager and its availability in the email client.

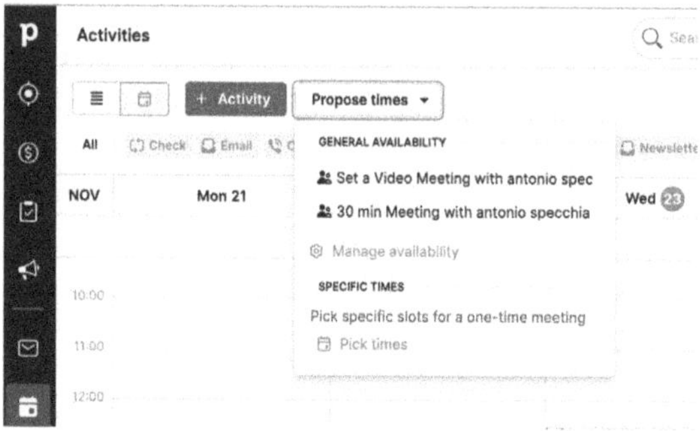

Fig 5.8.1. Set General Availability and Specific Times from calendar view (also possible in list view)

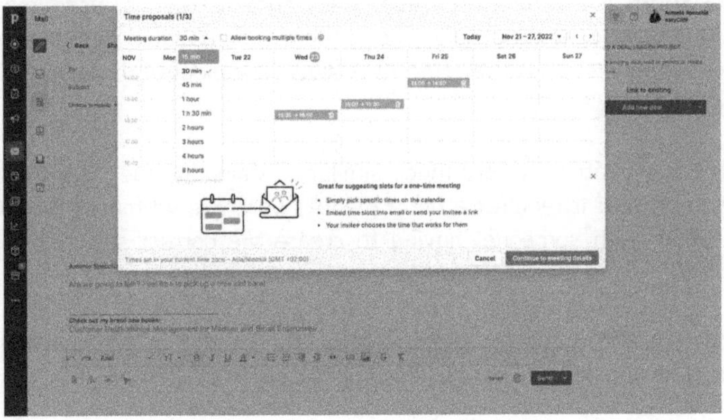

Fig 5.8.2 Creating a Pick times selection in the email client ready to be included in the message.

Create filtering of activities

The activities table-view is ready to generate selections likewise the people and organisations tables. Refer to chapter 4 on how to filter to create audiences.

This feature may be useful to segregate some types of activities or the ones performed in a certain period of time or even due into a specific period, the ones that belong to a user or have certain counterparts... The possibilities are many!

This feature does not affect reporting of activity that may be run in Insights, but may be useful to check, for instance, the effort applied to a specific deal or client for a given period of time.

Summary

We went through the logic of task management, as the effectiveness of the sales process relies on the tasks done.

- Recall of Activity Based Selling methodology
- Task manager
- Type of activities
- Creating activities
- Manage calendar
- Grouping activities analysis

6 DEALS- Managing Opportunities

Introduction

This chapter covers one of the paramount CRM features in running the sales process within a digital CRM. Pipedrive has achieved dramatic improvements in this area, well ahead and beyond many existing tools. Pipedrive focused on making the opportunities management smooth, effective, and intuitive.

In the CRM jargon, business opportunities are called Deals. A term that may be difficult to translate into other languages: in Italian for instance, deals has been translated with AFFARE, which does not really convey the prospective possibility. OPPORTUNITÁ (opportunity) might work better, and it would focus on a dynamic concept of something worth pursuing. In English DEAL is shorter, immediate and simpler to grab, something that English speakers appreciate a lot -even if it may be confusing as the word gets 6 meanings as a verb and 5 as a noun.

> Pipedrive users should have it clear: "...Deals are possibilities, opportunities ... to handle, to manage, to look after, to explore, to investigate... (*Oxford Dictionary*).

In this context, defining opportunities in a clearer way is of paramount importance, since they provide insight into the information that has to be handled.

This chapter will cover the following topics:

- What a deal is
- Data and information carried on a deal
- Working on deals one by one
- Working on deals in bulk
- Setting for the sales process

Let's examine how a digital entity "deal" is defined and managed in Pipedrive.

Opportunities or deals

Previously we discussed the entity **Lead**, which is a contact whose relevance has not yet been determined. Leads will become contact persons when they will be identified then qualified as MQLs. Once qualified as "possible Opportunities" it makes sense that the sales team establish a contact.

A MQL may not be in the position of actively searching for a solution that means to be ready for buying straight away. But it may be important to establish a relationship with all the MQL: understanding their specific situation, collecting information, helping them, nurturing the connection and making it possible for an opportunity to arise later on.

Companies with short sales processes, or a short term view, may be pressured to pursue only ready opportunities, neglecting the MQL nurturing effort. Long term view may suggest to put in place a stage for MQLs before entering them in the sales process, a relationship management stage that will pay off much later.

If they are actively looking for a solution they can be defined as **Prospects** and a **Deal** is (virtually) opened against them:

Deals are opportunities that we may pursue with a contact person on behalf of their company.

Let's see how Pipedrive enables deals management, first a paramount ability is to successfully grasp a useful overview of:

1. The company
2. The person(s)
3. Their situation
4. The expectations

The system is designed to enable users to develop information rendering into concise overviews capable of providing reliable data to decision makers.

Deal management is one of the most complex and crucial parts of a CRM for B2B, when well developed it is capable of enhancing the sales process effectiveness. And this sets Pipedrive apart from other digital tools.

Highly valuable platforms are quite complex to customise, implying relevant investments. Design a sales process management may be a complex team work: A multidisciplinary team should analyse the business case to design all the features required to be run by the digital CRM.

Pipedrive, with its focus on sales management, reduces the effort in designing features for sales process management.

A "digital representation" of a deal must include the following features:

- Gather **relevant** information

    - Focus on the information critical to close the deal.
- Enable salespeople to see the **big picture at a glance**.
    - Offer full scope of the entire sales process.
- Show the **history** with the contact persons related to the deal.
    - Track interactions, documents, information shared along the relationship and intuitively ease users to retrieve them at any time.
- Each stage should be set in light of the **circumstances**.
    - Each sales process stage should be unique and useful.
- Provide reliable data for **Reporting & Forecasting**.
    - Reliable data are properly collected by motivated and happy operators.
- Make sure to develop an accurate **valuation**, to have a good hypothesis of the **closing date** and to appraise the **probability of closing**.
    - Pipedrive empowers salespeople's control to proceed correctly and stay committed embracing more effective behaviours.
- Enabling sales people with **task management capabilities** to effectively carry out any action required.
    - With Activities Based Selling Methodology Pipedrive focuses on the mission of developing a tool to change salespeople's work style.

Proceeding we will see the basics of the deal as a digital entity as well as settings and features that will be applied to the sales process.

Deals formation

The process of creating deals when an opportunity arises may be a repetitive job for salespersons in B2B. Deals only exist inside a B2B sales process, their management is facilitated by the visual pipeline, which is the virtual rendering of the sales process itself. In the following chapter we will see the pipeline management, here we just focus on the deal entity.

How deals may be created:

- Deals can be set manually by users at any time.
    - Just digit period [.] on the keyboard from any view.
    - Creating a deal from a contact person page or an organisation page by hitting the green button
- Using Pipedrive's email client, deals can be created instantly from inside email messages if they are related to opportunities.

- Leads can be converted into Deals with the green button when they get qualified (MQL).
- Automation of workflow can create deals when triggered by an event.
- Deals can be created from another software application, which simply pushes the deals data into Pipedrive via API.

In Fig. 6.1 the mail view and its option to instantly create a contact person a Lead or a Deal

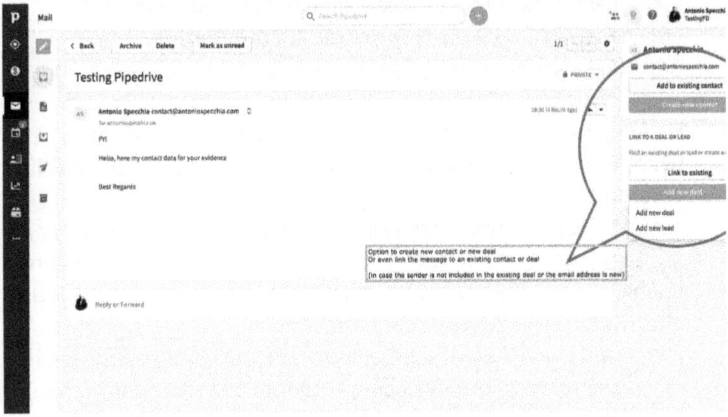

Fig. 6.1 - Mail view and deal creation function. Create a new deal or link to an existing one if the message arrives from a different email or person not yet included in the deal.

Let now look at the more efficient method to create deals in Pipedrive: from email messages

Deal creation from email message

Users who receive an email message from a person not listed in the CRM may create a deal by clicking the green button on the right. They create three new entities avoiding copying and pasting data.

We have four possibilities:

1. The contact person is not in the Pipedrive database
2. This email address is new for the person and/or not yet related to an that person in your Pipedrive database
3. The contact person is in your Pipedrive database but
    a. there are no deals open against them
    b. is not connected to an already existing deal

Here is how each case are managed within Pipedrive:

1. First option: the green button [**Add New Deal**] makes life easy, Pipedrive uploads the person's data creating three new entities, contact person, organisation and related deal.
2. Second case: If the user recognises the sender as a person already in the database but the message arrives from a different email address as Pipedrive shows if they exist (see Fig 6.1.1), the user can relate this message to the existing contact. Here the process simply explained:
   a. The white box is a cell: [**Add to existing contact**] when users click over it becomes a field box.
   b. Start writing the name of an existing contact person and Pipedrive suggests all people with that name or similar.
   c. Choosing the right person (checking the main information) connects the email address and the message thread to the person page-view.
3. Third case: The person is in the database and users may want to create a deal against that contact. The green button [**Add New Deal**] enables users to create a new deal directly. (Fig. 6.1.2).
4. Fourth case: This contact person is not related to an existing deal but for some reason the salesperson who received the email believes that it is worth adding this message thread to an existing deal. [**Link to Existing**] perform this, from this moment on all messages in the thread will be available in the Deal's page view.

Be aware

Users may decide to create a LEAD instead. An option may be worth exploring if the leads management is performed by a specific team in charge to qualify leads before input them in the sales process creating a Deal.
Both leads and deals include linked entities: the contact person and the company. The green button [**Add New Deal**] splits into two options: [**Add new deal**] and [**Add new lead**]. Pipedrive fills up the dialogue box that shows up with available data, users may add more information to contextualise the lead or the deal.

Fig 6.1.1 The dialogue-box that shows whether the contact person exists and what company they are related to.

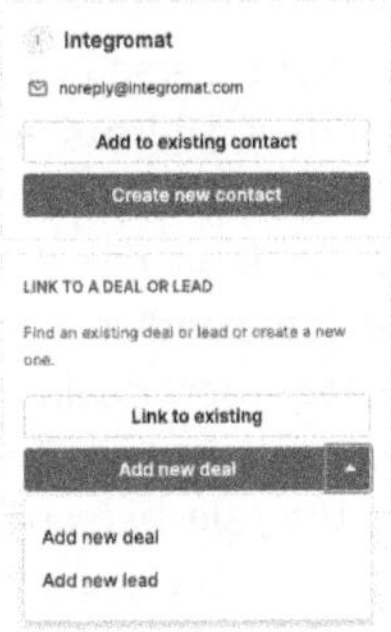

Fig 6.1.2 The dialogue-box' green button to add new deal/lead

Anyone who is used to spending time copying and pasting data will appreciate this feature.

Fig. 6.2 shows the dialogue box of the procedure of adding a deal, it shows how Pipedrive gets the main data automatically.

Fig. 6.2 - Starting a deal with all the possible options

Deal name

Pipedrive creates the Deal's name automatically, based on company's name adding the word - DEAL -

We suggest that you name deals in a more effective manner whenever possible including, for instance, the subject of the deal: what the deal is about - a service, a solution, a product...

Likewise for projects where the project's title matters, in sales if your company provides different products/services, deals' title will enable everyone to grasp immediately what the deal is about. But even better to create clusters, selection of deals related to the same product/service; then setting focused views of the sales process related to a particular selection of products/services.

Deals in company's processes

Deals are virtual entities that each company has to design for their own business needs. Setting what data each deal should include to enable salespeople to efficiently accomplish the miracle to bring it to success.

In Pipedrive the data set of deals is largely customisable, each company can set a vast number of fields to boost the informative power that digital deals should provide to the real world of sales.

We will see in detail later in Chapter 16: Data Architecture, now we just consider the possibility to add virtually any field[6] in the database in any of its tables to grasp the correct, necessary data to run the sales process.

Considering it, Pipedrive introduced a feature to control which field has to be shown in the "*Add deal*" view, and which fields should be always visible in the deal page-view. This is clearly a matter of the business processes requirements, the design of fields' visibility is also part of the implementation and its reason resides on the Less is More approach: showing all fields when adding an entity (deals or contact person) may be confusing and not efficient.

> Everytime when creating a deal, users will be able to fill in data fields according to business needs.
> Then they decide what stage and what pipeline -sales process- the new deal belongs to.

6 Verify each subscription for details

Some data may be relevant:

- its value
- the date of (possible) closing
- grades of probability
- anything relevant for the specific stage of the pipeline

Working with deals data

Many functions available for the People and Organisations tables are also available in deal table-view, including bulk editing.

Deals Table-views, likewise activities tables, can display fields from other tables to give a complete picture of the most relevant data. If you need to operate alteration on a number of deals, you just select a selection of records and operate on the appearing dialogue-box on the right the alteration you need.

Likewise other tables, users may only modify the fields that belong to the open table, in this case the deals table.

The deal table-view is available in the pipeline section. Users may switch views by the three icons on the top left corner of the screen.

They are:

- Pipeline view
- Table view
- Timeline view

Once in Table-view select fields visibility (columns) as in Fig. 6.3. Keeping only relevant fields for the purpose of the view then save the view as filter (query).

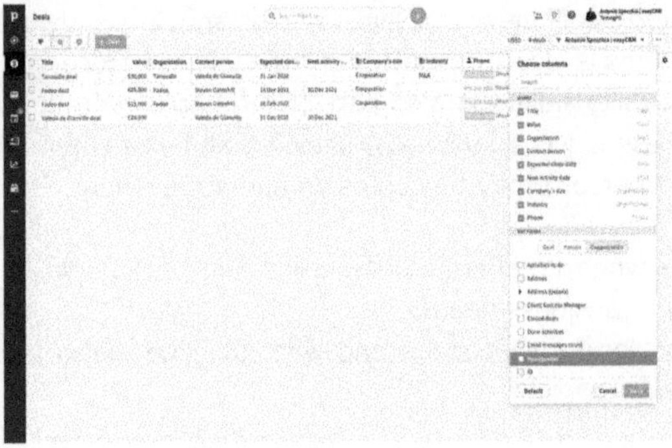

Fig. 6.3 - Deals table-view with data display options

In deals Table-view users may select records enabling some options:

- Bulk editing, each table field may be altered in bulk
- Sending group email, (up to 100) using email template or free message
- Convert them to Leads, generally a less useful feature
- Delete all selected deals, if you really want...

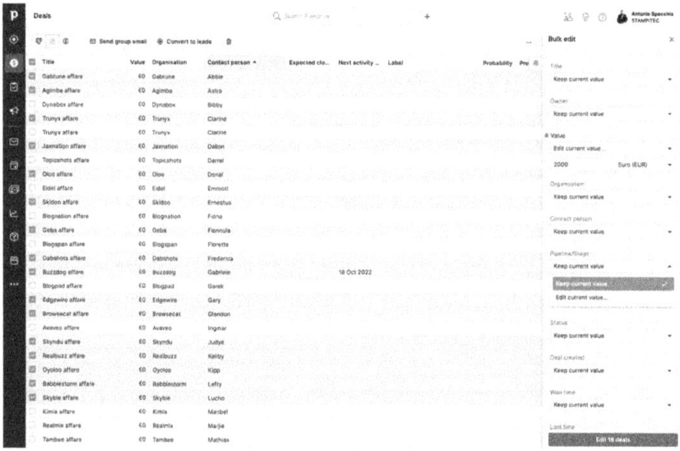

Fig. 6.3.1 Table-view selection. Once starting selecting deals (all or a portion of them) the BULK EDIT dialogue window appears on the right.

Note

All views imply a default selection of entities that belong to the active user. Often new users can't find anything, so changing the default selection to select Everyone ensures every user has access to the data.

Be aware

Setting specific selections of deals is essential for businesses to segregate the group where they need to operate. Users may create groups based on as many parameters as they need. This is a useful feature when it comes to:

- market analysis
- managing homogeneous groups of prospects
- checking how performing activities affect trends
- manage communication with prospects using Campaign

As we will see in the next chapter, this may be relevant for a more effective sales process management.

Deal's page-view

The deal's page-view maintains the same structure of both the person and the organisation page-views. This boosts familiarity with the views and the screen setting, providing a better user experience.

In this page-view, users will see elements associated with the Deal:

- All data of the opportunity: products, services, values
- Counterpart person data
- Organisation (client) data
- Deals history
- Deals journey timing
- Expected closure date
- Probability of a positive closure
-
- Every selected integration with specialised software: for instance Docusign control panel to manage creation, sharing and storing of electronically signed documents.

- The history of communication with any contact person related to the deal, as well as any thread of messages added (with the possibility to unlink them)
- A timeline including changelog data of:
    - ◇ Activities
    - ◇ Notes
    - ◇ Emails
    - ◇ Documents exchanged
    - ◇ Phone calls made
    - ◇ Invoices issued

- Commands to perform any action on the deal like change of status, change of stage, change of visibility group, ownerships ...
- Page-view enables access to all the data fields to work on them

- Same settings possibilities as described earlier for other page-views like settings the left side data column to focus on specific control boxes and their functions

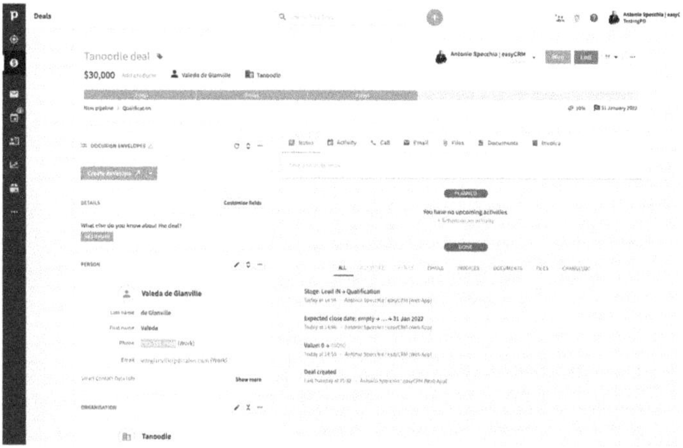

Fig 6.4 - The deal page-view. On first glance, it is similar to other pages: it allows for greater familiarity with the layout and allows for quicker learning.

As readers may appreciate, although the page layout is clean and bright - a certain degree of layout customisation is still possible. While not truly flexible, this approach prevents users' unexpected alterations from cluttering the view. Avoiding user interface customisation provides a predefined optimisation that makes the system easy to learn.

Control boxes

A series of boxes are placed in the data column (left side) related to each feature or function in use. Integrations with other software solutions, as well as the data related to the deal and each related entity, person and company are placed in dedicated boxes:

Please Fill

When important fields are in place, a dialogue window appears so that the users are reminded to fill in those data fields without stopping them in their tracks, -mandatory fields block the proceeding creating a workflow issue-.

If required fields are in place after the notice in the Please Fill box, and users try to proceed moving the deal to the next stage, Pipedrive will block it with another dialogue window.

Revenue

When payments are agreed on delay or the service goes under subscription, users may fill in dates and values useful to be shown in revenue forecasting and revenue cash-flow reports.

Participants

Anyone involved in the deal on the counterpart as company's employee or external agents can be included here. This functionality enables tracking communication with everyone listed as a participant in a specific deal.

Followers

Anyone involved in deal management on your own company's side. This includes colleagues and managers who are involved to follow the deal's progress. Any activity or action related to the transaction will be notified to those people.

Invoicing

When Pipedrive is connected to other software like Quickbooks or Xero, this box allows users to create invoices straight from Pipedrive and keep an overview of the invoice history with the client.

Integration panels

In this area will be located all the boxes managed by vendors that provide solutions integrated in Pipedrive. Users can perform several actions in those boxes, controlling the integration setting as well as their subscription to those services.

Details box

Deals data fields are shown when filled (less is more) it contains all fields of the specific deals table.

Person box

All person's data field, hidden if empty. The Smart Contact Data is not working (mock data wouldn't work), but in case of Pro subscription and real person data, Smart Contact Data will empower a view of the subject. If the person is known by Pipedrive and they added a picture it will be included in the box.

Organisation box

Same as before. To get at hand the major information about the company (the client) as the deal counterpart.

Setting the sequence of boxes is simple and effective, using the 3 dots option in the page-view (Fig. 6.4.2) where some controls also take place.

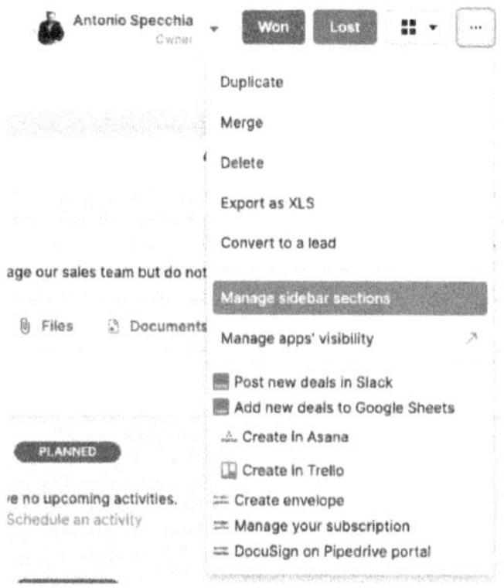

Fig 6.4.2 The control of the page-view panels list starts here: Manage Sidebar Section.

The list of control-panels or boxes may be reshaped and panels can be hidden by deselecting them (fig 6.4.3).

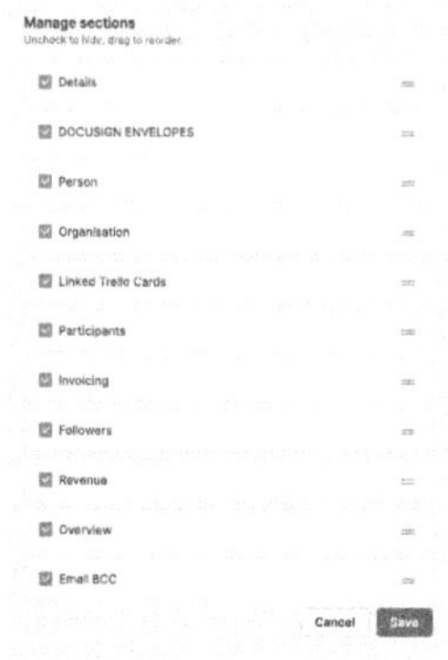

Fig 6.4.3 The setting of control panels sequence on the boxes column of Page-view.

Fig. 6.6, shows the deal Page-view and its data column. The {Customise Fields} option enables editing each field as well as creating new fields. Each entity panel, either a person or an organisation, enables switching to another entity or unlink it.

Fig. 6.6 - Deal's Page-view and the data column boxes to be organised.

Deal's fields manager

Deals details are stored in data fields. They contain basic information elements, listed and operated together to develop the purpose of the database: information shaping.

Each company requires a set of common data to collect, upon that basic index each business requires to add specific data-fields to store data business-specific.

In Pipedrive it is very simple to set up new fields, sometimes it may be considered even too simple! In fact users may risk creating way too many fields in lack of a proper plan. As a result, the effective locations of data may become ambiguous, and shaping reliable information may become harder.

Be aware

Sales processes may be effectively run with a limited amount of data. When data fields are too many, it affects data reliability.

Data-fields may be considered like Lego's bricks (fig. 6.4.4): they are connected to each other forming a shape.

The shape is the information, more meaningful than its bunch of data.

In this context, a professional design of the Data Architecture (chapter 16) may enable optimisation of the dataset to make it more useful and efficient for the specific sales process.

In Fig 6.5 the data-fields manager where Admins and Managers permission users may control the dataset.

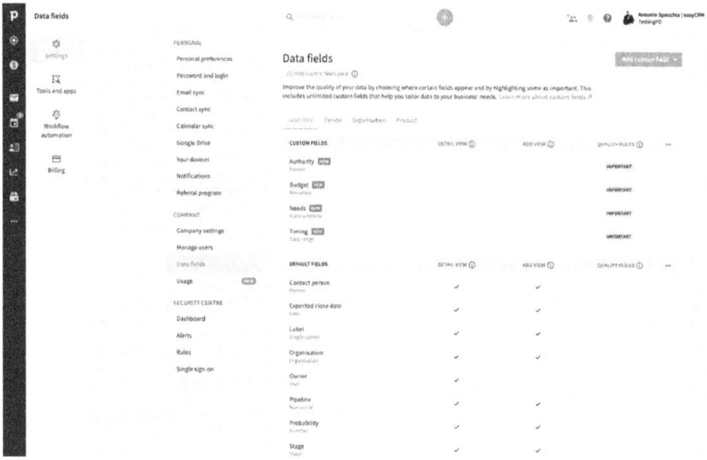

Fig. 6.5 - Data fields management window enables adding and editing fields, and locating each field API token.

When adding fields you may want your salespeople to use them. Some organisations use Mandatory Fields to force their salespeople to fill in them. By using the Important Fields, you nudge them that these data are essential to running the sales process.

> Since the beginning of Pipedrive the function "Important Field" was used instead of "Mandatory Field". Sadly, the market habit prevailed over the original idea that no field should be mandatory because no action should be imposed on anyone. The concept of educating salespeople by focusing their attention positively to something useful rather than coercing them to do something was, unfortunately, too good to last.

On a personal level we stuck with the idea that making a field mandatory might result in unuseful data being inserted. If lacking the correct information with the need to proceed forward, a salesperson can, with the positive intention of returning to it in the future, just add something randomly.

This happens quite often and most of the time gets unnoticed then later forgotten with the result that salespeople keep storing wrong data producing unreliable information and bad reporting later on.

As shown in Fig. 6.5, you can see that each entity table leads/deals, people, organisations and products have a set of data fields. Obviously, different datasets will yield different insights since different data will be collected.

Note

The system doesn't enable different data architecture / dataset for different pipelines. This feature has been announced for 2023, it should enable fields related to a pipeline, so they will be element of a specific sales process. If your company runs different businesses, or different markets with the same products/services, and needs different datasets by each market, today it may result in multiple data fields, but next year you may be able to fix this issue.

Summary

In this chapter, we delved into the heart of Pipedrive as well as the logic of CRM. An area which is the core value of the tool, designed and developed around the idea of improving sales process management and salespeople work at same time.

We went into this these topics:

- Deals in CRM, what are those "digital entities"?
- How to create deals
- Managing deals in Pipedrive Table-view and Page-view
- Bulk alteration of data
- What the main elements of a deal are

7 Sales Pipeline: the Sales Process Made Visual

Introduction

Pipedrive became popular mainly because of its approach on the sales process management using virtual pipelines: the **visual Kanban of the sales stages** gives a quick overview of the whole sales process.

In this chapter we will analyse it in detail so that the readers will learn how to set it up, how to use it to improve control over the sales management and then, boost efficiency in sales.

This chapter may also help as a guideline for the sales processes design: everyone will translate it into rules and methods that fit their own business. Using a perspective to enhance the sales process comprehension by mirroring it in the CRM to, ultimately, boost sales performance.

We will cover the following topics:

- About Sales Process management with Visual Pipeline
- Designing Visual Pipelines
- Pipelines setting
- Design a sales process in B2B
- Pipelines analysis

It is expected that readers will develop a clear understanding of the logic of sales process management with Pipedrive.

Be Aware

It may be helpful to depict the sales process more like a journey that needs to be performed together, the salesperson and the prospect.
This clarifies the relevance of the person on the other side of the table, the person you will be working with: the client.

Sales Process Management by Visual Pipeline

Pipedrive is a sales process management CRM. This must be very clear, as it implies that organisations with a clear understanding of their own sales processes will be able to extract real value from the tool. If the company lacks clear perception, it may be more complex to benefit from a CRM in general, not just Pipedrive. Often companies launch their CRM implementation projects without performing a proper analysis and it results in mismatch between tool performance and expectations.

Too often, when required to describe how sales take place, sales managers may begin stuttering, showing that they didn't consider sales as a repeatable process. The true story is that very often small, but also medium sized organisations, are not fully prepared to look at their sales as a process.

> The good news is that everyone can, or should, develop awareness over the sales process framework to improve effectiveness and boost the business' growth no matter the CRM or the solution they are going to adopt.

Another very good news is that this book can help in this purpose: providing readers with a comprehensive set of tools to understand how to slice and dice a sales process enabling companies to develop a clearer understanding of their own methods of selling.

The Process(es)

In B2C the petty transactional value suggests considering sales processes by purchasing archetypes, generally with little or no personal interaction. In B2B the transactions can be critical and highly valuable that results in a long and complex process.

B2B is a process that is a game for two, where the sales consultant engages with the client. The focus on B2B that strongly denotes Pipedrive implies the ability to support and facilitate the management of these very types of processes that take place in B2B.

Generally speaking it may be difficult for an organisation to define how sales take place. There is always clarity on the reason why: there are people out there in need of a solution. Then we should describe a repeatable process that conducts to sales: what should happen to provide enough support along the decision making process that the client is executing?

We can start to generalise more common processes by describing:

- Stages
- Activities
- Timing
- Defining information to exchange
- Setting milestones of the journey

- Clarify outcomes and their effects

We will explore each of these elements in more detail as we progress throughout the book.

When they are approaching a sales process management CRM like Pipedrive, organisations should be led into a deeper inspection, to develop their own know-how, with the direct effect of enhancing the organisational culture.

In fact, Pipedrive's sales pipeline offers the great opportunity to start thinking about each type of sales as a process developed by stages. And considering how many different sales processes may be needed by a company. It may lead in slice and dice elements of each process that matter for the results, and design each process rendering with a specific pipeline.

Clearly, salespeople can't make prospects buy, what they can do is to perform the best they can along the moment of truth of sales service. Doing this they may enhance the possibility to influence the prospect positively.

It is still unknown if the prospect will consider the solution presented as the best compromise for their needs, but without a perfectly balanced process of support to their decision making, it is more likely they will choose a different solution instead.

The Visual Pipeline

Pipedrive is the first CRM developed over a **visual pipeline**. The innovation introduced by Timo Rein and his partners is recognised as one of the most relevant innovations in CRM. The idea of creating an overview of the whole sales process and all deals from a single view was as simple as powerful, which explains why Pipedrive has been successful.

When the sales process is long and complex it can be easy to lose control over every single deal. When many opportunities are up in the air, with sales people juggling tasks, people and numbers, some balls can fall. Sometimes the counterpart comes back knocking the door to buy, but nobody can rely on that as a stable, repeatable process. Usually when this does not occur, the results are missing deals.

A well-designed CRM may make the difference. Pipedrive's visual pipeline facilitates control over deals in any stage of the sales process. The view includes warnings and signals about each deal's situation making it easy to notice when a deal is stuck unmanaged and some action is needed.

Sales CRMs should be able to support sales processes boosting efficiency: closing more deals because of a better process.

Designing Visual Pipelines

Pipedrive's sales pipeline's purpose is to mirror the sales processes inside the digital CRM. This enables a stronger sales management facilitated by the tool. It may dramatically enhance the tracking and reporting along the sales process while empowering salespeople in running daily duties more efficiently.

But the real challenge is: how to design a visual pipeline that works over a specific sales process? Let's analyse this.

The elements of designing become obvious when you are familiar with design thinking:

- Keep it simple
- Few, meaningful, clear stages
- A stage is a timeframe to perform specific activities, not a shelf
- Keep the pipeline connected to the process
- One pipeline for each sales process
- A sales process is a unique sequence of steps
- What matters is the outcome no how many steps
- Stages should come naturally, not implying more admin tasks
- Keep the focus on the client
- Clarify which actions the client expects to be performed to support decision making

Simplicity is powerful. Sales might be complex to achieve, this is why we must simplify everything around it. Organise essential information to easily grasp them at a glance, create and manage tasks easily, update data in real time, automate repeated tasks.

Service is the priority, neither the sales nor the admin.

When the sales process is designed by few, effective, meaningful stages it implies actions and outcomes. Each deal implies someone with whom we walk together along the journey, building a relationship, creating value with. The essence of the sales process is to escort clients in their journey to discover what is good for them, how can we better help them (than everyone else) and, ultimately, how they can better solve their problem.

About pipeline(s)

The first concept to clarify is when would it be good to set up one pipeline or more pipelines. Often users tend to set multiple pipelines to show different perspectives of the business.

For instance:

- one pipeline for each market
- different products involve different pipelines
- ...

Well, this is mainly wrong and can be set much more efficiently.

Let's analyse it:

Same sales process, different products and/or different markets
= one pipeline

Different sales processes, same products and/or markets
= different pipelines

What matters is the process and how it spreads in stages and activities, milestones and outputs, not the objects of the process. Essentially better to keep the same pipeline even when the product or the market change, but the sales process is designed the same.

On the other hand it is mandatory to create specific pipelines when sales processes differ even for the same product / market.

The reason should be clear: each sales process is made of different stages, different tasks to perform. One single product/service can be sold to different types of clients who rely on different processes to buy it. So, the pipeline that mirrors the sales process will be unique.

What is the pipeline really?

As the pipeline is the visual rendering of a sales process, then we wonder:

- What happens in real life when you meet a prospect?
- What does the person expect you to do, to help them in solving their problem?

Answering these questions enables us to describe the business' sales process in terms of stages to pass through and actions to perform.

- Meet a prospect (to investigate their needs) = is a stage which includes an activity.

A stage is a time frame where activities take place.

It is just another way to see sales: the pipeline represents a series of actions within a certain timing.

A great outcome is that managers who get confident with this method, become more likely to delegate the control of the flow to salespeople.

Pipelines settings: beyond just the 'default' option

Now is the time to master the rules before breaking them.

Let's have a look at Pipedrive's default pipeline: in fig. 7.1 readers will notice the elements of the main operational area, the Kanban view with the sales stages of the pipeline.

Fig. 7.1 - Pipedrive's default visual pipeline

The default visual pipeline is the view over the inventory of deals that sit in the process at a certain moment. The visual pipeline, which is a real-time view, may also show lots of subtle trends. Today the concept of Kanban is more common, so that readers can immediately see the benefit of a Kanban view to group entities.

How to set more meaningful stages

The secret is to describe what really happens in a real sales process with prospects in front of us. Users may set stages as they take place in real-life, not just adopt the default template as it is. Even if you are unfamiliar with the structure, please take the template as a guide.

From fig. 7.1 readers can recall the following stages:

- Qualified

- Contact made
- Demo scheduled
- Proposal made
- Negotiation

Let's start with the third stage: **Demo Scheduled**, not every business provides a **Demo**. And **Proposal Made** is certainly a parking place, as well as **Contact Made**, not much different it is **Qualified**. While **Negotiation** involves a two-way activity that should begin once the proposal is received by the prospect.

In order to shape an effective Visual Pipeline, we must follow that approach:

Stages are places where important things happen

Let's introduce a relevant concept for an effective visual pipeline:

Stages are not shelves where opportunities sit in hope to be picked up again later, rather they are crucial moments where performance matters!

Let's take the Negotiation, someone may assert how crucial it may be: in fact it is the moment of truth, a verification of what has been done before. Time when prospects check the provider on adaptability, flexibility, confidence, personal strengths and weaknesses and reliability.

We can infer a good rule from this example to define stages:

There must be critical tasks happening in Negotiation!

If important things take place within the sales process, then they are the critical happenings. The focus should be on performing those actions at the best, not in placing labels over some shelves.

Redesigning the pipeline according to the real sales process.

First of all we may think: what have we done with prospects that converted? What series of actions have been performed (and how) that possibly made the difference?

Now the game is to list that sequence of actions: plan the journey that has been successful. If the stages must drive action, their name should spark that intention. Revamping their names is not just "fancy" redesigning, rather is a decision to empower the meaning of the virtual pipeline leading salespeople to take action!

Let's explore each stage individually.

> Stages are not activities: "send proposal" is an activity that you can plan, execute and then it's over. "Creating proposal" is also not a stage if it doesn't take weeks, and if it does, then the stage may be something else.
>
> **Proposal Made**, is not an activity rather than is a parking place where something has been already performed: the proposal has been produced.
>
> *Then? What is the action that truly makes the difference?*

The title itself should be self motivational, not static like a shelf label, rather it should dynamically enable the actions to be performed. Those actions may be defined as the sequence of activities that successful sales have in common.

The stages we define are generally applicable to the B2B business model even if each company may alter the sequence of stages accordingly with their specific method of serving clients.

QUALIFIED

Here the MQL process should push new, fresh leads that have been considered qualified as possible clients. What is going to happen here? The name of the stage doesn't reveal much.

Once a MQL lead enters in the sales process someone has to initiate the journey. But this is something we know, not explained by the name.

Let's introduce this rule:

> **There must be critical tasks happening in this timeframe**

Leads Generation funnels push leads, "opportunities", that have not yet been revealed. Therefore, a critical task is to pursue the opportunity. But what does "opportunity" really mean?

> *Opportunity is the instant between not yet and no more!*

Opportunity, in Pipedrive's jargon is "deal", a possible deal that enters the sales process. In virtual terms, new leads entering the sales process, mean people who probably struggle with a problem we may solve. People who may be keen to explore a solution that fits them.

CONTACT MADE

By now, it should be clear what this label means: just a shelf. How could we define it more dynamically, implying that someone is doing something with the person? According to the rule:

There must be critical tasks happening in this timeframe.

How critical is the capability to bridge the gap between two people that have no awareness of reciprocal existence just a moment before? Extrovert people may state: "not at all", in fact, getting in touch with strangers, avoiding mistakes and instead, creating trust and confidence is an art. Performing the best action to engage someone just entering into the journey to make them happily say yes, is remarkable.

The contacting phase is a challenge in itself: from unaware unawareness to aware awareness, two people that didn't know each other are going to develop reciprocal trust! If you take this perspective, it may be quite amazing.

That's why, as part of the exploration process, tools like emotional intelligence, appreciative inquiry, master listening and effective communication are skills of paramount importance to engage in a meaningful and enjoyable exchange. The purpose is to gather information efficiently aiming straight to the next steps.

People buy from people: the whole sales process is nothing but a sequence of interactions that people perform with other people.

The art of sales lies in a deep understanding of what a person wants rather than just contacting them.

SALES QUALIFICATION

We can only make a good sale when we know the expectations of our counterpart, their constraints, their circumstances and, last but not least, their business. It is now clear how important this is for the sales process: it is not just about understanding what each prospect wants, but well beyond it, qualification serves to determine if they can become a client. How many times have we arrived at a negotiation only to find out too late that the counterpart does not have "*money*"?

We might say it was a missing budget, but learning it as soon as possible could save a lot of time.

In theory the *Qualification* stage could also take place during the discovering moment. To qualify an opportunity means also qualifying the company and the person behind it, centred around some parameters necessary for business:

- **B**udget
- **A**uthorisation
- **N**eeds
- **T**ime

This method, attributed to IBM back in the 1960, may be enhanced by other contributions on qualification, like *Hubspot's* paper on qualification.

> *Yet, the "**BANT**" acronym remains a pillar methodology in the sales practice.*

An experienced salesperson knows how to use them beyond a Go/NoGo, but rather as areas to investigate in order to identify differences and uncover opportunities. If BANT is not enough for you, then you might want to try out "MEDDIC" approach [7] or even 101 Hubspot's questions [8] -we just ask you to inform us how many customers will give you time to ask all the 101 questions...-.

> ***Because sales are also about timing! ... and time means efficiency***

Efficiency implies less resources to hit the same goal, while the most important resource is **time**, less time matters. A motto says: "On the road to success, there are no shortcuts". It is true, but neither running slow takes place on that road. We can see how velocity matters in business.

The final takeaway is: companies should develop their own way to perform the qualification process, starting from some framework and setting their own method: Asking good questions gently, collaboratively, and openly, is the main part of the method, but it also shows the power of engaging counterparts in a more effective and open negotiation which should take place at the right time.

As they actually are:

> ***... very critical tasks happening in this timeframe***

---

[7] Dick Dunkel and Jack Napoli at PTC corporation in the 1990s
[8] 101 Sales Qualification Questions, https://offers.hubspot.com/sales-qualification-questions

Then once the opportunity is qualified, you have a prospect! It depends on your sales method what actions you will do with a qualified prospect, but now that this company/person is a possible customer, it is up to you to start the core part of the sales: the effective selling part.

The *KERNEL* Stage

Every organisation needs to clearly define their sales process' **kernel stage**: this is pivotal for the whole process. During this stage your team will have the opportunity to demonstrate their most valuable sales ability:

> *Perform whatever is necessary to help the potential customer to: build trust, clarify benefits, overcome objections.*

Essentially helping them in feeling: *"My problem may be solved and the solution is here!"*

It is up to each company to determine how to name this "core stage," which is a matter of how they run their business. Whatever they decide, it is important to keep the end goal in mind: now is the right time to persuade the prospect. How to make it happen belongs to the art of sales.

For example:

- If a company sells very complex industrial plants, its kernel stage may imply a **visit** to a newly delivered factory somewhere in the world.
- If it sells bespoke software, its kernel stage would probably be the **feasibility meeting.**
- If it sells complex solutions, its stage may include **a meeting** where the prospect and other stakeholders involved in the project discuss it.
- If it sells anything that needs to be demonstrated, its stage will be just the "Demo" stage.
- If it sells bananas... Well, they probably don't need a CRM.

> *When business is about complex services the Kernel stage would definitely make more sense taking place before developing a proposal.*

In this case, this stage may probably be about depicting the right solution and the proposal will follow. Sometimes the counterpart may need time to evaluate the deal, especially with complex solutions. Engaging in a negotiation at the right time it is also very important: best to proceed further only when they are engaged.

If a formal proposal must be prepared after the main action performed in the kernel stage, then this is the activity that concludes the stage. If so, the golden rule is delivering the proposal at the right time.

So, when is the right time? That strongly depends on the specific market, industry, the brand positioning and a careful evaluation of specific circumstances. To hit this properly Pipedrive enables salespeople in setting the proposal's deadline as a task to-do then track its progress.

In sales processes where a complex solution must be built specifically for the client the kernel stage is the timeframe where client's requirements are reviewed and the final solution explained. This is why it represents a critical stage of the sales process, it is strongly recommended to give this stage the greatest focus.

Because:

There must be very critical tasks happening in this timeframe

Furthermore, a lot of what will be performed in this stage truly depends on the outcomes of previous two stages: at the discovery and qualification.

First: Information gathered in those stages will be very useful here.

Second: Experienced and well educated salespeople will be able to guide their counterparts in the decision making. Carefully considering expected features, functions and performance.

Third: by interacting with the provider, prospects will be able to anticipate how the solution will work in their specific context. For this reason it is imperative that prospects cooperate with a real expert who may properly explain how different functions and components will interact, redefining performances and effort.

This is probably the most challenging and demanding performance of the whole sales process, as this is "the timeframe" where prospects may anticipate the benefit of the solution.

NEGOTIATION

Last but not least, the negotiation begins. Sometimes. And at least its name is not static, according to the rule (say it with us!):

There must be very critical tasks happening in this timeframe

Despite the fact that negotiating is an ancient skill and negotiator is a specific, strongly educated professional role, even if sometimes they fail miserably (as for the Brexit talks). Negotiators are theoretically prepared and trained on the game of give and take, push to the limits and release the pressure. When negotiation takes place for someone it is a game of power, for someone else may be a leisure, for others just a pain.

Negotiation is not just a challenge, it is often the most in-depth interaction between the client and the supplier, between two human beings and their fear, beliefs and behaviours. Between two companies with their culture. When a client reaches the negotiation, there may be a real desire to reach a deal, but there are also lots of critical points to overcome.

This is the stage that, more than anywhere else, challenges the provider skills. Well beyond just the salesperson, the scrutiny is on the solution itself, the company's culture and its reliability. And it is also about the capability to build and manage a positive, win-to-win, relationship.

> During this stage, you may be on the verge of building a long-term relationship with your client; success in it brings happy clients on board, failure in it can throw all the previous effort in a bin or, in case or winning, it may bring on board clients that are suspicious and grumpy.

For this reason, during negotiations, the activities the organisation performs are also very specific, but one thing is sure: no additional stages are necessary. In the event of negotiation, there can only be two outcomes: **Loss** or **Win**.

A deal ends either won or lost; if neither happens we've got a problem. Perhaps something came up during the process and caused a decision delay. Something we are not aware of, or something inside the company's client, or in the market.

On the virtual pipeline it is a good rule to leave the deal where it was rather than adding a parking stage. A simple way to remind salespeople the deal is stuck may be using the proper reporting and the rotten deal rule[9]. Furthermore, the parking stage can turn into a dusty shelf that nobody really cares about.

A review of the pipeline: dynamic stages naming

Improving the default pipeline is not difficult, first is to focus on your real sales process, describe it by stages and tasks to achieve along the journey

[9] https://support.Pipedrive.com/en/article/the-rotting-feature

from unknown people (leads) to happy customers. We can evaluate the design considering two parameters: *efficiency* and *completeness*.

Completeness is when the process is well described, **efficiency** is when its description is clear and concise.

For instance, we could re-design the stage where the arriving leads enter after they have got qualified as MQL. They are QUALIFIED, but this attribute is included in the moving from leads process to sales process. We need to specify dynamically what will happen to them once they enter the sales process, and in doing so the very first task is to get in contact and understand their needs, their expectations, essentially to clarify the opportunity.

This first stage may be a discovery time frame, where the focus is on understanding the situation to prepare the following activities accordingly.

The name of this stage may be:

Discovery Opportunity

The Qualification of the Opportunity under the sales point of view is more effective once we know the situation and what exactly the client needs and the expectations around it. With a well run discovery session we may take the opportunity to investigate deeply into the prospect's real situation. And It enables understanding if the prospects are qualified from a sales point of view, and run the qualification stage.

In this stage the focus will be to clarify if the prospect can be a client. If we want to serve them, if they match with the Buyer Persona. For it we may investigate a bit more specifically on their intentions and attributes, to unveil the key parameters we decided matter for the good proceeding of the deal.

This stage name will be:

Qualification

Once it is clear that the prospect is in the position to become a client (SQL) then the sales process enters in its kernel: focus of this stage is to to develop the presentation of the perfect solution. The salesperson can add options and new functionalities to it, with the goal to engage the client into the process of defining the solution, its usage value, its performance, its overall cost... The solution presented may become more than just one. And this will be the effective

"Moment of Truth", when the seller and the buyer have to cooperate to design the solution and set its value.

This stage name may be:

Developing Solution(s)

When the solution for the specific case is clarified and accepted, or better the client is truly engaged in it, then the following stage is to discuss the conditions for acquiring the solution and the circumstances for the purchasing. On one hand the needs and possibility of the sellers' side, on the other hand the buyer's possibilities and expectations. Among them are the negotiation techniques and the representation of the different points of views.

This stage is the already known:

Negotiation

In figure 7.2 we can see a Pipedrive's window showing a re-defined, more dynamic visual pipeline.

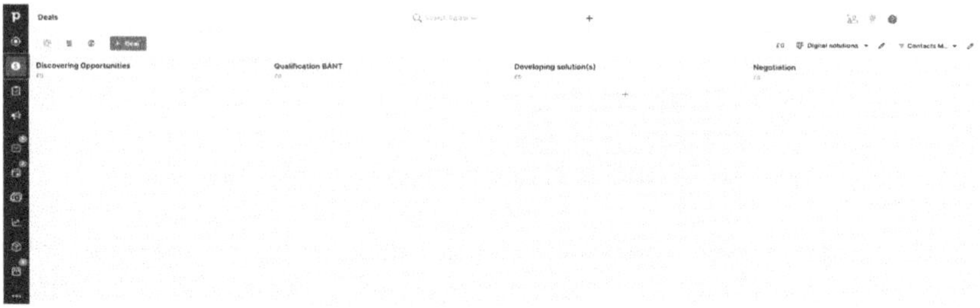

Fig. 7.2 - The Visual Pipeline redefined by dynamic names

Users may think their business is different, they require more stages to describe how they sell. Of course this is a possibility, but we challenge the idea that many stages are needed. Each stage is a container of several tasks, not a task itself, we suggest trying to be concise, effective and straight to the point.

---

4 Interactive challenge - Pipeline design

Readers can set a pipeline to render their own sales process design. There is no right or wrong, it may be a simple exercise, now that everyone is capable of using dynamic names.

The expected output should be able to:

- Mirror the sales process
- Dynamically engage action in each stage
- Include tasks expected in each stage
- Indicate tasks that may be automated
- Clarify outcomes of each stage

Readers are entitled to submit one result for the interactive challenges of this book. Anyone who would like to verify all the interactive challenges for solutions and explanations on what can be improved, may be requested to subscribe to the service.

More Pipelines

As we know there is a good reason for developing different sales pipelines: companies that have different sales processes need to mirror them in different pipelines.

For instance: returning clients differ from new leads.

We can focus on recurring clients or returning customers. Recurring clients are active customers who make regular purchases. In the logic of a B2B sales CRM, every deal is highly valuable and relevant, with minimal chances of closing it immediately. Do we really need to create a pipeline for recurring clients?

When it comes to returning customers, customers who bought previously that are coming back, it might be worth managing the process using a dedicated pipeline, especially if the deal is still complex and the process requires time.

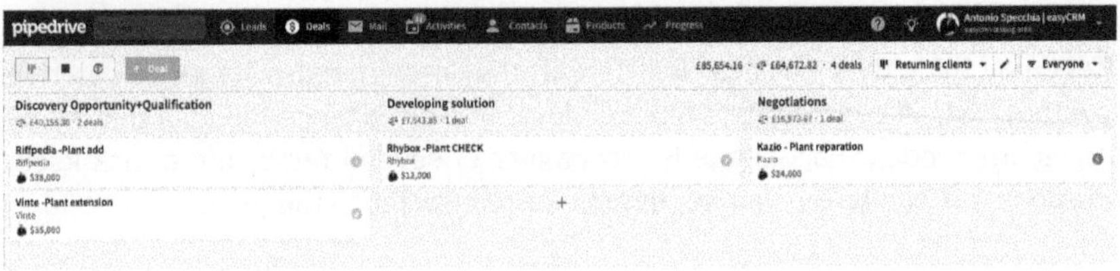

Fig. 7.3 - An example of pipeline for returning customers

For this we may need to include a few stages: - since a complex solution, or a critical product, needs to include the sales preparation within the sales process. The process implies a Qualification stage that may effectively be run in conjunction with the Discovery Opportunity aimed to clarify the client's needs and assess constraints for the specific opportunity. In doing so, it may be possible to check the expected investment (budget) and timing. Authority should already be clear. After that may follow the stage of solution development, or presentation, and the negotiation stage (Fig. 7.3).

Pipelines Examples

A pipeline is a visual representation of something real: the sales process. No two businesses have the same way to be on the market, everyone sells in a different way. Uniqueness is what makes you stand out. That's why it is important to design the sales process you effectively run. Developing control by creating the right rendering to empower the real sales process may be a real challenge. Designing a process may be less obvious than expected and making poor choices is easy. To achieve success companies need to define the why behind their CRM strategy before even considering the digital tools. Start with the logic, then apply it to the tool.

Start with why! [10]

By doing that, we prefer that the CRM tool does not dictate the method, instead the logic will shape solutions, even when the tool may have limitations.

The purpose of the following section is to check some examples of visual pipelines, analysing each one in the aim to help readers in understanding how to better design their own.

Example 1

This pipeline in fig. 7.4 was developed by a digital solution provider of a digital solution: a vendor.

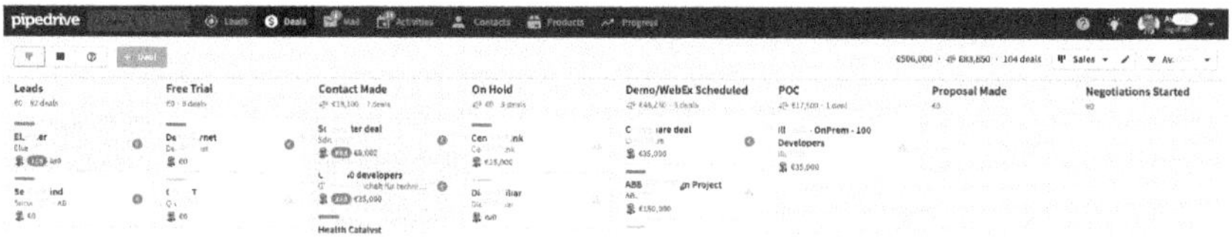

Fig. 7.4 - An example of pipeline adopted by a tech company (old layout)

[10] Sinek S., Start with Why, Penguin 2009 - www.startwhitwhy.com

Analysis

For one of their sales processes, the Israeli software company decided to run an 8-stage pipeline. We recognise these relevant stages:

- **Leads**. Here they park leads to be qualified.
- **Free Trial**. It is a stage where freely leads start testing the software solution. A salesperson may contact the lead if some parameters are in place (MQL verification)
- **Contact Made**. A salesperson offers support to clarify the solution usage by offering a guided demo.
- **On Hold**. Just waiting, the prospects keep testing.
- Demo. The prospect comes back accepting a demo guided by a specialist
- **POC**. Demonstrating the solution gives the opportunity to elaborate a Proof of Concept, this may be their most relevant stage: the kernel stage.
- **Proposal made**. It is intended to track the action of elaborating a tailored proposal.
- **Negotiation** discussing terms and conditions

Company's Rationale

As you may appreciate some stages have remained in place from the original Pipedrive template then they added some stages to manage their own process.

The sales process starts when users get a free trial, quite common for software vendors. In a B2B model it is important contacting leads when it has been clarified what company they belong to.

The next stage for them is just waiting. They allow the prospect to browse through their solution, testing it, using it and creating some value with it. Prospect may benefit from a demo with a specialist guiding them to unveil the value of the solution.

The proof of concept is tailored to the prospect's situation. Trying to engage the prospect in the value creation process. Then a proposal follows shortly and the negotiation may start.

Possible improvements

As you can now see all the names of the stages are just static. Salespeople have to decide to go to pick up some deals and take action. It is less self explanatory, or engaging.

Does the name "**Free trial**" require salespeople to do anything?

Would it be a bad idea to offer help? How to be sure they will test the solution correctly? Tracking the usage in testing mode carefully for instance, looking after what they do, if they are stuck, if they don't use some relevant features. Create automated warnings for those metrics and plan to take action when it happens.

What are the ***very critical tasks happening in this timeframe***?

Something like "Trialling" may be more dynamic: the prospect is testing the solution, we may be alert to give support.

Then "**Contact Made**", is this a parking place where leads have been contacted or is there something more that can be achieved in the meantime?

*There must be **very critical tasks happening in this timeframe***

As discussed previously, the contact time is a crucial moment for qualifying the opportunity and to check needs. Make sure they match our solutions.

"**On hold**": another parking place. If any action would be required they probably do not need a sales process at all.

*There are **no tasks happening in this timeframe***

Customers might flock, but they might also be helped to jump on board. Why passively wait for clients to decide alone to ask for a guided demo?

"**Demo Scheduled**": technically another shelf. What matters if a demo has been scheduled? What are the ***very critical tasks happening in this timeframe***?

How does a deal move from On Hold to Demo Scheduled? Because the prospect decides to ask for the demo? And once it is booked? What should happen? What is the outcome? In short, we go from zero interaction mode to a demo without qualification. The consequence might be to invest time with wrong prospects.

Then for some reason it is provided a "**Proof of Concept**", that seems more something like: "*Look how good my product is. Aren't you in love with it?*".

What are the **very critical tasks happening in this timeframe?**

If the prospect shows interest the proposal will be developed. Just to place the deal into another parking spot: "**Proposal made**"

*Where are the **very critical tasks happening in this timeframe?***

Then comes the "**Negotiation**". If it does... If the client fills their expectations. But which expectations? Not to mention about its capability/availability to pay for the solution.

Designing the virtual sales pipeline by clarifying the real process is the issue. We are sure the company was doing much more than what they designed on the pipeline, but they haven't been able to design it. Rendering the virtual pipeline mirroring the real process enables control, replication, spreading the method among the sales team, tracking and measuring it to improve.

Missing the opportunity to use the virtual pipeline in the right way may lead to developing the belief that the CRM is useless, or that Pipedrive CRM is poor while other CRMs may be better.

The reason why more than 70% of the CRM implementation projects fail, should be found in the lack of clarity about the tool logic and how much the tool's success depends on its design. And the design depends on the logic of the CRM.

Example 2

An Italian real estate builder. In figure 7.5, we can see the visual pipeline designed specifically (in Italian).

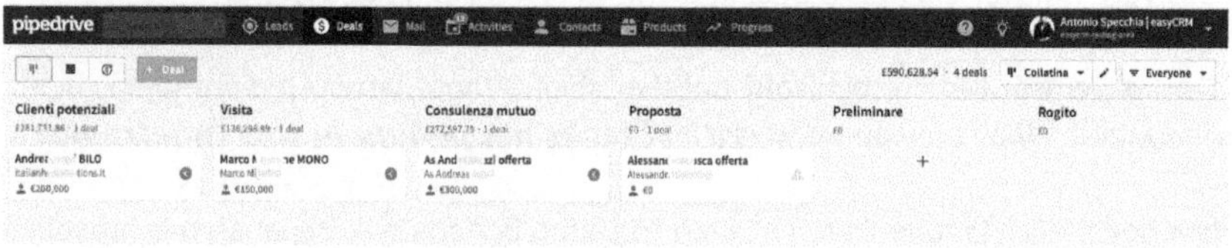

Fig. 7.5 - A visual pipeline for real-estate business (old layout)

Analysis

They aimed to create a pipeline for each new building under development. Then once all the flats were sold to close it.

They designed a 6-stage pipeline beginning with "**Clienti potenziali**" (prospects). People who contacted the sales team were, strangely, not considered unknown (leads).

Next stage is "**Visita**". This is where they show the jobsite and the sample-flats. They then call a mortgage consultant "**Consulenza Mutuo**", which is still an important step in the real estate buying process.

The "**Proposta**" (Proposal) is the complex stage that requires the salesperson to go into various options and features a client would want. (Unlike the UK market where it may be hard to stop builders from building a room wall when you may want to take it down later).

Then since clients purchase immediately, negotiation is unnecessary, isn't it?. Then the stage "**Preliminare**", which surprisingly (for Brits), but with respect for both parties, implies a pre-contract agreement that under rules and obligations binds both parties in the contract.

Lastly the "**Rogito**" which is the Italian legal term for a "Real Estate Purchasing Agreement" (This time Italian overtakes English in brevity).

Company's Rationale

This pipeline changed completely from the template. Since they receive people who are interested in buying a flat in the area, they move straight to show the jobsite and the possible flats. The sample flat is where they show the space and the available options. It is also the place where salespeople talk with the buyer.

Generally speaking, people who purchase homes take mortgages, for this reason an evaluation of the monthly cost may matter.

At that point an effective proposal can be prepared. If that converts, this document becomes the basis for the pre-contract, the Preliminare.

Once the Preliminare is agreed the first payment is settled, then it is only a matter of time before the Rogito takes place.

Possible improvements

This pipeline is just a list of parking places. They are phases where the deal may be stored, no operational activities are mentioned.

This type of lists are often perceived from salespeople as a burden, an admin control required to keep updated that does not add value to operations and does not facilitate the salespeople's daily job. Is not even a reminder of things to do!

Moreover, tasks have to be set manually to look after each deal.

On the logical perspective it seems that anyone passing by will be allowed to attend a visit to the sample-flats, regardless of whether they are really interested in purchasing a property or have nothing else to do. But let's assume they are serious buyers, are they the right buyer personas? And what are they really looking for? Actually in the real sales process the qualification takes place on the day of the visit.

After the visit, the pipeline goes straight into mortgage evaluation. But perhaps purchasing a property entails more topics than just determining whether the monthly payments are affordable.

Then comes the proposal. After checking the mortgage? Therefore, they should already be familiar with everything about the property, including the level of finishing, since they already have a price to check the mortgage. Then what the proposal stage stands for? It is just a store for prospective buyers to whom a proposal has been made?

And then, if they decide to proceed, they will hit another parking place at the Preliminare stage.

Lastly it will be a matter of waiting for the Rogito (contract).

We can see that none of the names used match the dynamic workflow approach, and that there are ***no critical tasks happening in those time frames****.*

Of course that's not actually the case! We know a lot of activities are happening across the real sales process:

- *The buyer's qualification takes place during the visit*
- *The property potential price is decided*
- *The client's ability to pay is confirmed*

Therefore the problem is not with the real process, but how it is placed in the virtual pipeline. It seems that the digital CRM is used to track where the deals are, just to provide administrative information. Something that salespeople strongly hate.

That's what this account was intended for: tracking numbers to take under control the cash flow. Basically killing any motivation in using the digital CRM by not only missing to help salespeople in their daily effort, but also by placing another layer of burden on their daily duties.

Example 3

The business service provider company developed this pipeline down under: Brisbane.

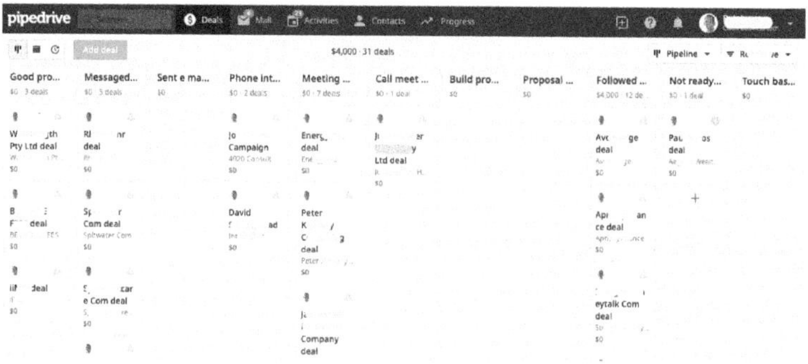

Fig. 7.6 - A pipeline for a Business to business long, complex sales process (old layout).

Analysis

Here we have 11 stages! This design aims to track everything with the purpose to keep each step under control.

From the initial introduction (Good Prospect), messaging in several steps (Messaged waiting reply, Sent email intro, Phone intro! Good Prospect) to arranging a meeting (Meeting Arranged), and confirming the meeting (Call Meeting Booked). Then comes the working stage of building a proposal (Build Proposal after discussion). Then a stage where the proposal has been sent and a follow up may be good (Proposal Sent - For follow up). Later, when the follow up has been made the negotiation will be started (Followed up- Negotiation Started).

At that point the prospect may not be ready for the deal, hence another touch base is considered to be good (Not ready - Nurture and future Follow up).

Then another contact (Touch base again - Check status)...

Readers may appreciate these 11 shelves to store deals. Don't you? There is no one single dynamic action included, there are absolutely ***no critical tasks happening in those time frames.***

In the next fig. 7.7 readers can appreciate the pipeline's structure, with its very long titles.

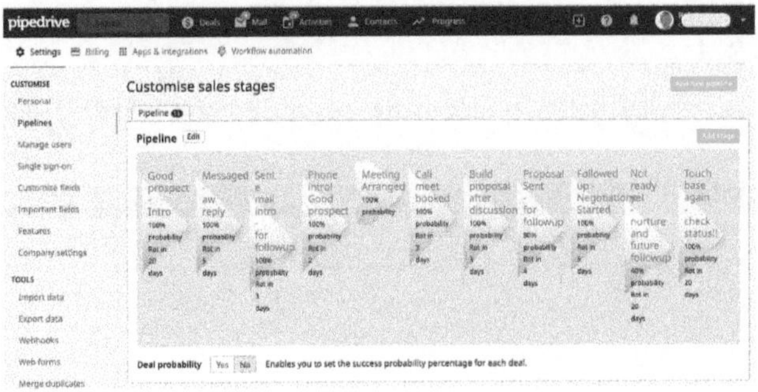

Figure 7.7 - The details of the stages names

Company's Rationale

The company was more focused on people's personal life than their businesses health, this implies a different approach and style. It was more a B2C business model, even if clients were business owners. What is interesting for us is its long and complex sales process, that matches the B2B complexity. The intention was first to start working, then checking deals' situation along the journey to keep track of the open opportunities. It wasn't much about using the digital tool on a daily basis to run the sales process.

Possible improvements

The pipeline begins with an already good prospect in place. That probably means a qualification has taken place. How? When? Nothing is mentioned. Probably it would make sense to design the qualification process before leads become prospects, considering what parameters make them good prospects.

Then we have 5 stages that actually are more "activities to-be-done" or, even worse, static locations where a deal is placed after an activity has been completed.

Finally, we reached an operative stage: developing a proposal. As there is mentioned "after discussion" it probably means that an idea of the client's needs was developed.

Going ahead, let's park this deal into a proposal sent stage, but with a follow up.

As a result of a follow-up, a negotiation has (already) taken place.

Consequently, the good prospect may delay any decision as it is not yet ready, (any doubt that wasn't so good?), which implies some sort of follow-up and nurturing that would be required. Then moving forward to the next stage "Touch base again" which probably is that "follow up/nurturing" already mentioned in the stage before.

We might assess how this pipeline is just a qualification process rather than mirroring a real sales process. It results in people delaying decision making. In fact the "negotiation" stage seems to be the timeframe where closures happen.
When a deal is lost an automation could move into another pipeline in which nurturing and follow-up are the focus instead of making them stuck. If so, the outcome would be: deal lost (tracked for reporting purposes). Deal moved into a new pipeline, "nurturing", while we will be waiting for the prospect's circumstances to change.
In fact, this pipeline has no qualification stage, they are assumed to be good prospects from the beginning, and then that idea of good prospects is going to be confirmed again after a series of interactions that are named as stages, instead of activities as they actually are.
*Here there is not even the doubt about which **critical tasks were happening in those time frames**.*
In reality this pipeline does not mirror any sales process. It was a genuine and honest effort, but it wasn't organised. We know they later switched to another digital tool. However, we do not know if the move allowed them to redefine their view of the real sales process, a missing point that resulted in a bad feeling against this tool.

Summary

This chapter focuses on the theoretical aspects of the sales process and how to improve it by mirroring it into a visual pipeline, including stages and outcomes, using Pipedrive.

We clarified the crucial contribution of the visual pipeline to sales process management.

Improving pipeline effectiveness by analysing each stage's content to facilitate the planning of salespeople's real job.

Even though the technology remains important, we focused on the logic of the pipeline in order to improve the sales process management from a business perspective.

We focused on the development of awareness about the logic of CRM. It is important to properly address the need to clarify the sales process logic before even considering any technical solution we may be keen to adopt.

This know-how can be applied to any CRM. Pipedrive brings several advantages in helping companies to design their CRM by forcing them to think to stages.

Finally we analysed examples of pipelines designed by users for their own businesses. We pointed out how those pipelines reflect their subtle sales processes, not how they might improve.

The know-how to design sales pipelines is not about keeping in memory a set of mandatory instructions. Rather, it involves learning how to read business processes, then apply rules according to effective business needs.

8 Workflow Automation

Introduction

Efficiency in sales is paramount, the management of the sales process aims to enable efficiency in salespeople daily duties. Tracking the efficiency trends is probably a quite difficult task. Everyone develops their own definition of efficiency.

> *We call "mad" someone who runs faster than us, while we are annoyed by slow drivers around us. Is it odd as we consider we are the only ones who always drive at the right speed!*

In this regard, determining the right level of efficiency may be hard. How much is too much effort on our job or when it is too little? How can a sales process be considered efficiently run? Is it really so complex to define the productivity of salespeople? Instead of determining it upfront, in sales we better seek for continuous improvement: set metrics, set KPIs, learn and search for ways to maximise things done.

Organisations can help salespeople in reducing repetitive tasks using workflow automation, something that Pipedrive includes in all types of subscription. Salespeople can keep the focus on the real value of their own job: selling.

Here you will find a few examples of what Pipedrive Workflow Automation can do, but first let's consider this: digital systems may offer way too many options, only the effective needs of the sales team should determine if any new solution should be considered to adopt. Too many options to evaluate may result in wasted effort.

Before thinking about what to automate, teams should run manual processes for a while after the CRM is just implemented, set the correct procedures, test them, verify how they work, what problems may incur, and what may benefit to be less structured and allow more human flexibility. Only then consider to automate procedures.

Consider first what are the elements of workflow automation:

- A trigger
- One (or some) condition(s)
- The action to perform

Triggers, Conditions, Action

Triggers are events that can ignite effects. The conditions determine the parameters to qualify the event. The action is what we want to make happen. Using the triggers' selection, users can choose events from 6 options: Deal, person, Activity, Lead, Organisation and Project. (Fig. 8.1)

Trigger may be selected among those options: Created, Updated, Deleted.

Conditions are specific parameters of the event: a person created who has blonde hair. Well, maybe not exactly like that... even if Pipedrive offers a comprehensive condition setting, around what attributes the subject may include (Fig. 8.2).

Action is the effect we want to accomplish, Pipedrive offers 10 different actions users may choose. (Fig 8.3)

Delay enables a delay of starting the action. Pipedrive offers some fixed time-delays in the intention to make it easy (we believe no fixed pattern of choices may satisfy all users), but at least now the action may be activated with a delay.

Workflow automations are focused on activities required throughout the sales process. Lately Pipedrive added its workflow automation even for its new feature Projects, enabling a more reliable accomplishment of repetitive tasks for both areas, sales and project management.

Setting a Workflow Automation (WA)

Let's consider a very simple one: for each deal won a new project will be set. Using your favourite project management tool you want to avoid copying and pasting basic information into the project platform leaving this to the machine.

Pipedrive enables a direct integration with external project management platforms as Asana and Trello, and even better with its own Projects.

Users may access the Workflow Automation manager by clicking the three dots icon in the vertical black belt on the left as well as by the menu under the user's name.

Once there, they can create a new WA by a template -a function that has recently been improved-, or create a new one from scratch by clicking on the green button " + Workflow ".

The first page user will be is where it is required to set the trigger (Fig 8.1).

In the trigger box there are 6 different types of entities and their possible events:

creation, **update** or **delete**.

For this WA, we choose the entity "Deal" and the event "Update". It results in the [Deal Update] event

As effect of this every time a deal will be updated this event will trigger this workflow automation.

"Apply trigger" green button moves to the next step: conditions

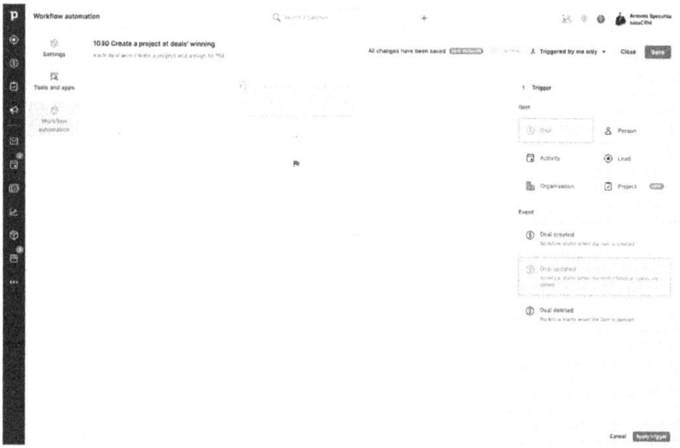

Fig. 8.1 - Starting a new workflow automation. Selecting the trigger.

Setting conditions is the method to avoid triggering the automation by any update of any deal. Only events that match the conditions will exert the action. For our WA let's set a condition for deals that matter on **data management**. (Fig 8.2)

Pipedrive enables many conditions to identify precisely only certain deals. The purpose is to enable users to select with no risks the kind of event and the kind of entities that ignite the action. In our case, the intention is to select deals that require project management. Let's "Apply Conditions" and the green button will move us to the next step: Action.

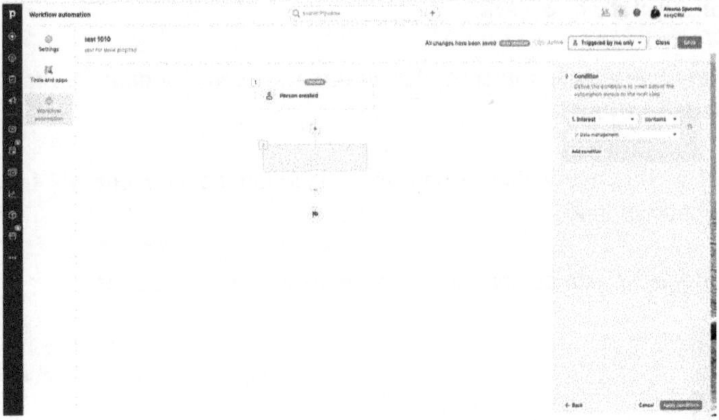

Fig. 8.2 - Setting the workflow automation. Selecting the conditions.

We are now ready to select the right action we are looking to execute any time automatically. Just before it Pipedrive introduced the possibility of adding a delay to the execution. We can then select to set a delay or select an action, or even set other conditions, clicking the green button again will make us proceed.

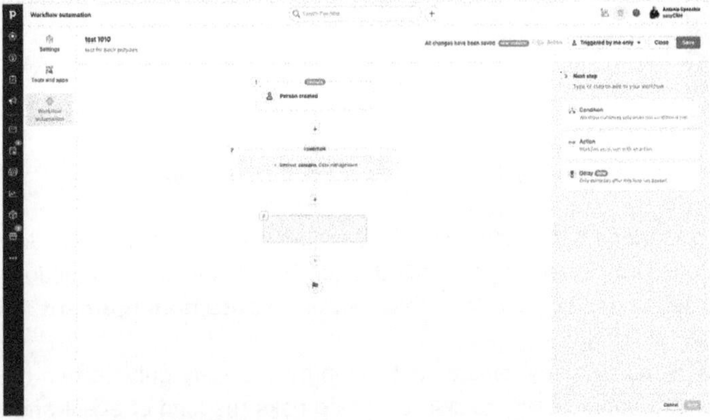

Fig. 8.2.1 - Setting the workflow automation. Selecting action.

In fig 8.2.2 we can see the delay setting, in the effort to make things simple, Pipedrive created a pattern of time-delay instead of a seconds counter that may be more complex to manage. Maybe your requirement falls into an option that is not listed. Just adjust your setting to the closer option.

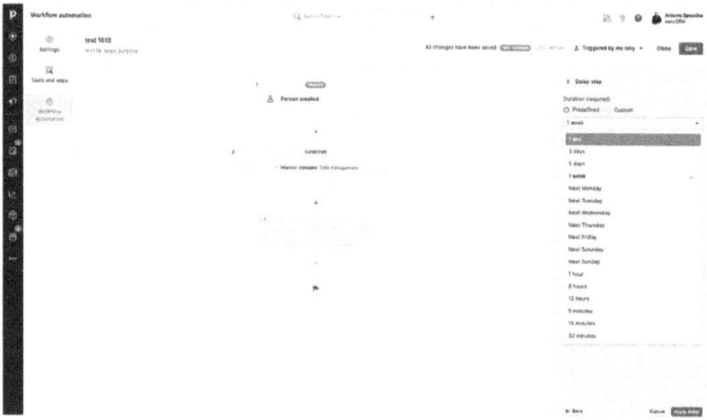

Fig. 8.2.2 the delay pattern available

Once a delay is set users go to select the "Action" so they will finally be shown all the possible actions to execute. Just select the one you need. (Fig. 8.3)

Fig. 8.3 - Setting the workflow automation. Selecting which action.

In the example we select: [Create project]. Creating a new Project's pipeline: the PM environment in Pipedrive Projects.

Note

Some annoying features:

In Fig. 8.4 readers may appreciate the "triggered only by me" default setting. This is an option easy to forget at time of setting a WA. It is an error that may cost a lot of effort to be fixed. This is because Pipedrive is missing a management of the workflow automation portfolio as well as a debugging tool. Later, when events won't trigger actions someone will need to investigate it, in lack of proper tools, companies may only rely on the descriptions if

they didn't write down a full workflow plan description on a document.
Nonsense ownership: WA are grouped as created by you and created by others, ownership can't be changed.
Lack of control: users can delete WA created by others but they can't alter them

In Fig. 8.4 and 8.5 we can see the settings when creating a new project environment, selecting data fields users want to bring over from the Deal.

Last three things are expected to do:

- Set "triggered by any user"
- Trig "activate"
- Setting name and description (carefully)

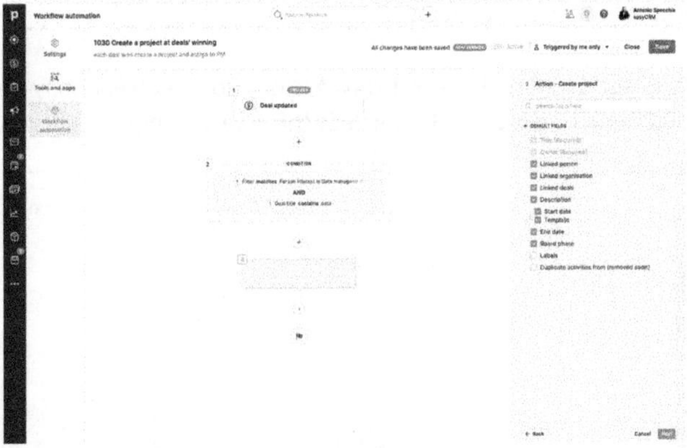

Fig. 8.4 - Selecting data to transfer when creating a new project.

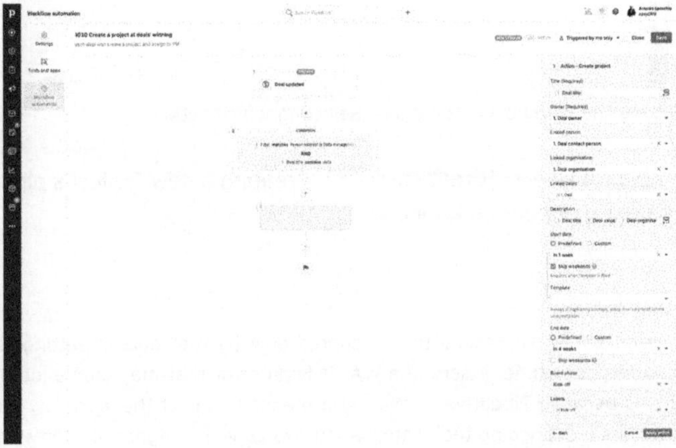

Fig. 8.5 - Setting the workflow automation. Defining dataset in the new project.

Just to check the most relevant cases we can see Trello and Asana are now really effective in the setting, in Fig 8.7 - 8.9 we can see the two options and how they may create new objects

Fig. 8.7 WA action to be performed into Trello.

Fig. 8.10 WA actions to be performed into Asana.

This may be a guide to clarify how to set automations for your business. The challenge may be to clarify what part should be automated in your sales process, which actions are repetitive, when and under what circumstances. Then you better create a plan, a document describing triggers, conditions and expected actions. This may prevent errors or getting lost when unexpected actions may be performed and, possibly unnoticed.

Unfortunately, a resolution of problems may be complex, as Pipedrive doesn't provide debugging features. There is no way to test or review a WA or even organise them.

Once it is set up, the Workflow Automations are great in helping salespeople save time, get more consistent in the output by focusing on relationships, and they will do what they like doing.

Automate it with…

To automate your work in Pipedrive you have Workflow Automation, for anything else …

Well, you may choose different solutions, as there are many platforms that support low code development of integrations between software solutions in different ways. One that is very appreciated in the developers' world is Make, formerly Integromat. This is slightly more technical but often offers a lot of options.

If you use Zapier you may benefit from the book **Automate It with Zapier**, by Kelly Goss, Packt Editions[11].

This book is a real bible for workflow automations: Kelly describes each one in great detail (570 pages!!), ultimately she can guide you to automate almost anything! The following Fig. 8.7 shows Kelly's use of Zapier to connect other services, in this case, a weather forecast, with Pipedrive.

I'm sure, when you will take confidence in automating actions with Pipedrive you will love what can be done with these tools and you may want to automate everything around you!

Fig. 8.7 - Kelly Goss, Automated It with Zapier. Creating workflow with service outside Pipedrive

[11] Goss, K., Automate it with Zapier, Packt, 2021

We will discuss later in chapter 19 the integrations via API and platforms.

---

5 Interactive challenge - Workflow design and setting

Readers may set a Workflow Automation recording each passage (also just a screenshot) and explain what they want to achieve. Our feedback will focus on missing issues.

Readers are entitled to submit one result for the interactive challenges of this book. Anyone who would like to verify all the interactive challenges for solutions and explanations on what can be improved, may be requested to subscribe to the service.

Summary

It is easy to create a lot of automations in Pipedrive, but it is also very easy to get lost in them. Be sure to describe each one on a plan, using the appropriate names and descriptions, then group them by a code in their title (1000, 1010, 1020, 1030).

- What is a Workflow Automation
- How to set it in place
- How to benefit from WA

9 Leads Generation

Introduction

What should I do to find new clients?

Small as well as new companies ask this question over and over again. Actually the matter is: how to attract new people to create more opportunities and develop a sustainable business? That's what marketing is all about and always will be: create the conditions to attract new business. But how can you meet this challenge in the era of digital everything?

Content is the answer. Good content that can create value to someone. The addressed audience is formed by people who are searching for a solution to a problem they are experiencing. Content brings awareness of possible solutions. How do CRM and marketing go along together?

In this chapter we will go on to check at the following topics:

- Leads generation today
- CRM and leads generation
- Leads generation tools

Leads Generation Today

Leads generation for B2B may be a complex process that includes many activities from different operators.

Let's super-summarise how it works by phases:

- Creation of interest in the market
- Engage people to interact with the brand
- Develop their interest on the brand
- Engage them in the sales process

- To create interest a brand nurtures the market by creating information, culture, sharing knowledge and values for an indefinite audience of people.

- To engage people a brand may develop a wide range of possible "catchy" moments, or lead magnets, elements where people may get benefits by starting an interaction with the brand.

- Developing interest in the brand is something that should be nurtured naturally: once people have already started interacting with the brand they will be open to receive more information and learn something new.

- People are now investing time interacting with the brand, experiencing samples, reading articles that support knowledge development, using content that improves their understanding; they are now exposed to messages that give them awareness of the problem-solution framework but also about the brand

- Engaging them in the sales process would be the next step: if those people are at the right time to purchase, the result will be a full engagement in the sales process.

The capability of creating interest by nurturing markets via "messages" involves a broad mix of activities that all together, and when well coordinated, enable the audience to develop awareness of the brand. Among these activities paramount is the content creation, that for B2B businesses is the way to communicate to people. While billboards may be fancy and advertising may be catchy, it is on more structured content that the best messages are supported.

Content is everything capable of transferring organised messages to recipients by any media: written, audio, video or whatever. It is by content that brands develop the knowledge sharing that audiences consume. Is it by content that values are understood and brands get appreciated in markets. The list can go longer but the idea is depicted: businesses need to be good content creators to be able to nurture audiences out in the market.

Once the content is ready, making it available for people is a media game. The right pattern of media and a correct budget for it. Once offered to the public, the content should be able to engage the targeted audience in a dialogue with the brand, that more often means to be interested to receive more information, more content to consume because the content is capable of transferring value (lifestyle, values, know-how, knowledge ...) from the brand. Developing this sort of interest makes people keen to "pay for", that often simply means unveiling their contact data. They start interacting with the brand by receiving and giving information.

It is at this point that contacts move from being unknown (audience) becoming contact persons (leads): they can be qualified as "interested" in the solution.

Being qualified under marketing parameters (MQL) means these leads (persons!) are consuming content about the matter, the solution. This denotes these people are in a position to be aware of the problem, they are collecting information about the problem-solution theme. Once this happens, they may be ready for purchase, so engaging them in the sales process is a natural result of the relevant effort so far.

From this point on Pipedrive provides the environment to execute the sales process: starting from qualifying the MQLs (contact persons) to assess if they are ready to become prospect customers (SQL); then run the sequence of activities that enables their decision making that convert them into customers.

CRM and leads generation

Pipedrive CRM is intended to support the sales process at the best, and in doing this it may be connected to other business processes in order to store contacts data in the same place. As we have seen, leads generation is the business process capable of generating the contact persons that will populate the sales process managed by CRM. In this sense the tool used for leads generation is expected to produce qualitative data then insert them in the CRM.

Tools may impact a lot on the way the work is performed at any stage of the business process. Either they are stainless tools or digital tools, their quality matters on the performance of the job done along the value creation process. The trade off between tools that offer strong focused value on one or free functions and tools that try to cover all the business processes often imply a not easy decision. Any result of this choice may close the gap on transferring contacts' data generated at the leads generation stage into the sales process tool: CRM.

Getting in touch with these contact persons (leads), when data are obtained via a well-designed funnel is correct as it implies a soft nurturing. And, as long as people perceive it as a valuable "conversation", they will probably remain engaged.

In this logic resides the kernel of email marketing: one of the many available media channels utilised to nurture relationships with audiences.

> Valuable information provided by brands, when they are perceived as relevant, results in a better nurturing of the audience that results in a more effective conversion process.

In this framework, email marketing is still relevant, even if a little bit worn, for the B2B business model, the challenge is to empower its use to match with the changed environment.

A key factor to succeed is perseverance. Markets are open and fast, people are better informed, but often impatient and critical. To develop brand awareness it is required to possess a clear, strong brand identity, good values, and real genuine intention to help.

Helping is the new selling

It implies that brands are available to clients providing valuable insights and useful support along the relationship.

- *Engaging unknown people to get in touch with the brand*
- *Offering useful support to expand what interests them*
- *Keep their attention by providing valuable content until they are ready to make a decision.*
- *Bringing them into the sales process to help them to decide*
- *Match their needs creating the most balanced compromise*
- *... and persuading them of this*

We can now clearly see where the difference between nurturing an audience and pushing for sales lies: building relationships over time to make sales possible rather than looking for buyers in the short term.

Marketing automation

The previous process, for the complex it may be, is something that companies are required to set in place for the best, and look after it continuously. It may imply a lot of human effort.

Marketing automation tools may provide efficient frameworks where content are properly managed along the media channels while leads behaviours are monitored supporting the best experience in consuming content.

There are many tools in the market developed purposely to manage this relevant business process.

Companies should develop their decision on this: how much value would be created by automating the processes in this area?

Having clear the differences between leads generation and CRM, companies can resolve the usefulness of a marketing automation platform to govern the leads generation processes while the CRM remains a tool that covers the sales process management.

Platforms like Hubspot may provide good value in that area, while the sales process management remains an area where more focused solutions provide more value. This is the reason why Hubspot is among the integrations available in Pipedrive's marketplace.

It is only a matter of time and budget to decide about how to run the leads generation process in your organisation, when it become clear that the amount of work required to look after the leads generation can't be held anymore by your marketing team, then will be time to start analysing what is available on the market.

Until then your organisation may benefit from a more labour intensive process management using less complex tools to look after the essentials of leads generation, the behaviours of recipients and how to respond to them.

Leads Generation Tools

While content production is still one of the most difficult challenges for many businesses, at least some processes may be facilitated along the whole process of generating new leads. Setting the content on the media is one part of the process, making them visible by engaging audiences is the next challenge.

Most of the tools in this area operate in the next stage: facilitating the contact point for the audience, then monitoring behaviours -preferences- on the kind of content they take advantage of.

Details about how to use the Leads Manager are in chapter 4.

LeadBooster

LeadBooster is Pipedrive's marketing add-on feature that groups already existing tools into one more effective, focused group of tools. The value proposed is to enable users in adding features when needed to facilitate the leads contact and dialogue: the lead acquisition. Several of these features may be subscribed from different vendors in the marketplace or even by integrating different solutions not listed by API or LowCode integration tools. For more details please check the vendor's knowledge base[12].

[12] https://support.pipedrive.com/en/article/leadbooster-add-on

Leadbooster includes **Live Chat**, **Chatbot**, **Web Forms** and **Prospector**. The last one works with a pay per use scheme, queries for searching contacts use credits that may be purchased in batches.

Live Chat

This chat-in-person tool enables organisations to add a simple chat window on the company's website. In general, this is one of the most relevant customer care tools, easy to use, immediate messaging that customers and prospects generally use when in search for more information or help. A live chat may be quite time-consuming for operators, when the company offers phone support or direct support of any kind a Live Chat is an effective and easy to use add on. Often, nudging prospects to release their contact data is a matter of providing value in exchange, and a rapid answer to everyday queries is valuable for many prospects.

ChatBot

The idea behind this is to provide leads with an immediate answer. A bot can be programmed to ask some questions then route people accordingly. The main benefit is the time saving for your company and not really on the value creation for prospects or clients forced to use it.

WebForm

Data collection is the gate for engaging leads in a dialogue with the brand, an interaction that should create value for both parties. The web forms are the tools that offer information disclosure in exchange of contact data.

Let's be clear: people are not in love with web form filling, people are there to find value on the interaction. If the webform is the gate to get that value then they are keen to proceed.

- Make sure your content provides real, tangible value
- Make it easy for people to fill in forms
- Be clear on what they will get
- Ensure GDPR enforcement (or similar rules) when required

Web form is a technique widely utilised, there are plenty of proposals in this area they are available in the marketplace as well elsewhere on the web. They are not better or worse than the Pipedrive's native web form, they may offer different features. Be aware when their vendors claim to be more engaging: engagement mainly depends on the value proposed, then by a minor portion on the appearance.

Prospector

Similarly to LinkedIn's Sales Navigator, it enables filtering of people's profiles and importing them in your Pipedrive's leads manager. Fig. 9.1 shows a query formation. It enables several parameters to run queries, resulting in lists of companies/people matching the criteria. Selecting a contact enables users to import it as a lead. Theoretically it enables users to reach thousands of people who match specific characteristics, with the intention of getting in touch and engaging them in a dialogue.

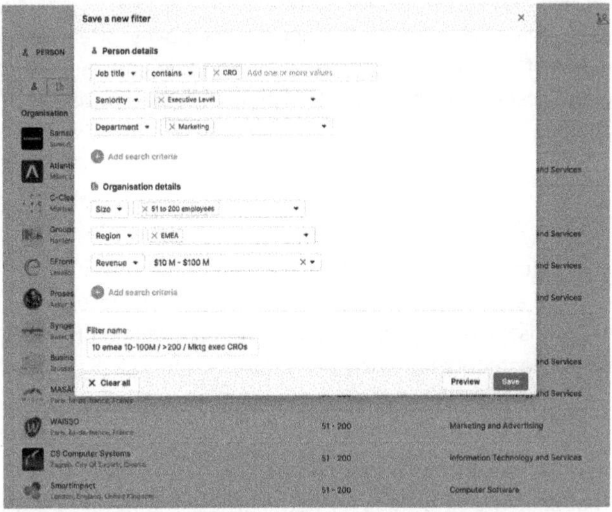

Fig. 9.1 - Prospector, develop a query for searching a target profile: CRO executive managers in EMEA companies, with revenues between 10M to 100M, and workforce between 51 to 200 people. (34 results)

Prospector is still an interesting method to check out new people even if, like Linkedin Sales Navigator, the capability to select a number of unknown contacts and message them directly, incredibly powerful when launched, is now under scrutiny. We wonder if an excessive exploitation resulted in a dramatic contraction of the general appetite towards unexpected communications.

Cold calls and out-of-the-blue emails are still widely used, and it probably means that they are still working. In this regard the quality of messages may be critical: to emerge from a low levelled, massive, often useless communication companies must develop remarkable messages and real, effective values.

People on Linkedin not only are withdrawing consent to show email addresses

-a move that disables the possibility to contact them- but even worse, many are limiting messages to paying members (INMAIL). (*You may wonder why they remain on a social network if they are not interested in developing connections*). A behaviour that may be an overreaction to the excessive use of Sales Navigator to fishing for clients, that resulted in crippling its effectiveness.

We believe that using Prospector with good intentions, remarkable messages and effective value propositions, may result in growing audiences if not in finding immediately new prospects.

It is one of the many contact-media any company should use, probably not expecting massive engagement by none of them singularly.

Active Campaign

A popular tool with a good balance between price, performance and usability. Anybody can use it without any coding knowledge. Active Campaign is becoming a marketing automation tool. Providing services in the leads generation area. Probably the price and usability of this tool have a role in its popularity. The usage isn't without challenges, especially on the data architecture. Active Campaign also offers a CRM function, with really basic features. On top of this, landing pages hosted outside your own website results in loss of traffic that may affect website ranking.

Autopilot

Digitally proficient users may design workflows, messaging routines, social media campaigns, chatbots, apps, blogs, and nurture audiences. Among such features it also includes website tracking, lead scoring, in-app messaging, Facebook retargeting, Google Adwords retargeting, as well as automation of repetitive tasks, such as assigning leads to salespeople, booking appointments, and following up on sales leads. Autopilot may be considered a LowCode solution that integrates with many applications. The tool is quite well supported, but is best for IT proficient people.

Leadfeeder

All the functionality of a marketing automation without the cost and the complexity. Leadfeeder provides full view of web visitors and their behaviors, enabling Pipedrive in slice and dice contacts developing high segementation. When your marketing has been able to produce qualitative content to engage people, Leadfeeder may enable outbound marketing retargetting engaged people resulted by inbound marketing. Definitively an app Must-Have.

Outfunnel

One of the most remarkable platforms tested for managing mailing marketing. It not only supports a well designed segmentation and lead scoring on website traffic but also generates data campaign management directly in the CRM enabling audience formation. Engage contacts to nurture them and lead them on 'visiting the website', 'tracking behaviours', and qualify audiences by 'showed interest in the brand'.

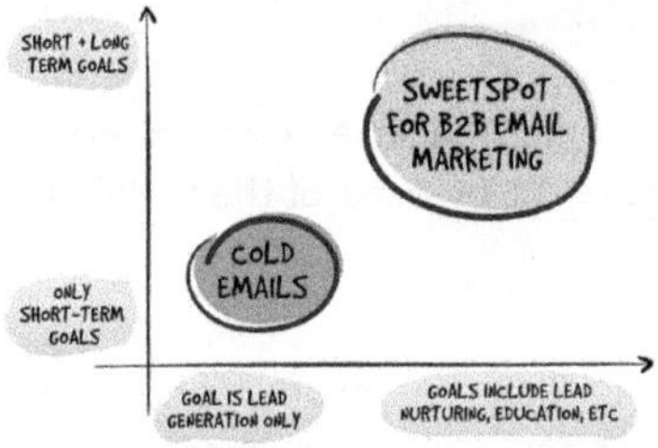

Fig 9.5 SweetSpot for B2B email marketing according to Outfunnel

Originally created as a two-way sync solution for Mailchimp users, Outfunnel developed its own platform as an integration into Pipedrive, creating a very strong app-panel. Well before Pipedrive's native app Campaigns, Outfunnel offered a well designed app where users can see all campaigns' data directly on the contact's page.

TypeForm

It offers a more engaging way to fill in forms focused on improving user experience. It integrates directly with many tools, Pipedrive included, and provides a useful free tier for small usage or testing.

Paperflite

A great amount of content can be difficult to organise, to make it available and deliver to the right person at the right time. This solution empowers sales teams in organising and sharing content with prospects. The added benefit is the tracking counterpart behaviour, which is exerted in nurturing then qualifying leads. Although it doesn't directly generate new leads, it can be helpful in nurturing existing ones.

LeadsBridge

Offers automation solutions specific to the marketing and advertising world, aiming to bridge the gap between companies' ads and sales funnels. If you're using Facebook Lead Ads, Google Ads lead form extensions, or LinkedIn Lead Gen Forms, you may benefit from interconnecting lead data transfer. Within the LeadsBridge platform users can create their own custom solution.

Summary

A wide range of tools are available in the lead generation, marketing automation, and email marketing arena. Although some of them are good, their primary focus tends to be outbound marketing: contacting contacts.

Lead generation should include managing social media campaigns, search engine campaigns, landing pages and data capture, together with leads nurturing, leads scoring and marketing qualification. Although few tools are capable of handling the whole process, it may be even better for a company to use different tools for those different steps.

Tools remain helpful when companies are capable of producing content with a clear strategy to engage audiences around their brand.

No business can afford to produce no content. All businesses should become media companies to boost their engagement and leads generation capabilities.

10 Gathering Data by Forms

The Blood Donation Form

As every blood donor in Italy knows, there is a procedure every time you go for a donation. You have to run the risk assessment every time. This procedure is understandably right as a donor could have risky behaviours between two donations. The medical doctor must clarify it and assess the safety of the blood they collect. Fine, no complaining about it.

My problem is that I get terribly bored filling dozens of checkboxes of stuff that I perceive useless and they are always the same. Just consider a paper form for both men and women, so you will find questions like: *"Have you got pregnant recently?" "Have you noticed any delay in your period lately?"*. Ok they could be just funny, but then you can also find questions like, *"Did you have sex in exchange for money?"*, which can be for both, men and women or some like: *"Did you hurt yourself with needles, or dirt of blood of someone who is drug addicted?"*. There is a long list of questions related to almost any kind of illness or physical problems you could have incurred.

The list is so long and you have to fill each checkbox one by one. Otherwise the doctor wouldn't accept it. You have to pay attention because from time to time you can find questions that you have to answer "YES" amid dozens where the answers are expected to be a NO. This has to be done using a pen over an A3 paper in the waiting room before entering the lab.

Well personally I *always* make mistakes in filling that form. I really can't keep attention for so long to something so useless. Last time I also totally forgot that I actually had medication, a minor check in a hospital with no consequences, but I should report that. It wouldn't affect my fitness to donate, but it is part of the information required by the form: *I simply skipped the question!* Why? Because I lose focus when I'm supposed to do something I feel is not bringing value to me and can easily be done in a more efficient way.

You will say, it is not useless at all: *"it's a very important procedure as it affects someone else's life!"* True.

But please ask yourself to whom it is relevant. Let's consider that: I'm the donor, I'm there to donate in favour of someone else, I do not get anything in exchange for it, just to be proud to give and to help someone, no matter who. I'm always sure my behaviour is correct and I do not have issues. Otherwise why should I go there?

Let's ask yourself: *Would you really go to donate blood if you had any doubt about your own conditions?*

If you answer yes, well then there is not much else to discuss about that subject. What I mean is that I wouldn't mind answering questions that assess the risk, because I'm considerate and respectful of the job of anyone who works in the healthcare service. But I can't suffer from stupidity and a waste of (my) time.

Let's consider an extreme example: Let's imagine that someone who is drug addicted, maybe also a prostitute, and goes to donate blood. Fortunately they don't, as there is no incentive, but let's imagine they would: do you really think they would fill the checkboxes as YES?

Hence, all the questions related to those topics are clearly totally useless. They are included as a means to take away the doctor's responsibility. Fine, it means they offload their problems to donors in a manner which **implies a greater effort for donors.**

Let's consider that the list includes many types of illness, possible physical issues and every kind of human problem, rendering the task mundane and difficult to focus on, resulting in a lack of interest and willingness that feels like a waste of my (precious and scarce) time.

I believe there should be another method to assess it, doing it in a more efficient way! If it would be proposed in that way, I wouldn't mind collaborating even better and deeper. Maybe I'm not alone in this view, but I am just able to speak out when many don't. Many just do it, quietly and calmly accepting the system and the rules as good citizens, but what happens when they are clients instead of donors?

As Jay Baer says in his book[12]: haters might be just good people who had expectations that the providers didn't fill, and because they are required to spend their own resources in dealing with a (bad) provider left feeling betrayed.

It is the same to me: I feel betrayed when I'm forced in using my time for doing stupid, useless things for someone else for the simple reason to obey their rules.

Why this story?

The example may provide an idea of the role of selecting the right information that really needs to be assessed. The method to collect data may often result incorrect in its purpose to engage your most valuable people: the client.

The method is inefficient, maybe legally correct, but it doesn't take into consideration the donor's experience. In order to donate, people are requested to pass through a frustrating, boring procedure.

---

[12] Baer, J., Hug Your Haters, Penguin NY, 2016

What if the donors would be enabled to fill forms faster, avoiding repetitive questions? Exposing immediately the areas of serious investigation creating a clear, fast overview of them?

The ultimate purpose should be to collect reliable information, not just run a procedure. Any method that would enable efficiency, reducing time consumption, I bet, will be greatly appreciated.

This is one great issue for organisations: overcome the idea of filling procedures (getting safe) instead of aiming for ecological goals.

Companies' data collections often leave a similar feeling: forms might be formally correct, they comply with the rules. But the customers' experience might be poor.

When forms focus on the data to collect, not on the customer's experience they do not engage customers and, even worse they are felt as useless and bothering.

Managers often say: "We need that data to give them the service they ask for...". Here the point is on "WE NEED", what if managers would suggest: "*Customers would feel the value of sharing those data with us*".

The outcome of a bad collection method, in forms to fill in or any other way, is often a lack of reliable data. Losing counterpart engagement and maybe also a waste of time in running controls of data that also impacts on the employees' feelings.

11 Case study

From Leads Generation to Sales

Buyapowa is the leading enterprise advocacy marketing platform, powering referral marketing for over 100 leading brands and retailers in 27 countries and 21 languages. Clients are active in telecommunications, banking, insurance, utilities, fashion, beauty, retail travel, grocery and gaming/gambling and includes big brands of each industry.

The solution allows brands to equip and incentivise their customers to recommend them to their friends, family and colleagues and offers incentives and rewards for genuine and successful customer referrals. Traditionally we know how unhappy clients are 5 times more likely to voice about their bad experiences with brands. Buyapowa allows brands to change that attitude and give voice to happy clients by spreading directly to their own acquaintances what a lovely customer experience they had.

The company is headquartered in London with offices in Vancouver and Berlin. Led by Gideon Lask, who formerly held senior executive positions at HMV, NBC Universal and LetsBuyIt.com, the team combines experience from leading retailers, brands and start-ups including uSwitch, Lastminute.com, HMV.com, Deutsche Bank, RBS, Glasses Direct, Home Advisor, Qubit and Salesforce.

In June 2021 we asked Peter Cunningham, marketing director at Buyapowa, to explain to us what actions they perform to develop their presence in the markets where they operate:

"Thank you Antonio. My view about the company's processes between marketing and sales is simple, we can also gather all these functions under one umbrella: the marketing, as marketing is about the whole activities performed by an organisation to analyse, know, understand markets then to act on them to perform business development. Sales is one of the marketing activities that any company needs to perform to stay in the market."

The Role of Marketing:

- Create awareness
- Get first touch point from the right people
- Help Sales to convince with arguments supported in well developed documents that convey qualitative contents.

The Role of Sales development:

- Qualify leads

The Role of Sales accountant:

- Show
- Convince
- Close

Which campaigns do you run?

"To nurture markets and generate new leads we mainly run marketing campaigns on social-media, mailing, SEM, listing but also organised events before COVID. Leads generation is still paramount to us."

How do you engage leads?

"In the leads generation funnel they mostly come inbound by requesting a demo or information on our website. We also have some email-gated content on our website and social media that enables email marketing. "

Once the data are in Pipedrive, what happens? How do you manage or treat data and who is in charge of doing that?

"Sales accountants and SDRs have their own Pipelines in Pipedrive and manage the contact, moving it back and forth through different stages."

What are your main parameters that affect the leads generation: quantity of campaigns, frequency, target audiences, content...?

"Referring to leads that respond to emails sent by Active Campaign, rather than leads coming via other sources.

The main factors are:

- ***The Quality of the Data**: contact the right person at the right company. Someone who would be interested in what we have to say. We can target different elements of the decision making circle with different messaging, but if the contact is the wrong person then we are wasting time even if it is the right company in terms of industry and size.*
- ***Deliverability** - sender reputation, both for your domain and the IP address used by the ESP. It is important to keep your data clean - removing bounces and unsubscribes and irrelevant emails.*
- ***Email subject line and sender** - these are the first things a recipient will see and so are important in influencing the decision to read, delete, unsubscribe or mark as spam*
- ***Relevance**: how can you quickly establish that you are relevant to a busy executive. Do you work with key brands? Are you referring to a hot topic?*
- ***Credibility of you as a business**: how can you get this across fast to a busy executive: look and feel of the email, address, client references, awards etc.*
- ***Language**: an obvious one, but you will get a higher interaction rate if you send an email to an Italian in Italian*
- ***Time of send**: this is important for an international database as an email*

arriving in the middle of the night is less likely to be read. We see that 95% of emails seem to be interacted with within the first hour of send or not at all

- ***Day of send***: *watch international holidays like Thanksgiving and Muslim countries not working on Fridays*
- ***Age of the database***: *due to the way in-boxes work, emails that are not engaged with will be moved to the spam filter. So you will typically see diminishing returns over time*
- ***Mixing it up***: *be prepared to mix in occasional tactical emails from different senders if response rates are dropping"*

How does this channel contribute to the company's growth rate?

"The growth of the company is driven by new client wins, retention of existing clients and upsells to existing clients. Sales to new clients is a large part of our growth, but our ability to grow within existing clients is equally important."

What are you thinking to change, alter or improve in the Leads generation process and why?

"We have experimented with different approaches over the years, and will continue it, particularly in new industries and territories. However, our preference is to do things in-house, wherever possible. We would like to increase automation. We are certainly open to finding a way to enhance the efficiency of the whole process, for this we may test some other solutions, then we will decide the best way to go. Nothing is decided, but leads generation is too important to be run with little efficiency."

12 Campaigns

Introduction

Nurturing markets is a long-term, challenging, expensive, and hard to measure plan. Often unavoidable for businesses, market nurturing includes challenges in content production, circulating, then people engagement.

The crucial part? Communicating with different audiences when they are getting closer to the brand, providing even more precise communication to homogeneous groups.

Once leads are unveiled as contact persons, it starts the effectiveness of Email Marketing Campaigning.

In this chapter we will go through the followings topics:

- How to set dynamic audiences
- How to create automated mailing
- How leverage audiences for nurturing

Pipedrive Campaigns add-on

The choice to include a native feature for email campaigns in Pipedrive CRM is not against the open source strategy. Clients who are into a specific tool can continue to use it, while the competition in the marketplace can only improve the quality of available solutions. The role of a native solution may be to smooth the process, and improve the data transfer. Pipedrive users can now see each campaign result both aggregated and in the contact's page-view.

In Fig. 12.01 we can see the main page, where all campaigns are stored with the main results immediately visible. Further details are available inside each campaign page.

As for Pipedrive Campaigns itself, it is now a well developed tool that offers almost anything required for the job.

Nurturing leads and contacts implies the capability to deliver messages at the right time. For instance, when some contacts download a white paper (a content) about a topic, this behaviour triggers another message (at the right time) to suggest some other content related to the same topic. This function takes the name of Automated Campaign - better known as Transactional Mailing.

- On one hand, we have direct mailing that a marketing person may design and schedule at the right time.
- On the other hand, there are transactional campaigns triggered by events, that are generally contacts' actions.

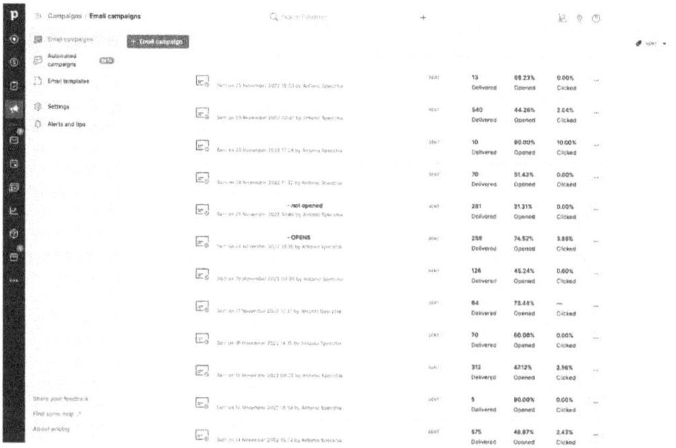

Fig. 12.01 - Campaigns sent list. The view offers main data to compare

Audiences management

CRM databases may contain a great amount of contacts collected along the marketing funnels and interested in the brand (MQL).

Wondering how they are "catched" by the brand may enable companies to create homogeneous groups around some relevant criteria, then develop different and more successful approaches focused on each group.

Creating audiences based on tags, implies to manage each tag for each contact while the number of contacts increases. Automating the process of inclusion improves efficiency reducing manual control on groups. Dynamic audience creation enables campaigning to each contact proposing a more interesting message and content according to their interest.

Dynamic audiences

In chapter four we saw the process of creating selections using the filter function in Pipedrive. Here we will go a little bit further in refining audiences.

Moreover, we would refer to the Data Architecture chapter later in this book to clarify the requirements to enhance the confidence in the system and the data stored in its database. Let us stress the importance of the data architecture: data quality, in terms of content of each field, is core to the reliability of selecting records.

> A good level of data quality cannot be achieved either by forcing salespeople to input mandatory data, and even less by punishing incorrect data input. (However, this may be the subject of another book...)

The filtering feature of Pipedrive is very well developed: users may create endless criteria selection to refine audiences in a very detailed manner. In fig 12.1 we can analyse a detailed filter to select the right audience.

It may be good to recall how this filter works as we last saw it in chapter four:

The upper part contains criteria that MUST be true.

> Only records that match all those parameters will be included in the audience.

The lower part of the filter builder accepts criteria that CAN be true.

> Using "ANY of these conditions" the output will show records that include at least one between the criterias. In the case of one criteria the list will be all records that match that criteria.

Filter Example 1

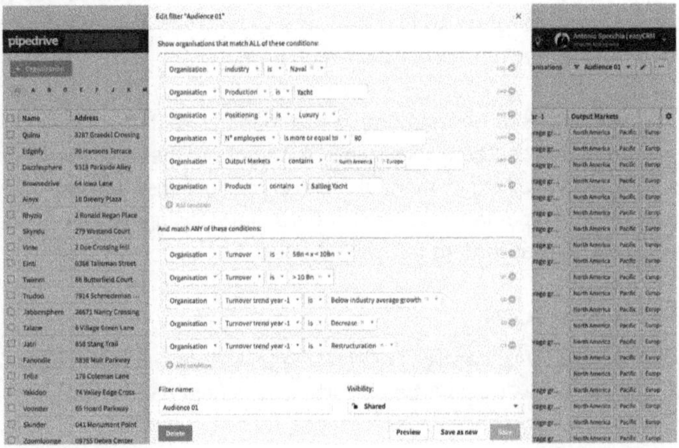

Fig 12.1 - Filtering audiences by many complex criteria

Let's analyse this case EXAMPLE 1.

In the conditions that **MUST** be true:

We have three criteria that define the **industry**, the **type of production** and the **brand positioning**.

Both **Industry** and **Positioning** fields are multiple options then condition IS is due to select the right option.

The **Production** is an autocomplete field where the content is free, the condition **IS** implies that ONLY the whole word is selected. If we choose the condition as "contains" or "starts with" that would enable selecting any word or phrase with the variable defined in this box: Yacht.

The **N* employees** field is numeric (maybe imported?), the condition here may be "is more or equal to" to select any company with 80 or more people in the workforce.

The **Output Markets** field has multiple options, here we can use "contains" as conditions and pick up the variables we need.

The **Products** is another autocomplete field, here using the condition "contains" enables to select all the words or phrases that contain [sailing yacht].

In the condition that **CAN** be true:

The **Turnover** is a single option field, the options have been defined in groups instead of using raw values. This may simplify the manual input. In this case we are forced to select two options of the same field.

The query is repeated to select the two possible contents.

The **Turnover trend year -1** field provides an information, someone or something (automated business process) created this information as the results of a relationship between more data. The information is qualitative, and it takes on the value of a word that describes it. Then we should have three queries for the three possible values, the words content we might want to include.

Filter Example 2

In fig. 12.2 we can analyse the filter to create an audience of 27 people, all managers of medium-sized companies in the automotive industry.

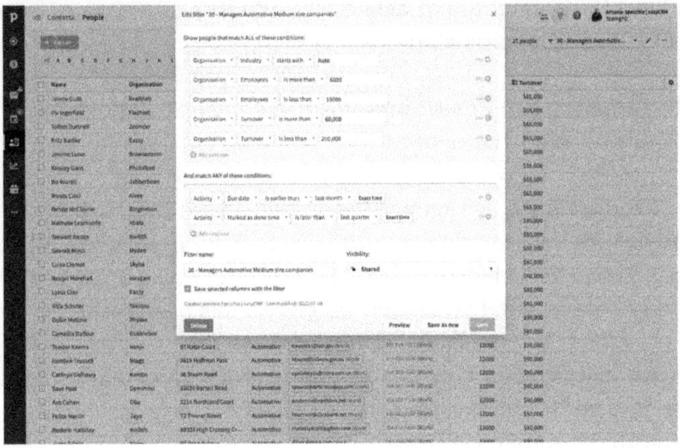

Fig. 12.2 - Filter to create audiences in people table

In this case we can see the different use of filter's criteria. They are parameters all related to companies' even if we are selecting people.

> **Industry** in this case is a free text field. Using a "starting with" condition may enable us to include in the selection any word related to [AUTO***]. This trick may help in case of risk of typos due to manual entry: *Automovite, autotive, automobiles*. All these words will be included in the selection.
>
> **Employees** and **Turnover** here are numeric and monetary fields. In both cases we have to create a double query to select the condition in MUST be true: first time every record MORE THAN a defined value; second time every record LESS THAN a value.
>
> **Activity** is a field from the activities database used here to select a range of time, last quarter, in which no activities have been run with this person. Even with this field, by creating two queries it helps in better defining the timeframe.

In these examples we know that a change of the audience will take place every time a data parameter changes in any record in the database.

Let's imagine data are regularly updated by a public list as the Companies House. Readers can easily adapt the example to other datasets that change even more frequently.

Companies that undergo either the number of employees or the turnover change can no longer belong to the audiences or enter in the audience if they were not included before.

To achieve it users will not need to insert or remove tags, there will be no manual control. There is no doubt that these are just exercises based on fake data.

> We can infer how the creating audiences feature using real-life data can be powerful, especially if those data change dynamically over the time.

Furthermore, we know how data should change by updating over time. A database that is not maintained, updated regularly and cleaned of wrong data will lose its informative power rapidly. This means that audiences always change.

In the effort to communicate to precise audiences it may be hazardous to not update data and lists of recipients ending up sending messages to an inaccurate audience. Those who will receive the communication finding it irrelevant will be ready to withdraw their consent. Hence, businesses lose valuable contacts for the simple reason of inaccurate selection of the message recipients list!

They are people who, instead, might be interested in receiving appropriate, valuable messages from the business.

Creating different audiences, it's best to organise them by code -a number and a name- so they can be easily found even when working with workflow automations.

Group emails

Using CRM lists to segments the population and build custom audiences may result in more efficient and effective retargeting campaigns[14]

In case the groups are smaller than 100 contacts, users may set up a simple email sending directly in the people table. In Fig. 12.3 you can see a selection of

[14] Baer, J., Hug Your Haters, Penguin NY, 2016

24 people to whom we may want to create a tailored message.

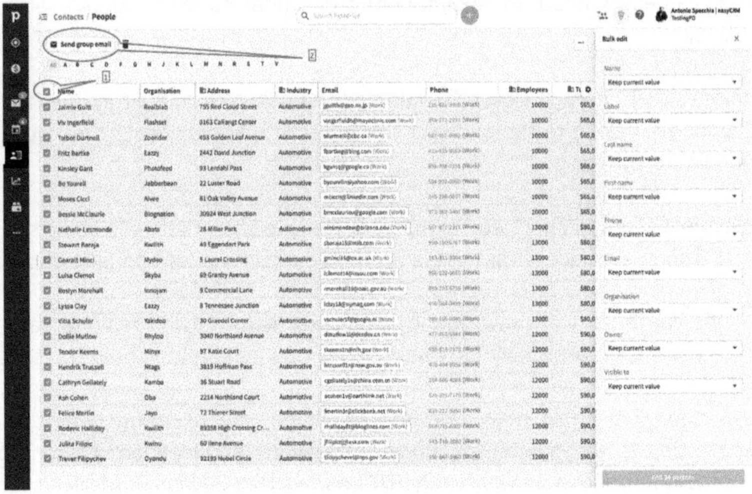

Fig. 12.3 - Audience of 24 contacts and its bulk email preparation

In this setting, users have to select all the contacts in the list by hitting the checkbox on the top of the list [1], then use the "**Sending Group Email**" function [2]. Group email function starts with the process of message creation. Users may create a new message from scratch or use an available template, eventually adapting it to the circumstances. In fig. 12.4 you can see the selection of templates.

Be aware

Pipedrive delays each message by 30 seconds, so if you have 100 contacts, it could take 50 minutes to send all the messages.

This feature is there to prevent the server from spamming blockage because of excessive traffic. Generally speaking, it is not an issue, but if you expect your contact to receive the message at 9.00 AM, be aware it might not happen.

Communicating to audiences

Next, we need to stress the importance of communicating the best tailored message to an audience, which is nothing new. Everyone agrees how powerful a message that reaches us might be when we are interested in that topic. While one of the most overlooked issues is creating homogenous audiences in email marketing. Too often organisations do not invest enough time in depicting different audiences by common traits. It is easier to shoot email to all contacts under the (wrong) feeling that "*...what we are gonna share is interesting to* *everyone!"*

It is more catchy the idea of sending thousands of (same) emails, even getting a tiny conversion rate that sums up to hundreds of conversions.

Probably also the idea of the *newsletter* sunk in, people are more keen to read short messages, very focused and straight to the point. Possibly actionable to produce value for recipients.

So, how do we create it?

First the topic of the message MUST be remarkable to every recipient. And it strongly depends on the homogeneity of the audience. Is here that a proper segmentation of the audience is key.

> Elements of the segmentation are the dataset, the quality of data and the strategy above all of them.

Businesses may know who their audiences are, what they are keen for. And to get there, in B2B, it often implies a marketing-sales common achievement. But once the audiences are well designed and the messages correctly developed, not only the conversion rate may improve, but something subtle will happen, often unnoticed: churn rate might decrease, but even more important the long term brand reputation rises. People find it useful to read the messages, and one day or another they might develop the intention to get more of it.

> Is there that the Pipedrive's capability to ease the fine segmentations needed to run email marketing campaigns aimed to very specific groups of people really makes the difference.

With the dynamic filtering, contacts can be added or excluded automatically along the way. While transactional mailing (called automated in Pipedrive) are mainly driven by events, dynamic filtering feature enhances scheduled campaigns that in a medium period of time they may see their audiences change accordingly to the change of some parameters.

The same filter used in Creating Audiences in chapter 4, now becomes extremely useful for Pipedrive Campaigns.

Composing the message

Here we will list some hints that may help readers in managing more effective direct messaging enhancing emailing effectiveness.

Dynamic content includes elements of the client's information in the email body. The correct use of data from the contact's record may improve the tone of voice, making the message really more personal.

- Adding variables in the message, well beyond just the personal name, gives the message a better personal touch.
- Keep messages short, straight to the point, tidy and clean.
- Aim to the purpose of creating real effective value for readers.
- Avoid pictures if they don't really mean something valuable to receivers.
- Rather than using a "newsletter" style, keep it clean and direct, as if you were writing to the person directly. It may increase reading rates. In general, the trend of discarding broadcasted messages is higher.
- Share web-link documents instead as attachments, even worse as editable format: messages will be lighter, faster and more importantly links may be tracked. Using links in shortened format by setting the URL on an anchor word.
- Keep email and link tracking enabled. The option is at the bottom of the email editor. You will see all the information about each person's behaviour directly in the contact's page!

Other Mailing tools

Outfunnel offers the great feature to sync campaign data in real time into contact's records in Pipedrive. The results of every campaign performed by classic tools like Mailchimp, Active Campaign, SendinBlue and also HubSpot are used to populate every contact's data and stored in each contact's page - showing behaviours along each campaign and enabling us to refinine the audiences.

Actually, the previous option of sending a list in Mailchimp required users to check for information of each campaign inside Mailchimp's dashboards, causing siloing of information. If you are still using Mailchimp, or prefer the marketing automation feature of HubSpot, then Outfunnel is a great way to connect the two platforms - bringing back data into Pipedrive automatically.

Mailchimp users may find it a bit more difficult to move into Pipedrive as the logic of the tools differ and Pipedrive enables more effective data management. Reshaping the data set may be required when planning to move your email marketing in the Pipedrive Campaign.

Summary

This chapter ideally continues the discussion of the lead generation chapter: MQLs may not be ready for a deal any time soon, but their needs might arise better in future.

This is the reason for nurturing audiences: staying in touch, offering relevant content, supporting brand's positioning, then keeping the position in prospects' minds about the offered solution.

Email Marketing Campaigning is not dead, companies using it under the correct framework may leverage another channel to nurture leads and contacts. Being remarkable, kind and providing real value the methodology may pay back.

Pipedrive Campaigns help to achieve it better and faster. And who wouldn't want that?

13 Projects

Introduction

The last arrival into the Project Management landscape, Pipedrive Projects leverages the same Kanban structure that made Pipedrive CRM a success. *-BTW the implementation of Project and Campaign were among the reasons for the delay of this book-*

Project management is a discipline with a consistent knowledge base, but it may be hard to discuss in this book. It would require a long discussion over the methodology and its big shift, including PMI and its foundation, to arrive at discussing Agile methodology.

We won't go in that area, which is significantly different from CRM. Instead, this chapter will only discuss some features on the Pipedrive's tool that may enable organisations to look after their projects for clients.

Another Project Management Software

The project management tools landscape may be quite crowded already, with Atlassian that offers the strong tool Jira, with significantly more complexities. Or on the other side, tools like Asana or even Trello (also by Atlassian) are less technical but still quite complex. These three tools all offer free tiers, but the real challenge of an organisation is not to save money - but to be effective when it comes to delivering their services or products.

Another issue with PM is that even if a well established knowledge base exists, no two companies run the same method, or use the same approach. For this reason, a tool on PM that includes all the possibilities may be very complex.

Pipedrive's approach is to simplify, maybe including less features and reducing complexity, but focus on what essentially matters to make project management easier.

Anyone who is familiar with Apple tools knows the difference between Numbers and Excel, or even our favourite, Google Sheets. The latters are much more powerful and complex, where users may develop extremely complex sheets to run really delicate functions. The problem is that they are still spreadsheets, while more complex and critical functions should deserve more stable and reliable tools than a spreadsheet.

With Numbers, users enjoy the simplicity to run spreadsheets easily, aiming for its specific purpose: calculation over columns of data.

When it comes to more critical functions, let's take for instance the CRM or even the Project Management functions, smart people do not use spreadsheets, but purposely developed software.

The same we can consider for Project Management: Pipedrive Project enables a simple, effective approach to running projects when the complexity is not the main issue.
Jira, to take one of the most reputable PM tools, is capable of running thousands of employees with hundreds of projects for very complex software development.

For this reason Pipedrive Projects is capable of ticking all the requirement boxes for many small and medium businesses when it comes to clients' projects like implementation, delivery and other services with a limited complexity.

To make it simple: If your company builds aircrafts, then probably your production team is using Jira already. That kind of complexity matters a great deal on the PM software that may support it.

But, the question is: *could the delivery of the aircrafts benefit from a simpler tool that doesn't deal with the complexity of the production, but is focused on facilitating the few stages and the (limited) number of activities and tasks that are required for the delivery?*

Maybe it is not the case to knock on Boeing's doors to try selling it -as it seems they are dealing with extremely more complex problems lately-, but every company may benefit from different tools for different purposes. Pipedrive Projects fits a precise niche of use. It is always about the *why*.

How it works

The tool benefits from a simple UX: clean, reducing any extra complexities or cluttering the view.

One of the first things to do, when a company tries Pipedrive Projects, may be to consider setting an automation to CREATE a new project when a deal is won. This functionality is covered by Workflow Automation (see chapter 8), but what matters now is the NAME of the projects. As we have seen Pipedrive names the deals, "deal", and we suggested to name them with a description of the product or service the deal will focus on. In doing so, your organisation will have better naming for the deals when they get won. So, adding them automatically to the project's name, adding the purpose of the project: "delivery", "implementation", or whatever matters to your business may be good.

Another task we strongly recommend, is the DESIGN of the project process. Likewise we suggested for the Pipeline, in order to mirror the real sales process, we suggest naming the project's stages according to the real process your company runs.

In doing so it would be beneficial, if your projects pattern includes different purposes that imply different stages, creating a project pipeline for each project type.

Furthermore, once you have properly shaped your project by tasks and activities to do, save it as a template. Templates repository is simple and useful and each template is associated with a Project Pipeline.

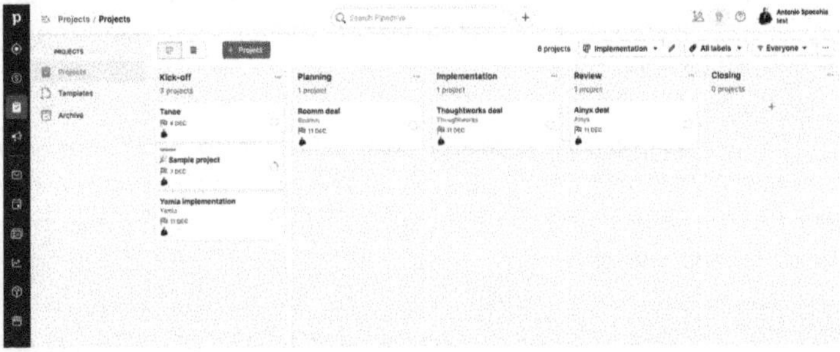

Fig 13.1 Pipedrive Project overview: like the Kanban pipeline users may get the project portfolio at a glance

Pipedrive default is quite good, but as we said before, each organisation adopts a different approach for PM, make it yours to be more effective!

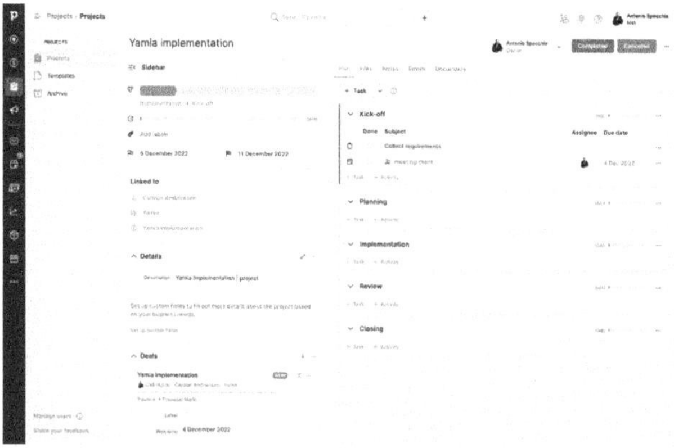

Fig 13.2 Page-view of each project, on the left the data column, on the right the operational space.

From the projects' portfolio view, users may drill into each project page, finding it very intuitive as it was for the CRM.

Activities and tasks of the project may be populated manually or, even better, automatically by using a template. When in place they are listed on the right side of the page, a chronological order can create very intuitive results.

More interesting still is the feature of Tasks that differs by Activities by appearing in the To Do list, but not in the Calendar. Similar to the [Check] task in the CRM, that appears in the calendar but doesn't block the time slot, here the task type doesn't even clutter the calendar.

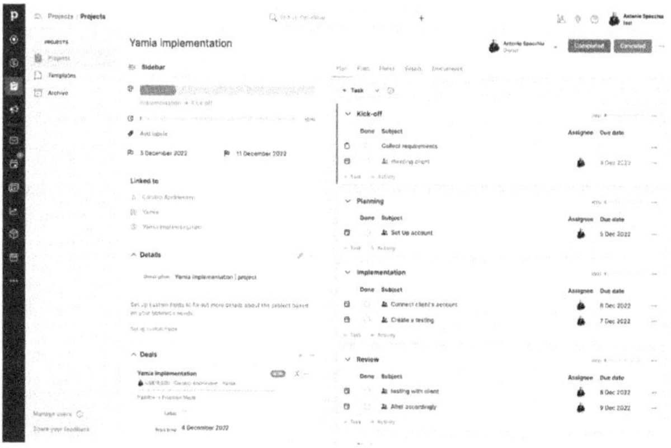

Fig. 13.3 The project page populated by activities

A project needs a different dataset from a CRM deal, so you can find the projects table' fields manager alongside the other main tables of Pipedrive.

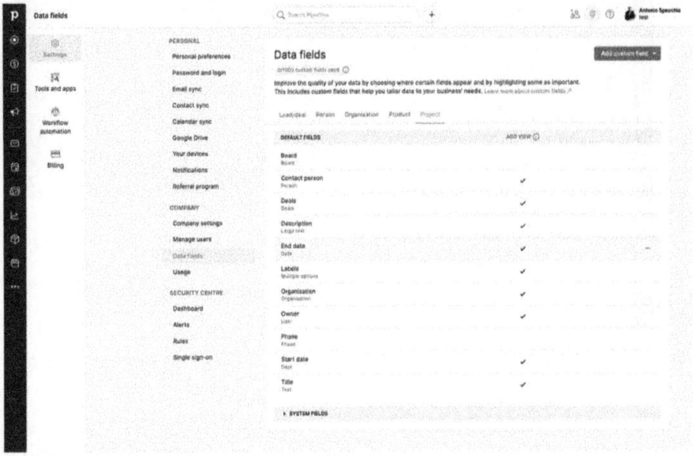

Fig. 13.4 Fields manager of Projects.

Want to know something equally fascinating? The last stage Closing is a dynamic stage, projects there are not close yet, when they are closed their status changes. This takes them away from the pipeline while they can be visible again using the, now well known, "Filtering" feature. Selecting Completed. In Fig. 14.4 one way to complete a project: drag and drop it on the page bottom, selecting the dropbox Complete, likewise for the pipeline's deal management in the CRM section.

Filtering is also fully functional here, likewise workflow automation, email sync and reporting.

Pipedrive just announced a task manager function dedicated to Projects that will be available from Q2 2023. This will enable users to keep the two types of activity together -in case the role of the users implies both, sales and project management-, or keep them separated when the person's role differs, or the organisation of the job may benefit from this.

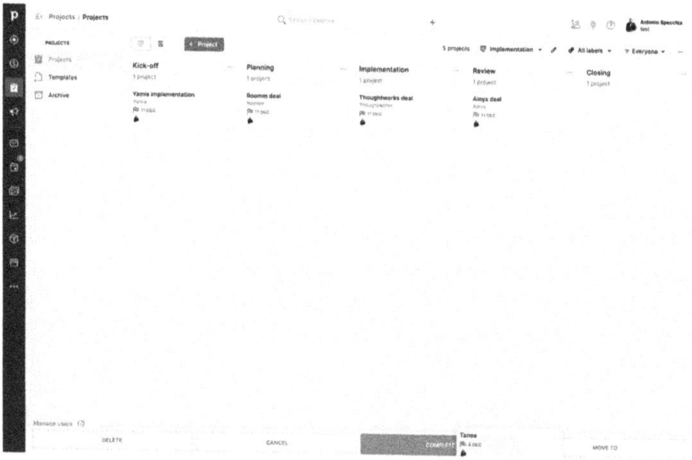

Fig. 14.4 Close a project once the stage Closing is completed: drag it and drop into the dropbox COMPLETE.

Completed and cancelled projects may be made visible again by filtering alongside Open projects.

Archived projects will be moved away from the pipeline, as they will be parked. They remain available in the Archive for further necessities, but they won't be part of the reporting on open, cancelled and completed projects. This function is very similar to cancelling a project that, instead, leaves the project in the pipeline, where it will also be tracked by reporting.

Deleted projects, meanwhile, will be erased completely.

Summary

Overall, Pipedrive Projects fits quite nicely into the Pipedrive suite, creating a value for users who may benefit from a simplified project management.

The main benefits, beyond simplicity, are the smooth integration with the pipelines of the CRM that enables an effective data transferring, the automation of the Kanban board and, likewise for the pipeline view, the overview of the whole projects portfolio at a glance. For now, only about each pipeline, but Pipedrive is working on revamping the pipeline system and it may result in a possible multi-pipeline view.

14 Reporting

Introduction

Many factors can determine business success or failure, the reasons behind success are always more complex than the simple straight view depicted by the latin motto: "*Post Hoc Ergo Propter Hoc*". Which means, -because such a thing happened before the event, that's caused the event-. For this very reason, a method to build a better awareness of processes is to track all the activities that took place in the process, and in doing that, create a reliable and detailed reporting of them.

Understanding the sales process trends may enable us to clarify what activities have a greater effect on the output. Doing that we can alter the activities performed along the process and measure changes.

> **If you don't measure it you can't improve it.**

Thus reporting is more than just keeping track of the past, but it enables us to learn the interaction between activities along the process and results.

> According to Jurgen Appelo's Celebration Grid: "**Success can also happen by doing bad things**"[15].

> In Peter Senge's "The Fifth Discipline"[16] : "**...any effect we perceive depends on the complex interactions of multiple factors**".

In "The Fifth Discipline" Peter describes the System-Thinking, as an opposite approach to mechanical-thinking. Mechanical-Thinking is when we believe that an event is just the result of a linear dependance cause-effect. When observing an event we infer a direct cause in something that happened just before the observed event. And by doing it we are missing the complexity of the real world.

In the real, complex world, factors that affect success and failure can be difficult to determine. This is also true whether they are business-related or at a personal level. The good thing is that, in business, tracking methods may help to identify several of the many causes that may concour in triggering an event.

---

15 Appelo, J., Managing for Happiness, Wiley, 2016
16 Peter Senge, The fifth discipline, Random House, 2006

CRM allows companies to collect data on a daily basis, then combine data to illustrate trends and tendencies.

A number is just raw data. Among other data, a number may convey a meaning. The relationship between data sets is what builds information. But then, the reliability of data is a crucial component of reporting processes: creating charts displaying unreliable trends is probably worse than having no reporting at all.

Later in chapter 16, we will discuss how data architecture is essential to develop an effective CRM. Here we want to emphasise how the quality of the dataset strongly depends on data architecture.

Identifying problems and developing solutions should begin with understanding the nature of the existing issues. In other words, if we develop analysis on bad data, the analysis is not only useless, it is actually dangerous for the business.

It is true that reporting could be developed over any data, so the R&F shouldn't be affected by the data architecture. In fact the organisation of data, its architecture, should be clear to analysts who investigate. But more than that, the quality of data input is affected by the design of data fields and the data architecture. As a result, the data architecture directly impacts the Reporting & Forecasting.

Sales support

Sales can be quite complex: squeezing an amount of tasks into working hours being able to remain effective all time. Using an efficient approach and tools to manage daily duties is then paramount.

Reporting over the sales process is then vital for any business, but it also requires the correct approach to it: reports can't develop reliable information on rubbish data!

For instance, salespeople may tend to shortcut managing activities and track wrongly, one thing we often observe are hundreds of tasks not closed, as they have not been done.

"***No activity exists if it is not recorded in Pipedrive!***"
This way a business owner has managed to set the salespeople's engagement. Not much to discuss.

In **Getting Things Done**[17], David Allen encourages readers to set a plan, act, then report on a daily basis as this leads to boost productivity.

> Pipedrive provides a great environment to salespeople's task management with the purpose to boost productivity that ultimately affects results: more deals closed.

This was the reason-why behind the development of Pipedrive: in search of a salespeople effectiveness boost.

Reporting in Pipedrive

With Pipedrive CRM, companies can easily create reports based on their CRM, displaying trends over the most relevant market data. Pipedrive's reporting tool, Insight, makes it easy to develop charts about many key parameters' trends.

Be aware: We use a more standard naming here than Pipedrive. Chart is the graph while a Report is a more complete and complex set of information.

Charts

A key component of Pipedrive reporting are the charts, they are graphs rendering to visualising data.

We will analyse some of the different options of charts, while later in the next chapter we will discuss how to build dashboards with different charts. Within Insights, users can choose chart templates or create a chart from scratch. In Pipedrive, the chart builder is simple, but its options can be confusing.

> With so many options, we strongly recommend that you plan your output: determine what trends you want to control. It would be helpful to start with a simple drawing to be able to build them with clarity.

There are two basic types of tracking and reporting:

- Reporting over activities, tasks done in a broad sense
- Reporting about deals' progress

It may be useful to clarify that "reporting over activities" may provide a better understanding of the effort required for sales. Tracking the effort on an individual level, related to results, enables sales managers to plan for a future goal knowing

[17] Allen, D., Getting Things Done, Penguin Books

the effective effort required to achieve it.

Tracking also supports the understanding over changes: how marketing policies execution might affect the sales effort?

Tracking and reporting over the sales process is more specific showing the deal's journey. How long does the journey last? How long does each stage last?

> Gathering this information means that companies can finally figure the sales process effectiveness and efficiency trends.

A relevant topic to discuss is compensation: has the result come from greater efforts or a smarter approach? Is success due to commitment and effort or pure luck? How do we reward one versus the other?

Reporting over Activities

Activities tracking is also the basis of Pipedrive logic via the embedded Activities Based Selling approach.

Tracking activities as it implies awareness of task accomplishment, is already a strong support for productivity. But it is the reporting that provides a definitive view of the sales process endeavour. The effort, individually tracked but analysed cumulatively, supports the company's culture development by connecting output and people work. This makes it possible to better plan for a future business expansion by knowing the amount of human work to add.

Using Pipedrive builder users can create reports for activities, deals or forecasting (Fig. 14.1)

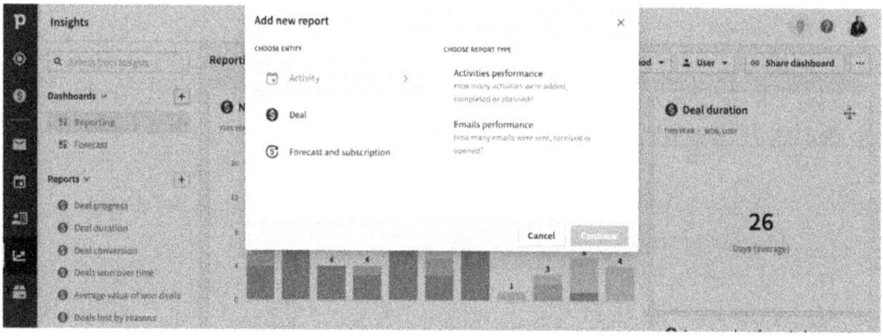

Fig. 14.1 - Creating a report in Insights

In the attempt to ease the process, Insights builder provides a default view (in Fig 14.2), capable to displays on the Y-axis:

- number of activities
- number of activities grouped by type

While along the X-axis:

- time period

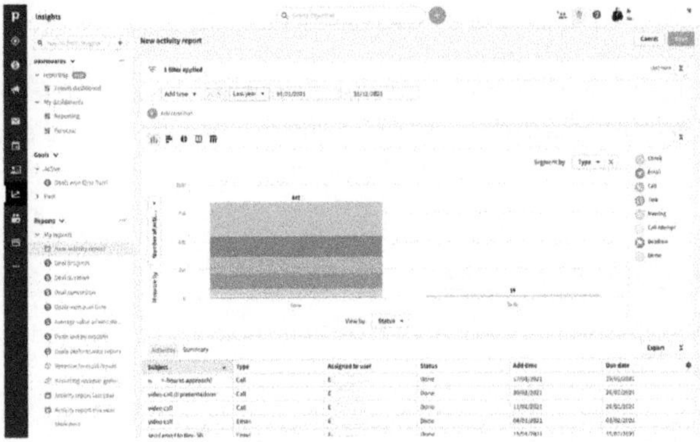

Fig. 14.2 - Standard chart at the very first setting

You can easily adjust this chart by changing the criteria: on the upper side, it offers a filter, which enables users to select the criteria to refine the chart rendering.

The filter works over:

- Users
- Pipelines
- Status

And using the Professional tier it may also work on custom fields. In Fig. 14.3, some of the available parameters are shown.

Once the data are selected, the builder enables three more dimensions:

- Measured by = Y-axis
- Segmented by = Y-axis
- View by = X-axis

Visual representations can also show three views:

- Histograms
- Pie charts
- Value

Different visual representations have a stronger meaning than just being entertaining.

> The use of pie charts instead of histograms could be more informative for some type of data selections

When users are looking for new ways to interpret data, we suggest experimenting with parameters and views.

But it is important for users to be aware that the lack of a clear plan on what they want to analyse, and playing around with chart settings may lead to confusion.

Fig. 14.3 - Filtering the data along some parameters to perform selection

During the process of building the chart, data will be displayed in the table-view below it. Moving the cart in a dashboard implies only the chart will be visible. But all the charts are drillable in the dashboard: by clicking the chart the data in table view will become visible.

The chart may paginate if the rendering becomes too large. A set of a year data grouped by weeks, for instance, cannot fit in the view. Users can scroll pages laterally in the dashboard view.

> Charts may also be created to slice data for specific analysis: rather than checking general trends, users may want to focus on a specific dimension.

A study over a long period of time could reveal how many activities have been carried out against an organisation. Or the trend of activities in months, when seasons may affect businesses or some other reason to be understood.

For example, if your company serves a few big clients among many small ones, being able to track the effort required in dealing with those clients, over turnover and across years, may provide some insight into how profitable they are.

In Fig. 14.4 it shows the distribution of activities where some clients require more effort.

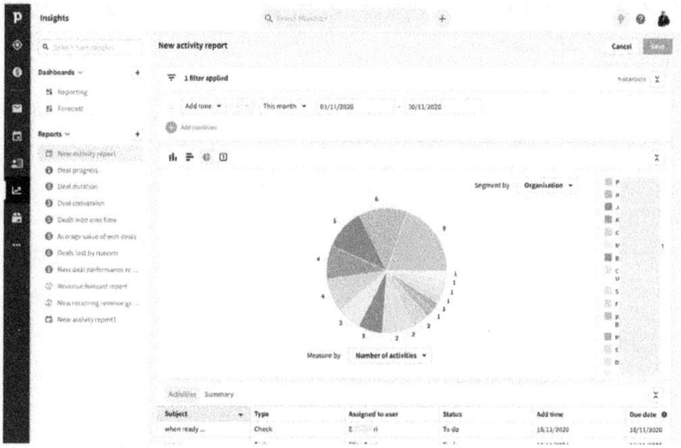

Fig. 14.4 - Segmenting (grouping) by organisations' names in pie view.

This reporting implies that people manage activities with care: open, accomplish and close them, establishing rules in the organisation with the clear purposes of creating benefits to everyone will make it easier.

Operators will have to:

- select type of activity
- choose the time and due date according with work loads
- define the time slot of activities (start and end)
- relate it to each counterpart: person, organisation
- set activities related to deals
- mark it as done when checked and decide to move
- never leave activities undone

By doing so, everyone will produce better, more insightful reporting, related to what has been done on a daily basis.

Decide how many charts your business should develop, depends by your ability to define useful metrics avoiding the mistake of celebrate vanity metrics[18]. Once your company embraces Activity Based Selling methodology the need for better reporting about activities will arise and answers will be found.

It is vital to clarify how reporting contributes to decision making, prioritising efforts, forecasting future business and workload. When done correctly, salespeople and company management benefit from it equally.

> Using Pipedrive to stay tuned on the activities reporting of a team's daily effort will enable sales managers in learning the metrics that matter the most for the business.

Insights has a section on reporting over emails. Email is believed to be one of the most important contact media with potential clients in B2B. Business managers can decide whether or not that metric is relevant for their business. Our advice is to avoid using this metric to determine whether salespeople are committed to the work they do.

Reporting over Opportunities

Trace the sales process proceeding in time, effort and results is particularly important, it provides insights on how the business actually performs and enables managers to clearly understand subtle trends that may be less evident in absence of a structured controlling system. In Pipedrive a company can easily develop an appropriate set of charts to provide an overview of the sales process trends at a glance: a tool that every experienced sales manager desires.

An appraisal of the sales process involves several dimensions. According to its structure and the deals' journey stages, it may be appropriate to slice and dice data to highlight trends and enable comparisons across time and locations.

This is how Pipedrive works: each chart can be easily adjusted around several parameters, enabling it to spot trends that any sales manager needs. On the other hand the setting of charts may be less intuitive to catch when someone approaches it. Of course having a clear understanding of what you are looking for and setting a plan avoids getting lost in the many options.

---

[18] Ries, E., The Lean Startup, Crown Business, 2011

To create a chart (Pipedrive defines them "Report"), the procedure is still the same we have seen for creating activities charts, just selecting deals instead. The purposes of each chart will be refined in the next window by selecting the 4 applicable layouts:

- Performance
- Conversion
- Duration
- progress

We can refrain from those options with a bit more sense as a guideline for what you are going to develop.

Performance Analysis

Analysis of Performance of the sales process shows the situation of the cumulative value. Using Weighted Value the chart highlights the actual value of all deals in the sales process (a possible turnover).

Fig. 14.5 provides two pictures Q2 and Q3 each of them shows:

- The total value of all deals started in the period
- The value of every stage for that period

deals are filtered per:

- Pipeline: - pipeline -
- Timeframe: deals created -year-
- Deal Status: Open

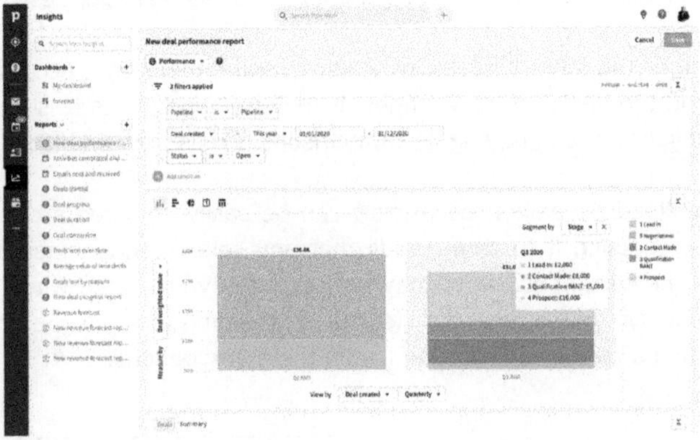

Fig. 14.5 - Performance report setting

1. The X-axis shows periods -the year divided in quarters
2. The Y-axis is value, summing up the value of each deal, cumulated per stage, then summing up stages to the whole amount of the sales process

The segmentation is selected per STAGE, Mouse over shows the value of each stage

How to highlight Trends, the relevance of knowledge.

This chart shows how opportunities in the process changed position over two quarters.

In Q2 it pictures 10K in the very early stage, Lead In, while 26.8K in Negotiation.

In Q3 the situation changed to: only 2K in Lead In stage, 8K in the Contact made stage, 5K in Qualification stage, and 16K in Prospect stage.

This view provides two static situations, Q2 and Q3, it doesn't tell the sales manager what caused the change, it is the sales manager that should be aware of causes or at least be able to investigate this trend.

These mocked data applied on a fake sales process do not set a case history and probably make very little sense. But let's play this game:

- May the 5K in Q2 *LeadIn* stage moved in Q3 into the next stages of Contact made, Qualification and Prospect (this changes Weighted Value)
- The 26.8K in *Negotiation* disappeared.
- Another chart must be checked to clarify if the deals in *Negotiation* have been closed, won or lost.
- *Lead In* only summed up to 2K in Q3. It was 5K in Q2.
- In Q3 there are no deals in *Negotiation*.

Then is time to place proper questions to investigate:

- What's the short term trend? (Q3 and Q4 Turnover)
- Is new business shrinking?

Being able to question the visible situations pictured out in properly developed reports is key to highlighting trends and find out reasons for them.

Reporting doesn't tell you directly what is going on in the business, reporting is agnostic, it just provides an overview of how numbers move. It is the knowledge of the sales manager who should be able to investigate details to explain the observed changes.

Conversion Analysis

This chart may highlight the deals' closure trend. Fig. 14.8 provides some hints as:

- What percentage of deals moved to the next stage
- The percentage of deals winning on the total

The sales process' deals are filtered per:

- Pipeline: A Pipeline
- Timeframe: year (mandatory)
- Deal Status: Open, Won and Lost

In this chart the readers can see the percentage of deals that moved to the next stage. In this example:

- 100% have moved from Lead In to the next stage Discovery Opportunities
- 78% of them moved to Qualification
- 71% of them moved to Developing Solution(s)
- 40% of them moved into Negotiation

Then they were all successful

Pipedrive assesses the sales process effectiveness as 22% (out of 9 deals opened, 2 converted).

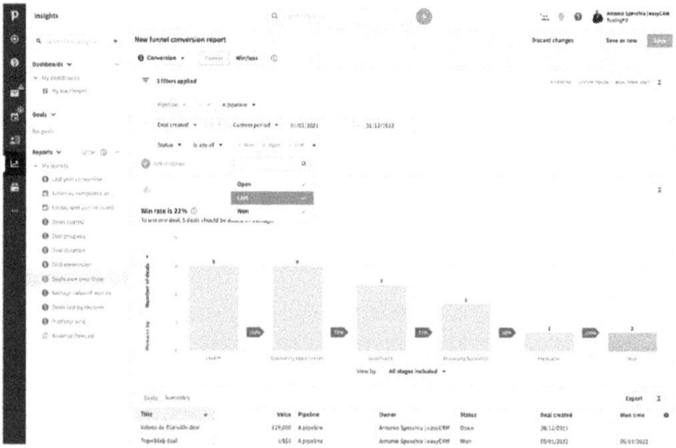

Fig. 14.8 - Conversion funnel chart, the trend per stages of deal that proceed along the sales process

Be aware: This chart doesn't include DELETED deals. (If someone deletes deals instead of marking them lost, this analysis will fail).

This chart may be easily altered to show Weighted Value or Net Value of deals, in this case instead of the number of deals per stage, the aggregate value would be shown.

In the chart setting we can see in the chart builder (fig 14.6), the button to change the chart type switching to different types of charts, **Performance**, **Conversion**, **Duration** and **Progress**. In Conversion mode two types of visualisations are possible: **Funnel** and **Win/Loss**.

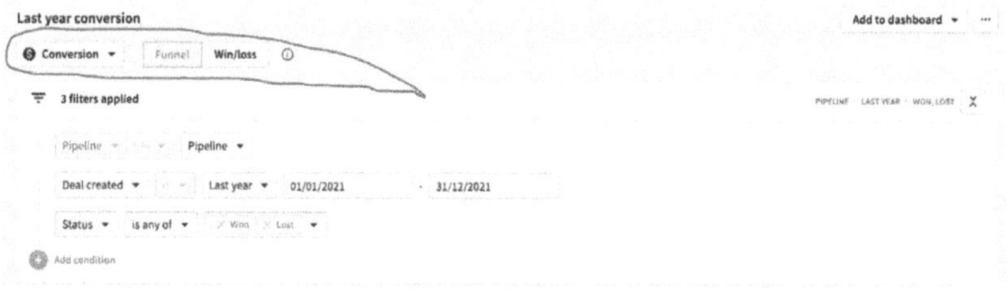

Fig. 14.6 - Details of chart development

The selection between Funnel and Win/Loss views is now working properly [19], users can choose the previous view (fig. 14.8) to analyse the funnel between stages: *how many deals proceeded*. Or they can select a differential view (fig 14.9) where they can analyse the relationship between converted deals and lost deals: analysing this chart may be more complex: the percentage of deals won and lost is related to the number of deals per stage.

Let's clarify, this time on real data of fig 14.9:

Leads IN: has a 9% success rate it means that only 9% of the deals that were in this stage (in the whole year) have been closed successfully (9% overall success rate).

Discovering Opportunities: 17% of deals passed through this stage have been successful. While 75% of them failed to convert.

Qualification: 17% of deals passed through the qualification process have been successful. While 67% of them didn't convert.

Developing solution(s): 70% of deals passed by the stage of deciding the proper solution have been successful. While 30% of them failed to convert.

Negotiation: 44% of deals that went in negotiation succeed. But 50% of them failed to convert.

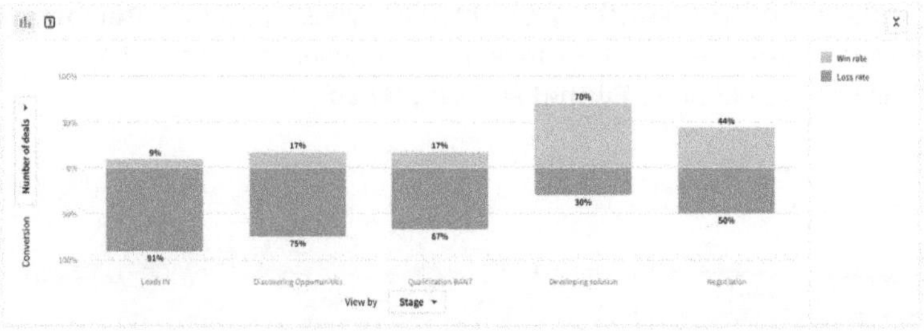

Fig. 14.9 - The Win/Loss rate view may bring on the table an interesting perspective.

Note

If the numbers are not clear to you, don't worry, the error happens if the chart setting includes OPEN deals. Open deals should be deselected. But deselecting the OPEN deals creates another problem that Pipedrive doesn't explain: probably deselecting open deals by

[19] We noticed a bug last year in this function then Pipedrive fixed it.

this chart excludes them from the total number of deals entered in the sales process.

Let's see what different information the win/loss rate shows when the main parameter considered (Y-axis) is the deals' weighted values.

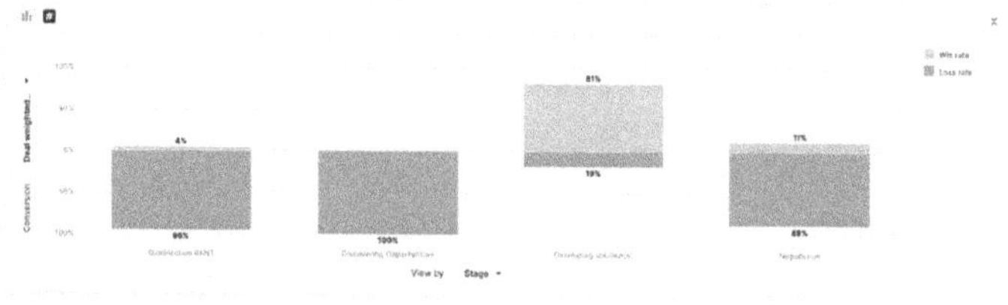

Fig. 14.10 - Win/Loss rate by deals value

Pipedrive may show problems in listing stages. Then, to add more complications, to know each deal value salespeople need to clarify what is the solution.

Discovery solutions: 100% of deals lost. This problem is due to open deals not included in the total number of deals in the sales process.

Qualification: 96% of the valued deals (in value) didn't convert. Only 4% converted.

Developing Solution(s): 81% of deals (in value) have been successful, 19% went lost.

Negotiation: 11% converted while 89% didn't.

This chart may be very helpful to develop powerful questions about the situation depicted here. As said, the chart itself doesn't provide reasons for trends. The trends are clearly visible to trained people, who may then develop questions to investigate causes.

---

6 Interactive challenge - investigating the sales process trends.

The challenge for the readers is to develop 5-8 powerful questions to investigate trends you can recognise in the previous two charts.
Alternatively, and maybe easier, readers may work on their own pipelines, in this case please send over screenshots of the charts developed that you need to investigate.
Readers are entitled to submit one result for the interactive challenges of this book. Anyone who would like to verify all the interactive challenges for solutions and explanations on what can be improved, may be requested to subscribe to the service.

Duration analysis

Keep under control the time of deals' journey: how long the sales process lasts (on average). The chart (Fig. 14.12) provides some hints as:

- Average time between initiating and closing deals
- How long they last in each stage
- How long it takes for each salesperson

deals are filtered per:

- Pipeline: pipeline
- Timeframe: year
- Deal Status: Lost and Won

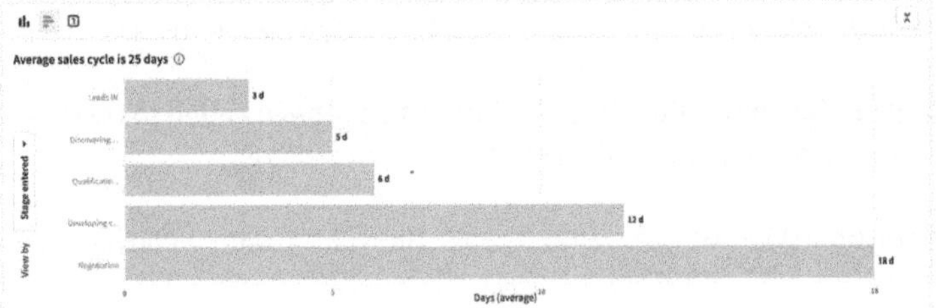

Fig. 14.12 - Sales process analysis for all deals status per stages

Fig. 14.13 shows the sales process timing using other parameters. We can see the different length of the sales cycle comparing just two salespeople of this sales process.

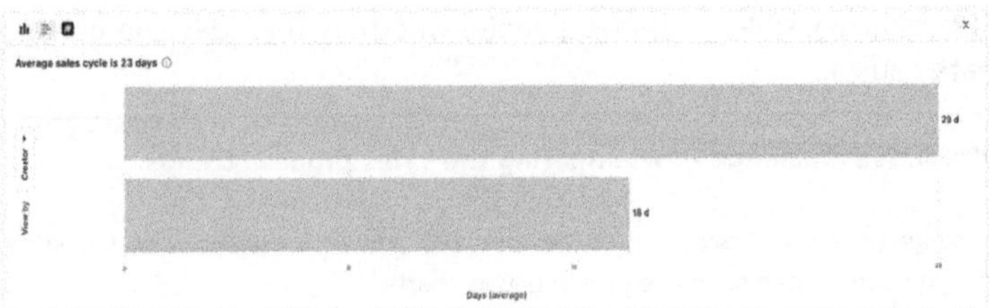

Fig. 14.13 - Sales people average time of sales cycle

The analysis of duration of sales cycle may show some valuable information:

- Which stage requires more time, or in other words, where the process is stuck

- The efficiency of the process under certain parameters
- What is the product/service differences in sales cycle
- The financial cycle: the cash flows cycle that affect financial needs when the business grows

Also in this analysis what matters the most is the capability to investigate causes with the best approach. Becoming able to place more powerful questions.

Progress analysis

This reporting chart's purpose is to keep under control the deals' journey by its stages: how many deals have entered in each stage during a timeframe. The chart highlight the topic:

- How many deals were in each stage at a certain time

deals are filtered per:

- Pipeline: pipeline
- Timeframe: years

First Case of Progress Analysis

The fig. 14.14 shows the trend recorded for a small business over the whole year. We can see the amount of deals that were in each stage per each month.
The situation month after month may highlight unexpected changes in how deals moved into other stages.

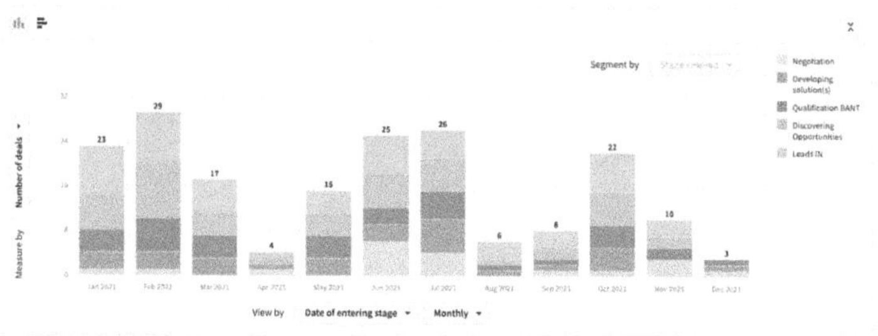

Fig. 14.14 - Progress of sales process along the whole year

The progress analysis of the sales cycle may show some valuable information:

- The composition of stages (density of deals) per month
- How each stage changed from previous month
- The effect of those changes on the business turnover (need another chart)
- The effect of changes on the people workload (need another chart)

This analysis provides elements to investigate over causes using an improved approach and guiding users in placing powerful questions.

Let's try to set some questions:

1. Jan, Feb and March were months with a high number of new deals - Was the business growing steadily?
2. In April not only new deals dropped, but also every other stage went dry - What caused it?
3. May, April and June recovering was great, in June a big number of deals entered the Negotiation stage. The sales cycle seems very variable, the Developing solution(s) stage varied too much between May and July - What caused it?
4. August's shrink may be seasonal, but a shrinking of all stages and followed by a very low September - How was the turnover trend in those months?
5. A great October has brought several new deals in Leads In, but also in Discovery Opportunities, Qualification, Developing solution(s) stages. - Having so many businesses in the first 4 stages at the same time, could it be caused by a short sales cycle as they have almost gone in November.
6. November is still having some deals in Negotiation, they probably remain open from the previous month, but the wave of new deals seems drying out. - The business goes by seasons or there is some other problem?
7. December records a small amount of deals in the sales process, and none in the first two stages. - Is that expected? Is the business affected by seasonal trends?

Evaluations:

We can appreciate how unsteady the business is: the median should be 22,42 deals at any time in the sales process. This business shows 5 very low months, the average number of deals is just 15,66. The cycle variability appears in line with general small business trends, where a small number of deals can easily double or halve the monthly revenue.

In order to understand the business profitability, we can change the Y-axis parameter: from Deal Number to Deal Value, or even better, to Weighted Value. Looking at that view (not shown here) you could appreciate the business' real dimension and, by knowing the company's financials, have a better understanding of its sustainability.

At the same time as investigating the effect of changes on the turnover and peoples' workload, this has to be done using other reports. They are available in Pipedrive but they are not shown here about this business. The purpose is to clarify that an investigation over a business needs reporting over many dimensions. Defining the set of charts to use involves the planning of the reporting and for this purpose Pipedrive offers the dashboard: a container where different charts may be included for a quick check.

Second Case of Progress analysis

In the fig. 14.15 we can see another progress analysis of a business' sales process. This view shows the weighted value of the sales process (Y-axis) per deal status (X-Axis).

The chart shows that this business is still counting **90.5K USD** of deals in its pipeline (open deals), while **50.0K** have been won, against only **18.0K** that have been lost.

The business appears healthy with a high rate of conversion, it is still a small business, but the numbers are promising and if the trend is confirmed growth can be faster than what they initially planned.

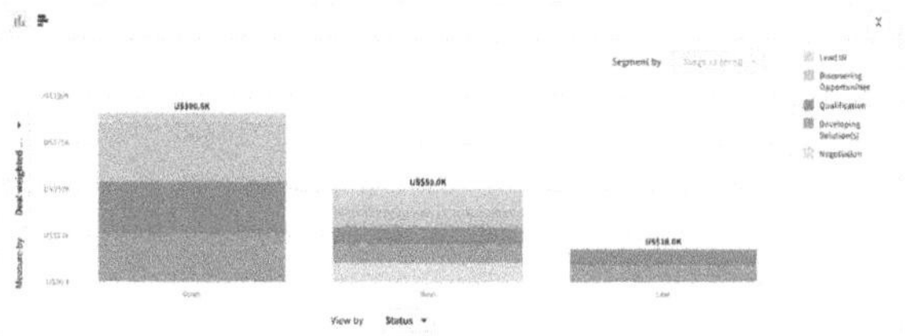

Fig. 14.15 - Sales process situation at today's time per deals status

We can set some evaluation about what can be seen in this chart:

There are 90.5K of open deals distributed mainly between Discovery Solutions, Qualification and Developing Solution(s) stages. There are no open deals in Negotiation. Which may seem odd.

In the same way we can see how winning deals happen in all the 5 stages, also Leads IN, which is a shelf where deals are picked up by sales people.

Additionally, we can appreciate that losses occur during Qualification and Discovery Solution(s) stages.

Clarifying the why of those "trends" may seem trivial but is not. It is the essence of the business, analysing its sales process may provide many opportunities to understand what really drives the business to success (or failure).

---

7 Interactive challenge - investigating the sales process progress.

The challenge for the readers is to develop 5 powerful questions to investigate trends you can recognise in the previous chart. (fig 14.15)

Readers are entitled to submit one result for the interactive challenges of this book. Anyone who would like to verify all the interactive challenges for solutions and explanations on what can be improved, may be requested to subscribe to the service.

Third Case of Progress Analysis

In fig. 14.16 this chart provides a rendering of two years, grouped quarterly upon sales process stages.

A seasonal effect in the first quarters is visible. This business appears more stable, and its volume of deals is higher. The analysis spanning two years may provide further areas of investigation.

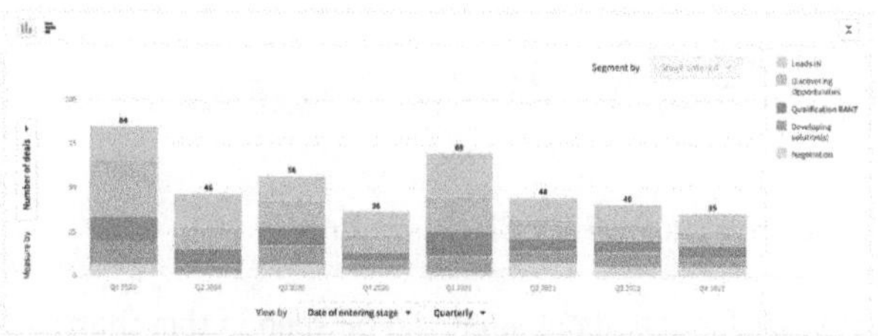

Fig. 14.16 - Two years analysis of stages progression

The main pattern of strategic questions we may set is:

Stages are oddly not subsequent: the Discovery Opportunities stage is always predominant. We may expect a growth of the Qualification stage in the next month, after the first two stages were crowded. The shortfall in transferring deals into the qualification stage may highlight a high level of disengagement of prospects at the very beginning of the sales process.

- Why only a portion of deals move into the qualification stage?
- What are the activities performed during Leads IN and Discovery Opportunities stages?
- Who and how performs those stages?
- How does the LG funnel really engage MQL leads instead of just unqualified leads?

Summary

This chapter investigated INSIGHTS, the reporting feature native in Pipedrive. We approached the logic of how businesses may use reporting to improve decision making.

In this chapter we went through activities reporting and opportunities reporting, two aspects that Pipedrive covers quite well.

For some it may seem complex, however, we encourage users to get some help to design their reporting to avoid ending up lost in so many features.

Small businesses may not take reporting into consideration. They often believe they already have control over the business and the effort to set up reporting do not add any value.

We suggest users to review this belief, and make a plan to set up a reporting within 4-6 months, set some simple charts then improve, get some hints over the situations, learn how to spot trends and then see if that is useful.

To rely on the sales process reporting, businesses will unveil that they need qualitative data management.

Using good and clean data may also impact positively on the business.

Two points to add last minute:

Pipedrive is going to add a feature to export **Dashboards in PDF**.

Useful? Definitely. Not because you should share reports and charts in PDF, it may be, but the real value of dashboards is to be LIVE. No, the value of the export dashboard might be to store them.

Let’s see: every month you check the results, your dashboard shows trends and tendencies. But next month you probably don’t remember what the trends were, and in the meantime the dashboard changed. This is even more true when it comes to Forecasting. Trends change and previous figures may be forgotten.

Insights is expected to include **Campaigns reporting**.

At the moment we could test it and we can’t report any positive result. We are sure the pipedrive team will fix it soon, but at the moment the performance is below the expectations.

15 Forecasting

After much debated work on the forecasting functionality we decided to delete this chapter altogether.

We believe Pipedrive will revamp the forecasting soon so discussing it at this point doesn't really matter. The existing functionality is below the expected performance of a CRM leader of the market.

The good thing is that many integrated tools are available (see next chapter 19) so that users only have to choose their favourite one and plug it in.

16 R&F Enhancement

Introduction

Not too long ago reporting in business used to be run on a monthly basis, mainly by printing a "picture" report: what has happened in that month. Today dashboards are real-time data rendering, mainly visual, where business managers can get an overview at a glance.

Charts are developed to highlight the trends based on several variables, their values are measured within a selection of parameters to make metrics truly relevant for the business.

An important value of adopting a CRM is the capability to work on real-time data. There aren't many companies that haven't moved digital yet, but effective use of a digital CRM tool is nowadays becoming fashionable, and too often first adoption doesn't bring the expected benefits.

But what companies need is a tool that smooths their processes from data collection to data usage. When data input and data rendering are well designed and connected, all the data consumers and the decisors, can improve their decision making and reach a better outcome.

In this chapter, we will see what other possibilities are available to improve dashboards effectiveness by using integrated tools. Assuming that Pipedrive offers an easy to use tool, Insights, but some users may require advanced tools to perform deeper analysis.

Through the course of this chapter, we will cover:

- Information that matters
    - ◇ What data are useful to collect
- Improving Reporting and forecasting
    - ◇ Some integrated tools that may help rendering more information

Information that matters.

Organisations should design their CRM database by starting from the minimum viable dataset required to run the process they need to facilitate. This goal may be achieved simply by placing two questions:

- For a salesperson to close a deal, what information cannot be avoided?

- Are the data absolutely relevant to support the sales process?

The logic should be to keep it simple: **less-is-more**.

> The information that a salesperson can collect about a client might be quite a lot, however, if we ignore non essential information, how much data are actually needed?

The correct amount of data fields really depends on each business. On top of those minimal data we can add information required in order to define audiences or useful for any other purpose designed for the CRM.

But we suggest staying on the sales process management, and clarify what data are absolutely unmissable. The goal is to keep data collection to the minimum. This rule may help to improve efficiency in the whole process.

Improving Reporting and Forecasting

The great benefit of systems that are not intended to be fully comprehensive frameworks is that integration with more specialised solutions may actually be extremely better than a fully integrated system. In the last few years great names of the CRM industry moved to an integration friendly environment, in the belief that nobody can be great at everything. Keeping focus on the core business is still important, even if vendors complete their offer with added features. Users should be able to select different tools that may fit their specific needs better.

As we stated, relying on good reporting and forecasting is important for businesses. To make it more efficient there are several proposals available in the Pipedrive marketplace that can strongly enhance this feature.

Let's discuss some of them.

Dear Lucy

Developed in 2018 as a product this funny named company's greatest feature is the really enhanced rendering of dashboards. It may be of great effect when you set them to web sharing: the feature of including a video in the background really boosts the engagement of a public show.

It has probably been developed with that purpose in mind: monitor showing a dashboard into a salespeople open space to boost engagement.

The capability to develop charts is pretty good. Thus, the solution is young and under continuous development, we noticed some minor issues, like the sequencing of Pipeline Stages that was organised by alphabetical order. Also, the API connection that was only available for the Deals database, something that hinders reporting about organisations and people. With that said, we believe that the company will soon improve it if not already in place when this book will be in your hands.

In the next screenshots, we can see some style of reporting in Dear Lucy.

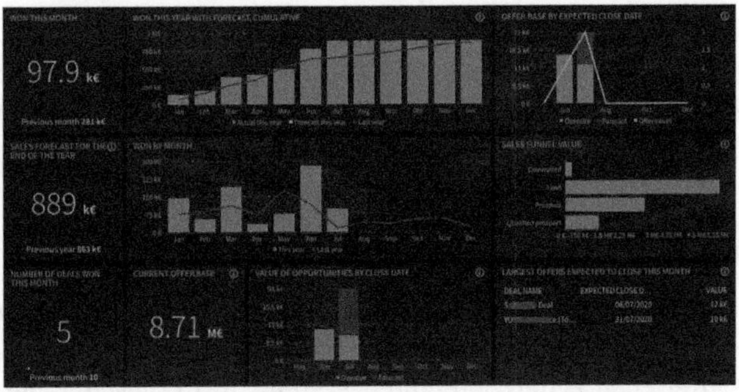

Fig. 16.1 - Dear Lucy Standard Dashboard

Second option of dashboard looks like:

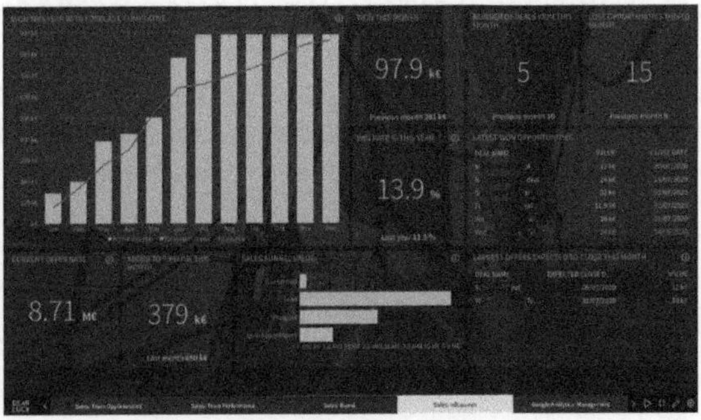

Fig 16.2 - Different view of the dashboard in Dear Lucy

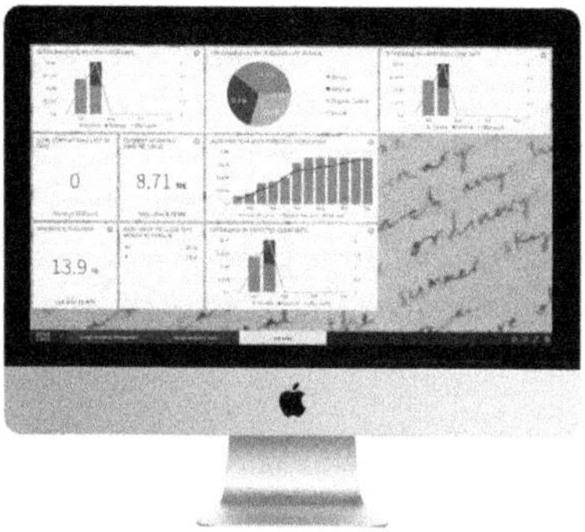

Fig. 16.3 - Dear Lucy reporting dashboard ready to be shown on public screens

Dear Lucy provides companies with a user-friendly reporting management platform that visualises data from many CRM systems. Its connector works smoothly in Pipedrive. And its implementation is a no-deal.

Dear Lucy appears to be a good compromise of features and performance especially if your purpose is to show dashboards on big screens to keep teams updated and motivated. Refreshing data on an hourly schedule is a pretty good balance between real-time and longer, even daily data refresh. The value of this solution is positioned in the higher side of the market as it leverages on a good finishing of the charts rendering. At the time of testing we appreciated a connection into Pipedrive limited to deals database. For us this was a serious limitation and a flaw on the logic of R&F. We are sure the company is about to fix it.

Slemma

Slemma is one of the most flexible solutions capable of empowering organisations with deep data analysis. The analytics capabilities are closer to a BI tool than just a reporting tool. Slemma is capable of smoothly connecting almost everything, from Google Analytics to spreadsheets, from Quickbooks to Facebook advertising. Its integration into Pipedrive is fully developed and it works on every database, Deals, People, Organisations, Leads and Activities. Slemma is a professional tool that is great when you have a know-how of what to do and how. This tool is less appropriate for beginners as its setting requires quite a bit of knowledge. Companies may benefit from buying it in outsourcing: a system integrator can run the setting, the dashboards development and also provide dashboards in Saas to each organisation.

Slemma has a complex, whole system of data analysis with almost every option to data mining and reporting. As any powerful tool it needs to possess the proper know-how.

The limit of Slemma is on its rendering capability of fancy options and finishing. The web sharing is fully developed and it can also be set under access control. Dashboards can be fully informative and shaped to be clear with simple graphic options:

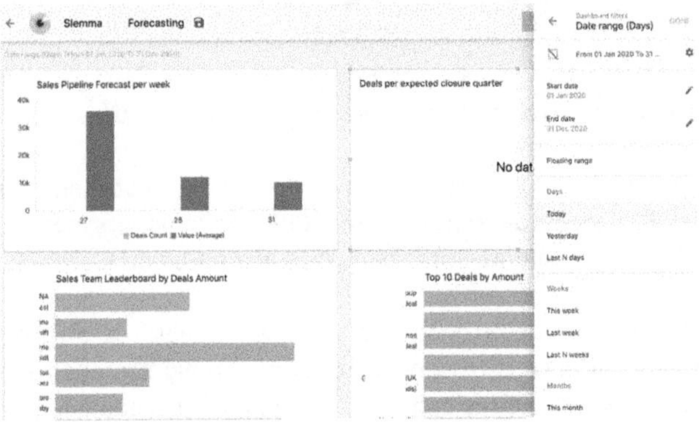

Figure 16.4 - Slemma charts development tool

Slemma refreshes data on a daily basis on its low-cost plans. To get hourly data refreshing, it requires a higher plan.

Web shared dashboards may be absolutely less effective under daily data refresh when a dashboard is intended to be shown on the sales dept as a real time refresh is expected. The daily refresh of dashboards may be ok for the company's management.

Tableau

This software owned by salesforce is a powerful BI tool. Positioned on the highest side of the market, consequently it has a premium price.

The skills required to manage Tableau are articulated and its learning curve is quite long. If you are a company with large, very complex sales, then hiring a consultant specialised in Tableau is definitely an option. The presentation is absolutely professional and the tool allows you to slice and dice data according to best BI methodologies.

To see what can be done with Tableau, please check this list prepared by Amit Sarda[20]:

- *Sales and conversion rates by geographic region, visualised on a map*
- *Performance of salespeople and identifying opportunities to learn from one another*
- *Deals inflow rate and patterns in deals inflow*
- *Deals progression through the sales pipeline and identifying bottlenecks, if any*
- *Health of your sales pipeline and sales forecast*
- *Uncover reasons for losing deals*
- *Deals conversion by enquiry month*
- *Days to close deals*

"You can think of combining any of these insights to build a new hypothesis. You can then test this hypothesis by digging deeper into the data to analyse one or more segments at a time.

A couple of resources to help you understand what I mean are mentioned below:

- *Here's a sample Tableau Dashboard that I built using dummy Deals data from Pipedrive: https://bit.ly/Pipedriveinsights*
- *If you're new to Tableau, this tutorial should help you get started: https://bit.ly/ioradtableau"*

Power BI

This tool is still an option if you have a Windows server in place. Like Tableau, you better not approach it if you lack strong skills on BI or you can't hire well prepared consultants. Pricing can be surprising, before starting to use the tool in its almost free version, better check the prices structure carefully before your business grows.

On the other hand Power BI is really powerful and flexible, you can build almost any kind of analysis and reporting on data from everywhere. Something to consider.

Summary

In this chapter we talked about four tools that may support stronger reporting and forecasting in Pipedrive. They are just a selection among many possibilities,

[20] Amit Sarda, PipedriveTableau, Gumroad

it is up to each company to experiment what works best for them under their specific budget.

Creating a dashboard is quite simple when you have a clear purpose for the information requested.

We suggest avoiding cluttered dashboards with all-in-one, but instead create concise dashboards with chunks of information.

Using a plain structure and avoiding excessive graphics effects (Ban PowerPoint, Jeff Bezos, 2018), and keep each chart clean.

Design dashboards with purpose and audience in mind.

Keep information clean and focused, avoid an informative excess.

Fancy finishing in public screens can be strongly engaging for salespeople, comparing goals and results, often seen in a modern environment. We suggest users to think carefully if the company really benefits from it.

17 Data Architecture

Introduction

Companies use data repositories, not just to store data somewhere, but to elaborate data, and aggregate them in order to provide structured information to the data consumers. Information, as we have seen, is developed upon data and serves to feed the decision-making processes at any level.

Unfortunately the reliability of information this time, doesn't depend on which news channel you watch or the editor of the newspaper you read. In this domain, good information just depends on the quality of data collected on the field.

> What's a simple way to clarify what data architecture is? It may be useful to think of CRM architects like building architects: their purpose is to construct a solid but useful shape. Great architects employ the design to facilitate use of the building, rather than considering it their primary objective.

The first step will be to clarify:

- What are "data" and "information"
- How to build "information" over raw "data"
- How to design datasets to collect the right data

Readers who get familiar with the basics of data architecture may develop the ability to leverage data architecture to design a more effective CRM for their company.

If this chapter had a subtitle, it would be: **the Secret of Designing an Effective CRM.**

A secret that relies on the following topics:

- Understanding data management
- Defining data, information, and knowledge
- Exploring how data collection can generate problems in CRM
- Information for the sales process

Understanding data management

"Using modern database tools, just about anyone can build a database. The

question is, will that resulting database be useful? A database won't do you much good if you can't get data out of it quickly, reliably, and consistently. It won't be useful if it's full of incorrect or contradictory data. You can address all of these potential problems by using modern database tools, ..., but only if you understand what those problems are so you can avoid them." [21]

> The process of developing a digital solution may be similar to the process of building a house. Would you start building anything without an architectural plan in place?

However, developers and entrepreneurs are often pressed for time and they just want to go ahead. IT operators may believe they can develop anything they like just by starting to code, then patch and fix it to provide the expected functions. We have to admit that is something much harder to achieve in real estate. Additionally, development is measurable: something is developed every day, boosting productivity! People discover too late that lack of design may seriously affect the output.

Back in Chapter 1, Rod Stephens was discussing databases, and CRM is just a database with a software layer on top. Rod's words apply even better today on CRM, since many entry-level CRM and No Code platforms encourage every user to build their own CRM from scratch. Yet, Rod Stephens' question remains: "*... will the resulting tool be useful?*".

To make things even more complex, there is the simplicity of the purchasing process: any organisation just subscribes to a SaaS CRM and starts developing it. Small companies may find it expensive to hire consultants to lead the design and implementation project: "*Why should we? The CRM is ready, just to plug in and use.*" And perhaps this is also true!

However, Ernesto Sirolli brought up an important point: no one can manage every aspect of business. What it takes to build a business are:

> *"You have to do only three things: create a fantastic product, build tremendous marketing, and be outstanding in looking after the money! The only problem is that no one can do all these three things".* [22]

Operating a successful business is a considerable achievement, why should successful entrepreneurs spend time dealing on how to set up tools to run a

---

21 Stephens R., Beginning Database Design Solutions, Wiley, 2009.
22 Sirolli, E., Shut up and Listen, TED Talks.

function of their business? Companies need to optimise their (limited) resources and foster velocity, being able to go-to-market faster, engaging clients in the most effective way.

Technology is essential today, businesses need to learn to govern the technology, but then they better outsource from specialised providers instead to make it in-house.

Defining data, information, and knowledge

Let's define "data" and "information":

DAMA defines: "***Data are the representation of facts as text, numbers, graphics, images, sound or video.***" [23] We can break it down by considering data like bricks. Many bricks, properly arranged, can build a wall. Several walls can support a roof. Walls with a roof may shape a building, or a house.

In the same way, organised data develops a piece of information. Information as the result of row data in specific contexts can shape a meaning. Meanings based on properly arranged information, sets knowledge.

A huge simplification with the purpose to clarify the differences of the terms "data" and "information".

Information is created using data.

[23] DAMA (2009) DMBoK 2, https://www.dama.org/cpages/body-of-knowledge

Data, data, data. Not just data please!

Data alone have no significance, the way in which data are organised shapes the information itself. This is why the motto: **truth is created, not represented**.

Let's assume we have some company's data: **50.000.000** and **130**. Those numbers are just raw data and they need a little bit more to get a meaning.

Now we define them as turnover and employees.

Turnover is a key metric that contributes in defining the financial dimensions, while the number of **employees** is a metric useful for physical dimension.

> Combining the two data enables a first idea of the business. (= a company with a value added per employee of £ 384,615.38).

Then, according to the purpose, analysis may require a lot more data. That's why we start collecting data, which implies first defining the dataset required.

> Deciding what data to collect and how to store them may seem simple, but it is not.

In the intention to improve prospect profiling, many organisations may tend to collect more data than they really need. It results in inefficient data management. Assuming that some data are specific to a business, the right balance between the amount of data and its manageability is at the kernel of the data architecture.

> Designing an efficient data structure, "data architecture"[24], really depends on the business needs. Making sure the CRM will be enabled to render useful information is an element of the implementation project.

We should then recognise how data collection may present some challenges.

Data collection and possible issues

The most common problems arising from incorrect data design impacts the information rendering, which in turn can result in a lack of value of the information developed and a crippling of the ability to analyse cohorts. Those problems include:

---

24 https://www.dataversity.net/what-is-data-architecture/#

- Suboptimal data fields quantity
- Redundant or superfluous data fields
- Lack of constraints in data input

In order to avoid errors in number, quality, and type of data fields, CRM architects investigate the purpose of the database: what information it should provide? What aggregate of data composes the expected information? How are reports, forecasts, and cohorts' analysis of populations developed?

Let's look at these issues in detail.

Suboptimal dataset

In regards to the informational power of the CRM, it is logical that too few data fields will lead to misinformation: assuming incorrect hypotheses that may imply fallacious decision making.

> The risk is to implement a sort of Rolodex, with names, phone numbers, and e-mail addresses, which may be fine, but isn't a CRM.

Beside Pipedrive standard fields, users can set custom fields: each organisation should determine what fields they require based on specific needs.

Redundant or superfluous data fields

On the other hand, all too often the creation of custom fields lacks design, leading to clumsy databases.

Pipedrive users may fail this task since it's extremely easy to create new fields. The Pipedrive mission is to make it easy for anyone to set up, customise and adapt their CRM. This simplicity may lead managers to add fields without a plan and in lack of a specific preparation in data management.

> The purpose is to store relevant data. The result is a duplication of data fields, scattered pieces of information may end up in different tables, same data stored in different fields, loss of bearing on what should be stored and where.

Users building queries over audiences for cohort analysis or bulk actions may find it hard to locate the right data. Logical data architecture simplifies cohort segregation. A flawed data architecture makes selections too complex and inefficient. The use of a simple Tag, here called Label, only provides temporary peace of mind, losing any benefit of dynamic audience selection, something that requires a solid data architecture.

Smooth, simple features are the emergent results of good design.

Unreliable data results from lack of structure, redundant data fields and from unclear purposes. In consequence, even complex queries may not provide reliable information.

Lack of data input constraints

Data-input may probably be the weakest part of any operations. Either in manual input as well as for database import, the data quality is an everlasting problem for organisations. Limiting typos and control errors may help in reducing garbage collection.

GIGO is the acronym of **Garbage In = Garbage Out**, effect.

Data validity should be constantly verified, as well as records erasing that may break relationships creating orphan data.

There is a range of controls in Pipedrive when it comes to type of data fields:

Address field is geographically referenced = Users may easily see locations in Google Maps. A powerful feature that may help prevent mistakes like "**London, UK**" instead of "**London, ON**".

A type of field where Pipedrive provides effective control is **value**. For instance, the value of the deal must be a value referring to specific currency. When creating custom fields, users should avoid the temptation of just using text fields. The following options are available to control data input:

- Text (within 255 digits)
- Large text (more than 255 digits)
- Single option
- Multiple options
- Autocomplete
- Numerical
- Monetary
- User (someone else in your organisation)
- Organisation (a company listed in your CRM)
- Person (a contact person included in your CRM)
- Phone (in missing of a control)
- Time

- Time Range
- Data
- Date Range
- Address

Text and large text are the first found in the list, and are the types of data fields to be used with care as they accept anything users may write.

Pipedrive announced for 2023, the introduction of three big things:

1 More types of fields. It means a better control over the dataset and the (possible) input in each field. This matches the idea that caring about the data architecture is important for a better CRM performance.

2 Calculated fields! Maybe not everyone notices the lack of this feature, but some companies will strongly appreciate this. Finally, Pipedrive will enable clients in managing mathematical operations on the numeric and currency fields. Something that now is only possible using the table Product, but with a lot of limitations.

3 Sales Process specific fields. If different pipelines are aimed at different sales processes, then probably the dataset required are also different. This will be possible starting from 2023.

Note

At the moment we register the lack of control for the Phone field, this is because of the original idea of enabling users to also input Skype names (a once popular tool for video chat...). In fact, this choice misses the opportunity to avoid the GIGO effect. We hope next year also this issue will be reviewed.

Information for the sales process

Designing a database architecture aimed to facilitate the stage of collecting, managing and rendering of information is important to define the subtle purposes. Each entity, whether a person or an organisation, has dozens or even hundreds of possibly interesting data. The data architecture discipline is also about decision over the type of data which is efficient to store.

Deciding what type of data fields are required is the ultimate challenge.

For the purpose of describing an object for **storage** purposes, maybe it will be enough to collect the shipping dimension, its weight, the article code and its value.

For the purpose of **selling** it to a consumer, it would be necessary to use additonal data such as its price, name, description, availability, characteristics and compatibility. While shipping dimension and weight may not be so relevant anymore.

Generally speaking: "*These data are included in the product's tech data sheet and are automatically stored in the ERP at all times*". Absolutely right. But the question is to define the specific purpose in order to clarify which data we need.

An enterprise customer relationship management system is not a database of products. Filling it with all the possible data to cover every possible need or application may be an excessive effort and in any case it won't be efficient. In a products' database technical data can be easily stored. But CRM involves living persons and organisations. First of all, data are valid within a timeframe, then information about each person or organisation is massive, and the dimensions (raw data) that shape those information are huge.

Some good questions to ask ourselves may be:

- What are the unmissable information required to accomplish the process?
- What minimalist set of data may clearly frame the information?

While CRM in B2C markets uses different sets of data, we only refer to B2B purposes.

Let's analyse some purposes of a B2B CRM:

Sales process

- Qualifying leads
- Developing solutions
- Performing sales service
- Long term clients satisfaction

Information

- Analysing market trends
- Performing upselling, cross marketing, cross selling.
- Designing homogeneous audiences
- Support to decision making
- Strategising by data
- Invoicing

While a software can run the invoicing process using just a set of raw data, other topics are more complex to achieve and require a degree of tact. The human touch is therefore considered a valuable asset that may be facilitated by Pipedrive. How? By empowering people who run human-based sales processes, and data consumers to receive real time information reporting based on data renderings to support decision making.

Qualifying leads

When it comes to determining if a lead can become a prospect, the information to be collected is crucial. Each business has specific criteria to determine the "ideal client". Pipedrive aims at different audiences, enabling companies to implement each specific need. When companies define clear criteria, they can add custom fields to collect and compare data for this purpose.

This stage is about collecting data that shape information about the lead - contact person- to enable the qualification process.

Among those data we can find:

- Does the contact persons' business have the traits of the "ideal client"?
- What factors determine the success of the deal?
  - ◇ Budget
    - YES [it matches the price]
    - NO [not (enough) budget]
  - ◇ Authority
    - YES [he or she decides]
    - NO [deciders are others]
  - ◇ Needs
    - Are their business needs achievable?
    - Are the requirements consistent with the budget?
  - ◇ Timing
    - Expected/Possible timing achievable

- How does the counterpart assess the value of the required solution?
- How critical is the solution for them?
- What is the greatest pain they wish to solve?
- What if they cannot find a solution?
- How challenging is it to find the solution for them?

We appreciate these questions can't be answered just by raw data. The questions require qualitative information. The possibility of composing them provides a great advantage in storing and retrieving records for audience creation purposes.

Deconstructing information in elemental data enables booleans and maths functions in retrieving information over multiple dimensions. The information rendering is essentially based on data.

Let's analyse this very simple example of information:

> *"In the last three years, the business had performed a growth rate of 30% but the added value per employee remained stable around $350 K"*

We can clearly see how this simple information is based on data, but the storytelling of the company's trend may say a lot to those who may consider this business for different reasons.

In this case the readers can easily dismantle this information in the type of raw data that composes it. But nobody can really guess the original data.

The essence of straight, concise information usefulness doesn't rely on the completeness of data but on their aggregation and simplification.

What's more, knowing the exact numbers that represent the turnovers over the three years as well as the numbers of the employees in each year, we can simply shape the information above.

But what if the information contained the series of values that demonstrate how the value added per employee per year changed from $348 K, to $352 K, and then to $349 K would it be really important?

According to some specific purposes of the analysis it may be relevant to be able to retrieve each piece of data, but most of the time it is not. Information matters when analysed in a relationship: 30% of growth is the result of a relationship between the turnovers of two years.

What is important is to store those raw data, then combine them with the purpose of shaping different information according to each analysis:

> Knowing the turnover of each year as well as the number of employees enables the previous evaluation as well as the evaluation of the exact dimension of the company.

Here we are extending the foundational BANT model without entering yet into specific business needs. Furthermore, slicing and dicing information to create a useful dataset will improve later capabilities of more precise cohort analysis.

Developing Solutions

Another powerful question is about investigating the process to create a proposal; what information does the salesperson need to know?

To find an answer, we must relate to the specificity of the business:

- What do we provide?
- How do we provide that?
- What is the level of service we provide?
- What impact does the solution have on the client's business?
- What risks are associated with the solution?
- Who else may provide similar solutions?
- What are the differences between the (possibly competitive) solutions?

Tailored solutions are very common in B2B. This is true well beyond just services, providers are even more called to match different client-specific requirements.

The process of the proposal development leverages the client's requirements. And should aim to render as clear as possible the imagined solution. For this reason a well exploited stage of gathering information will provide a more accurate sense of the subtle needs.

The main focus includes quantitative data such as:

- What (product/service)?
- How many and when?
- Prices
- Related costs
- Duties and exemptions

And qualitative information such as:

- Why?
- To do what?
- To whom?
- As an alternative to?
- Connected to what?

One of the major challenges that salespeople face every day is to be able to collect all the information in a reliable manner, while keeping the counterpart engaged and happy to contribute with the information.

Performing sales service

In order to evaluate the quality of the sales service we can only consider the client's perspective, as we all know very well, **quality is only what the clients' perceive**[25]. So an investigation on the service provided during the sales process can be performed by using the following list of questions:

- How does the sales experience differ from other companies?
- Does the sales service provide an experience capable of adding value to the transaction as well as supporting the brand's positioning?
- What information is required from salespeople in order to perform the sales at the planned customer's experience?
- How effectively do salespeople collect information?
- What does the client feel, perceive and experience during the information gathering process?
- What do salespeople do to ensure a pleasant experience for the client?
- How does the sales process improve each client's overall experience with the company?

Among the required information we can find some client-specific qualitative information, such as:

- Risk aversion
- Outcome of previous experiences
- Usage purposes
- Personal lifestyle or brand character
- How the solution is perceived Mission Critical

Those relevant information may only be collected during the interaction between the salesperson and the client person. An interaction that takes place within the sales process. Salespeople are probably well aware of how relevant these information are in deciding how to develop a proposal for the prospective client. But the "how" information gathering is performed under the human perspective matters a great deal, affecting the experience for the prospective client.

Once the deal is signed, the information and data required for the service deployment can be gathered, as it is time to perform the service. The habit of collecting information in advance may be a source of problems in the relationship.

Being able to empathise with a counterpart asked to provide subtle information long before a decision is made, is a crucial skill of good sales people: as it's

[25] Grönroos, C., Service Management and Marketing, Wiley, 2000

imposing to share information not felt relevant for the sales process - leading to a rebuff of the interaction, either partially or entirely.

When it happens, clients are not mad, they just react to the vendor: they perceive a bad approach, wrong behaviour and uncaring beliefs. That's why a client may suddenly become snappy without the need to explain why.

This may suggest the **extreme sensitivity of the information gathering** within the sales process: it is not trivial to plan for it aiming for the best performance. Neither you nor your salespeople would be able to fully clarify what works and what doesn't, but when the process is performed at its best, people will recognise that something great is happening.

How can data architecture facilitate this?

It is a matter of defining the best architecture of data fields - one that enables efficient collection of the minimal, optimal data: designing what salespeople should be capable of collecting, with minimal effort for both salespeople and prospective clients. The essential data to shape the information needed is not massive. Less is more, being capable of getting concise information is first and foremost an art of living, and also an art of CRM.

Reviewing market trends

Analysing markets to catch subtle trends and, consequently, adapt their sales policies, is an essential function that CRM should facilitate. Companies of all types develop their own market understanding and, likewise for CRM, that no business exists in absence of it, the same happens about market trends: no business may endure without an understanding of market trends.

Using a CRM digital tool, like Pipedrive, doesn't enable organisations to develop market trends analysis if they don't have it in place already. But it may really facilitate it!

Companies often have a number of questions related to market trends. They may allow managers to develop a more precise understanding of the targets they decide to work with, which means to improve efficiency in the market management process.

What companies are more likely to adopt ... (technologies or solutions)?

- What do they do?
- What results do they achieve?
- How do they position themselves?

- For which of them (the solution) would we be more effective?

We can see that there is a mixture of quantitative and qualitative information to collect. Defining the best comprehensive data set with a minimum quantity of fields is the ability of the data architect.

> Analysis of market trends based on information collected from a variety of sources is yet a very powerful and perhaps mostly overlooked CRM function by small businesses.
>
> Most small businesses find the process of market analysis too complex for a limited return on investment.
>
> By comparison, medium-sized companies are more likely to exploit market analysis in the effort to protect their own investments and continue to stay afloat in the face of a stormy environment (i.e. strategic planning).

These kinds of activities are not focused on single contacts, they are analysis performed on big audiences as a whole. The capability to infer trends among as much data as possible is connected to the ability to design audiences, cohorts, groups of contacts with similar attributes.

And queries or filtering databases is an important know-how strongly enabled by powerful tools.

Performing cross marketing / cross selling

Cross-marketing involves the following:

- Campaigns attempting to persuade prospects/contacts/clients to purchase something related to what they have already purchased.
- Audience nurturing aiming to communicate to groups of homogeneous contact "prospects" or "clients" proposing to them some content, information, ideas or solutions that may be interesting to them and keep them engaged in a high valuable connection (nurturing relationships).

The selection of correct audiences of homogeneous subjects is the key to execute these actions successfully:

> Sending messages to someone is risky. If the message isn't right for the recipient, companies will lose the relationship in seconds.

Valuable messages for the recipients may be noticed. Messages with poor value or wrong are immediately noticed, and deleted.

Be noteworthy for the audience, be remarkable[26], and don't be obvious.

Data management

CRM data are not static: data changes and dies. A healthy database is a value for any business, but also a never ending job. Problems in using wrong or out of date data may affect any of the CRM purposes, from contacts management to audience settings, from trends analysis to reporting and forecasting. The importance of database maintenance is often overlooked by businesses. Small businesses are even worse, as they have limited resources and they may be capable of extracting little value from the data.

Once a CRM is in place, its database needs to be maintained, not in terms of functionalities but in terms of data stored. And how to look after data changes is the kernel of the database maintenance duty. Using dedicated tools allows companies to go through data, check errors and (most of the time) any lack of clarity among data. Anyone who has experienced data analysis reporting from a variety of databases knows how messy data can be.

Not everyone knows that messy data impacts the CRM, the people's productivity and, ultimately, the relationships in the market.

Unfortunately data management and business intelligence are a gold mine for companies that provide consulting services and tools. Small businesses are often left alone and have limited or no access to effective know-how in this area. Here we discuss two solutions that enable Pipedrive users to maintain better data storage, avoiding mistakes with contacts that may be hidden and highly costly.

Insycle data management

Companies all around the world struggle in keeping data clean and updated. When data are manually inputed, human errors are there. When data are collected by other sources, errors are still there too. Duplicated, or badly formatted data are extremely common, but also wrongly inputted or mistakes. This may lead to the conviction that looking after the data as a whole is a job itself. For this reason we believe every company should develop a data management strategy and stick with execution.

---

[26] Godin, S., Purple Cow: Transform Your Business by Being Remarkable, Gardeners books, 2004

And to do that, you need a must-have app.

With Insycle, looking after the data becomes simple, even for non-data educated people. Entrepreneurs and business people may have no idea or little time to control their CRM data, and is here where Insycle offers the greatest value: scheduling analysis of data that results in warnings that enable intervention by just following some clear instructions, is an opportunity not valued enough!

In fact we are surprised by the extremely generous free tier (up to 5k records) that this solution offers to any client. And this freeware use is not fully compensated by highly expensive subscriptions, on the contrary. The honest pricing for bigger accounts, may not completely balance out the benefit that many small businesses might get by using this solution!

However, we believe that Data Management is at the same time undervalued by businesses and absurdly priced by vendors. Insycle shows that data management doesn't have to be a trade off between qualitative results and cost of the service.

Plus, Insycle is, by no means, THE data manager that any company MUST have.

Knime data management

Data analysis is so important that it may be better to be done outside Pipedrive. If you are tech savvy, you may connect an open source data management software. It may be challenging to deal with Open source software for data management, but for very techy people is not an issue. Maybe it involves time (hence money) and a knowledge of what CRM data are and how they must be verified -and how often-. But the possibilities are endless, and tech savvy people may find it very interesting:

KNIME is a low-code data science and data preparation platform that makes understanding data and designing analytic workflows accessible. KNIME suite includes:

- **KNIME Analytics Platform**, a desktop-based tool where analysts and developers construct workflows.
- **KNIME Server**, enterprise software designed for team-based collaboration, automation, management, and deployment of workflows.

KNIME Analytics Platform is a free tool full-featured and powerful for building data prep workflows of any level of complexity.

Whether you need to connect to Excel files, a Snowflake database, process audio files, analyse images, or build an interactive dashboard, KNIME can do it. Its drag-and-drop interface allows developers to connect data, perform manipulations, create interactive visualisations, and much more — without coding.[27]

Google Sheets and other data management solutions

Even just using spreadsheets like **Google Sheets** may enable data management. De-duplication, analysis of data congruence and segregating data by pattern may be doable, enabling a first level of data maintenance that any small business may do with just a bit of effort in developing spreadsheet's know-how. This method may be more familiar to everyone used to Excel, but since Insycle may perform the same function, even better, and in less time, we believe that is a no-brain decision.

Summary

Throughout this chapter, we looked at data architecture design, showed what it is, and how it is more than just setting up a number of data fields.

By implementing a proper data architecture, everyone can produce better reports and cohort analyses, remain more effective in contact management and ultimately boost their businesses growth better. For this reason it is relevant to plan the data control for each field, not just simple text fields to store bad data. The GIGO effect is dangerous. In order to understand the role of data architecture, we explored the purposes of information usage in business processes, how CRM may support processes' facilitation and how to build those information by data.

Throughout this chapter, we examined information pertaining to sales processes, qualification, performing services, and market-trend analysis, as well as audiences' creation for cross-marketing and cross-selling purposes. Having understood how a CRM data architecture should look, you can begin to develop your own.

There are a lot of software programmes out there to perform great data analysis, business intelligence and data visualisation in the market. Companies of any kind can find the solution that suits their needs. It is only a matter of clarifying the correct budget for it.

Pipedrive is going to add more data types in 2023, so we believe there will be

[27] https://www.phdata.io/blog/getting-started-with-knime/

even more possibilities to design better datasets. Hoping they will finally adopt the E.164 standard format ditching the idea of the (old fashionable) Skype name in the same field.

Be aware

More control may imply less freedom for users who may feel constrained by a more rigid protocol, but for data fields it may be easy to trick the system using an open text field instead of the phone number-dedicated field if someone really wants to keep that freedom. Be aware that this would cripple system performance. We can't have it all, bad data doesn't make a system work well, constraints do, but they may require users to become more aware of the data quality. If users do not care about data quality, they are free to use open text fields but then, shouldn't complain that the system doesn't perform some functions.

Take the phone number case, for instance. Even if, at the very beginning, a team doesn't use VOIP and find the E.164 standard annoying, then later change their mind and decide to adopt an application like Aircall or Channels to record voice calls - the mess of phone number will stillbe a problem to resolve to make the system work.

This last example clearly shows how Data Management is a critical part of any business, now and in the future. Whether you have millions of records or just hundreds, you'd better establish a data management system to look after your most valuable asset - data. Make the data grow healthy, and you can extract value from it.

If your company has plenty of resources, then highly priced Business Intelligence tools may be the way to go. A safe choice. If the resources are under control as well as the vendor lock-in risk, then try other tools that may also be valuable as an energy-enhancing solution. Most of all, developing data knowledge and data know-how in house may be a method to preserve the value of your most critical asset.

---

8 Interactive challenge - Data management

Verifying how to analyse data is the challenge. Output can be transferred to us by screenshot of your (masked) data. Explaining what you want to achieve and how you think to treat data in your CRM to keep it efficient and effective.

The expected output should at least be able to:

- Clarify the data meaning
- Identify data duplication and possible mistakes in data

Readers are entitled to submit one result for the interactive challenges of this book. Anyone who would like to verify all the interactive challenges for solutions and explanations on what can be improved, may be requested to subscribe to the service.

---

18 Products

Introduction

In this chapter we will explore the use of the feature Products. We start seeing how this function is intended to support the overall CRM functionality.

Pipedrive introduced this feature from the beginning and improved it a few times. We are sure there will be even more improvements ahead.

In this chapter we will see:

- Use of products in Pipedrive
- Setting and product table use

Note

We may warn readers that the "Products" feature is not fully developed. As a result users may feel odd in using it, lack of clarity and missing functions may frustrate the good intention of a useful tool. Plans to improve will probably take place during 2023.

Products use

Products function in Pipedrive is not for inventory purposes. It is intended to facilitate proposals creation by a list of products or services ready to be included in each deal. Via specialised solutions, like Pandadoc, users can push products' data into proposals' templates, creating personalised proposals faster. It allows a standard pricing on deals: including the right product/service will include description and price in the deal.

As a result it may dramatically enable forecasting reports including content under offers that may be useful to unveil future trends.

Product Table

This table is similar to any other tables in Pipedrive where users may perform views of selections and segregations. Then, by selecting one record users may open it in a page-view where users can find any related deal where the product has been included and their status.

The "product" record may host a file, as the product tech sheet or whatever may be useful. If a team is in charge of looking after some product change then adding them as Followers will inform them about any alteration or changes of the product data.

In Fig. 18.1 we can see the products list.

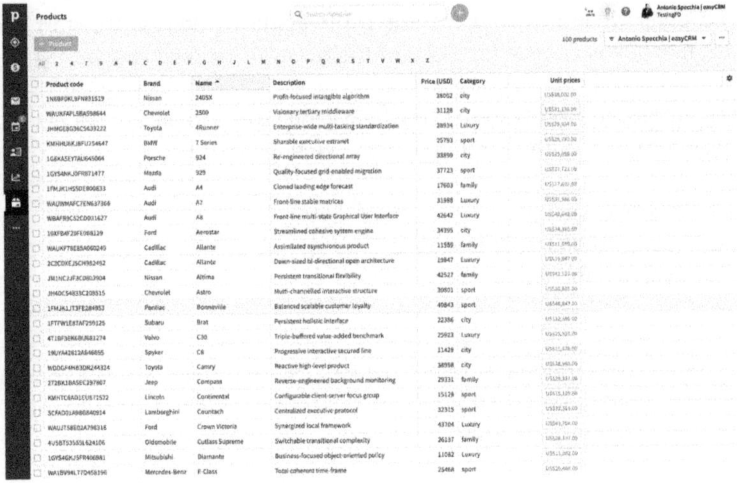

Fig. 18.1 - Products list-view

The list is organised by NAME, but users can set a view by code as in fig 18.1. The process to include products into deals is made easy. Once several products are included in the deal, the list has the maths function of sum producing the total amount per the deal value. Fig. 18.2 displays the procedure to add a product in a deal.

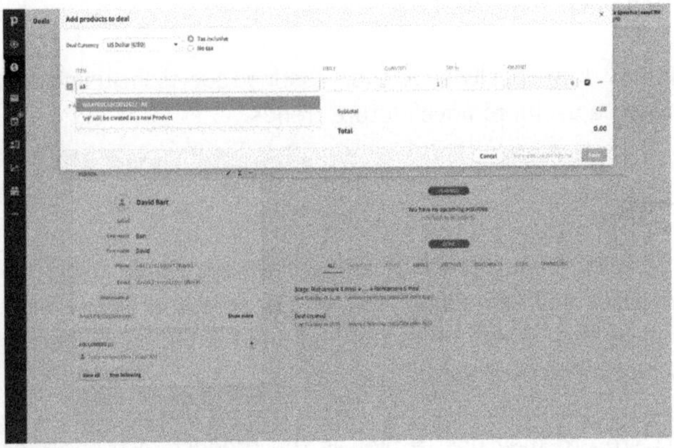

Fig. 18.2 - Adding a product to a deal

Summary

Users may set up the product list with the purpose to develop automated proposals within the CRM, or to improve forecasting. It may be done without substituting the function from any of their existing tools: ERP, Inventory or invoicing system. This feature may be useful for very small businesses, especially if focused on services, in this case no need to duplicate data or to connect ERP via API to keep data aligned.

19 Adding functions

Introduction

Dozens of different software solutions are used on a daily basis to run a company, Pipedrive as born as a part of an ecosystem is naturally open to be connected with any other software solution a company may use.

To make the best of all of them, integration should enable data to flow between each software creating efficiency in the use of each solution. Integrating the sales process and the customer care process, where existing and recurring clients may be followed and tracked, to perform a better customer experience altogether. Companies that are still running customer care processes separated by sales processes are now able to connect them. Which software a company may want to connect only depends on the purposes and the business requirements. Which implies a rising degree of digital transformation.

In this chapter, we will discuss CRM that connects all processes: leverage integrations. Considering the possibilities to connect all software, keeping the benefit of each one by centralising access, data management and control.

Embracing Digital Transformation

Embracing the digital transformation is not an option, businesses all over the world are facing it inside and outside the company. Internal processes as well as on clients' side: engaging, onboarding, retaining clients by a qualified digital capability. CRM technology is now at the heart of digital transformation and Pipedrive was born for this era: fully integrable at many levels.

"This Digital Transformation is not going to be an easy task, but CRM offers a lifeline and can help to resolve some of the pain. It achieves this in two different ways by utilising these points:

- *Traditional companies have a customer base and market knowledge.*
- *Traditional businesses have a vast amount of data and information they could leverage.*

Many customers that I have met and been engaged with in recent years are facing competition from digital disrupters, and many have started to realise the full potential of the digitalisation of their existing application landscape. Through that, they have begun adjusting their business model accordingly. We will ...

discuss how to overcome the challenge posed by high-tech start-ups and big-tech companies." [28].

Generally speaking, managers of companies with no digital CRM find it hard to understand the digital transformation. Missing this tool may be a sign of a lack of digital confidence.

Digital transformation is more of a journey now and as for many things it involves business logics, strategies and management first.

> *Digital Transformation is: The integration of digital technology into all areas of a business, fundamentally changing how business operates and creates value to customers. It's actually a strong cultural change and for this reason it requires organisations to continually change, run experiments, embracing Agile methodology to face failures and rapid implementations.*[29]

Pipedrive's open source strategy

Pipedrive was born as a focused solution: its kernel was, and is still, on sales process management. As a system Pipedrive was set as open-source to integrations of any kind since the beginning. Instead of trying to cover all possible features in house, they decided to build an open source environment enabling faster coverage of many features.

This strategy is of great value for users -readers can recall Apple-. It opens competition on the very same feature from different vendors, everyone with different approaches and perspectives, different capabilities to grasp the users' need and different ways to solve the problem.

Later Pipedrive started developing some features in house, expanding the system possibilities. This expected move didn't change the integration first commitment, first because it may be complex to catch up with specialised vendors already capable of performing great features and UX.

Second: not all the needs are the same, so having more possibilities of solving the same "problem" is good for users. Different positioning, prices and functions is only good for users.

Ok, maybe it may be more difficult to reach an effective decision making. Too

[28] Fatouretchi, M., The Art of CRM, Packt 2018
[29] The Enterprisers Projects, https://enterprisersproject.com/

many possibilities may result in a more difficult selection process.

Pipedrive loses 1 feature but wins 2: three notable cases.

- VOIP
- Email Marketing solutions
- Project management

The first feature, **Voice Over IP, a voice call function** from inside the CRM is now going to be abandoned by Pipedrive. The reason resides on its poor performance and the probably unexpected relevant complexity of this feature that lead to show the limitation of developing it in-house. Aircall for instance is taking over that feature having developed a strong infrastructure capable to match business needs.

The second, an **email marketing software**, was once a go-to for Mailchimp. The challenge to Mailchimp has been set only last year (2021), and it results now in a shifting of the market from that historically acclaimed -first developed solution- into the new Pipedrive Campaigns. This big success is offering the opportunity to split CRM and Campaigns into two close, but almost independent, products.

The third, was honestly a very difficult challenge. **Project management tools** are around for quite a long time, quite well established in the market. Many different approaches were already offered, its main complexity resides in the almost unique way to manage projects that almost every organisation develops.

Pipedrive integration with Asana was quite good, and the dominance of that tool was difficult to discuss. The good thing is that often, tools that become too complex, may become less effective. The complexity is not always easy to manage and more possibilities doesn't mean they are good for everyone.

Pipedrive Projects, thanks to its simplicity, appears to fit better what organisations need in order to run after their projects. This product is definitely on the way to become an independent tool that users may adopt no matter the CRM.

Pipedrive's possibilities enhancement

Here we will list some features that may be enhanced by integrating different tools capable to perform on different areas of MarTech. Lot depends on each company's needs, expectations and capabilities. Each solution sets a degree of simplicity against complexity, completeness and cost effectiveness.

Marketing Automation

This area that dominates the leads generation may be relevant for businesses as they grow and want to set a pattern of automations around their own marketing campaigns to boost their investment ROI.

Some companies have integrated **Hubspot** and Pipedrive to perform high dominance of their content distribution, engagement and qualification.

Leadfeeder, already mentioned, is a must-have solution. Its cost shouldn't discourage anyone. Small businesses can afford it, medium companies shouldn't think that such a small investment may provide little value. On the contrary, LeadFeeder is capable to provide a great value, under the condition that your website is capable to receive lot of traffic.

Other possibilities are with low cost tools such as **Active Campaign** or **Autopilot**. A rising star may be **Outfunnel**. Marketing automation shouldn't be confused with email marketing, messaging or leads generation itself, being more complex and covering most of these functions.

Document management

Proposals, contracts, NDA and generally any type of official documents a company wants to sign with clients is a function that is moving digital. There are many solutions to this, from simple **Google Doc** up to more completed functions like legally guaranteed signatures in most parts of the world as **Docusign** offers. In the middle users can find several solutions for almost any budget, like **PandaDoc**, intended as a fully functional tool for creating, editing and sharing documents for signature, like proposals. Lately **Pipedrive SmartDoc** -available for Pro and Enterprise tiers- offers a quite comprehensive suite for creating editing and sharing documents. Based on Google Doc or OneDrive Docs by relying on Docusign e-signature embedded. **Docusign** can also be used stand alone or integrated in Pipedrive directly.

Project management

The need to run projects is typical of service based businesses, while products based businesses are not involved in it. According to each company's purposes, different tools of project management may be a better fit.

Asana for instance enables free users like clients and external players. It offers a complete free tier, and makes things "fancy". Easy to set up may be useful offering many views including calendar's view as well as the "old fashionable"

GAANT view.

Jira is the IT professional tool, it also offers a free tier. Its environment is so complete but strictly organised that may result in frustration if the usage is not for Software development.

Trello, once a free toy with its Kanban tool, is today a professional software, since Atlassian took over it has been revamped to become much more seriously effective for different types of projects.

Pipedrive Projects, last to arrive in the PM landscape, Projects leverages the Kanban structure native to Pipedrive. Its UX and simplicity is honestly clean and with no extra complexities it may be a good solution for organisations that may require simple projects. Something that won't fit in Software dev, but may be more than enough for delivering customised solutions for clients.

Voice and messaging

Tracking communications on multiple platforms inside the CRM is getting more relevant, not only for quality and training purposes but also for future referrals along the relationship with clients.

When voice is the most powerful way to communicate, but the phone is siloed, teams may waste time logging calls and searching for context. Or simply they don't do it.

Many solutions are available for it and especially now that Pipedrive caller is sunset, users have to explore more vendors to find out which may fit their needs. This feature is not an easy pie. The technology is on rapid change as transferring voice over the internet and then to voices on phones improves and messaging may include or not some channels. Generally speaking one player that fits all may not be the best at everything. Using different tools each strongly developed to perform one feature may result in more effectiveness.

Channels is a small polish company endeavouring the VOIP service in many countries with a good balance of pricing and performance of integration in Pipedrive.

Aircall proposes an ecosystem of apps to easily connect with other technologies, helping to amplify the power of communicating by voice. They declare their mission as to make phone systems easy to manage - accessible, transparent, and collaborative. Pipedrive integration enables in seeing key contact caller details.

Several messaging platforms operate this service while Pipedrive integrates **Twilio** services. It results in a quite user friendly tool inside the CRM.

Calendars

Pipedrive improves the effectiveness of its internal calendar by integrating natively both standard solutions **Google Cal** and **Outlook**. On the other hand, Pipedrive time scheduling and time availability are quite essential features. while **Calendly** is a bit more advanced.

Collaboration Platforms

Pipedrive does not support internal messaging between team members or organisation's wide. **Slack** can be the integrable solution that enables this direct communication without using email.

Summary

Many solutions empower Pipedrive to go beyond its capabilities matching many business requirements. Pipedrive is then capable of exchanging data with a plethora of tools focused on governing different functions.

In this chapter, we went through a number of integration options to support awareness on possibilities.

Small businesses should carefully consider the benefit of integrating more specialised tools, controlling performance and costs, enabling in changing any tool when better options become available or their requirements change.

Budget is the main parameter here. Everything is possible, it is up to users to decide how to make it.

20 LowCode and Api Integration

Introduction

Some solutions, typically highly business-specific, need to be integrated in the CRM and there is no reason to develop a connector for a single solution.

In this case, users can rely on the possibility to connect Pipedrive directly with their software.

Two options are available:

- LowCode technology
- API

The latter is most suitable for developers, a strong connection owned and adjusted ad-hoc. The former is almost possible to anyone, with the benefit of simplifying the API connection via dedicated platforms.

Low-Code Options

Low-Code also enables non-programmers in developing integrations and lately also applications for specific purposes that go under the definition of RPA. The vision implies that programming can be simplified by the software itself. Avoiding tech tasks such as connecting APIs and commands and controls.

A great boost to LowCoding comes from the previous high shortage of developers. Maybe in the near future there will be less demands from big tech companies, but lowcoding remains a big opportunity.

Saving development time, thus shortening the time for project deployment by enabling speeding up development.

MAKE

Previously INTEGROMAT is a strong, well developed platform that enables easy connections between thousands of software solutions. The following fig. 20.1 shows the scenario development. The environment that hosts the connection development and run that users need to set up.

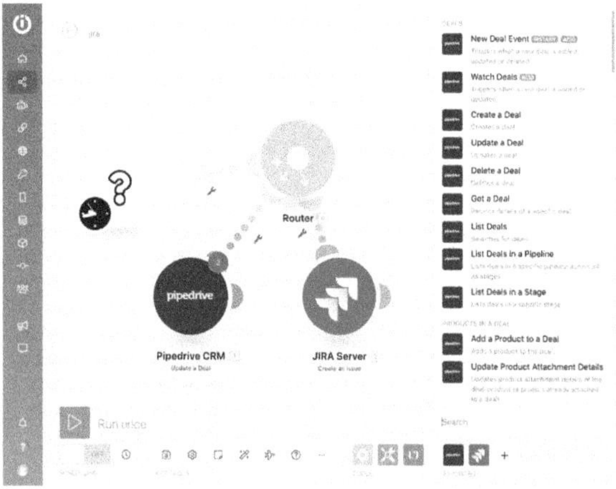

Fig. 20.1 - A view of the Integromat setting to connect Pipedrive with Jira

In the following screenshot we can appreciate the possibilities of connections offered ready to use into MAKE.

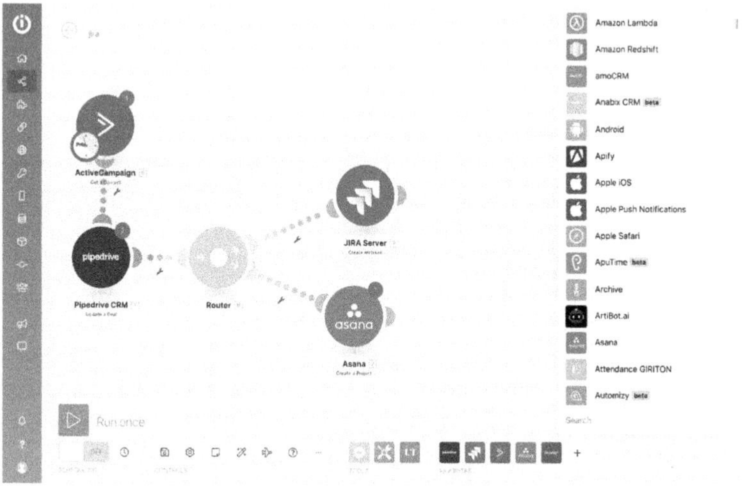

Figure 20.2 - A scenario. Example of possible connections.

This scenario is an example just to show connection. Processes can also be split in different scenarios then a trigger on an event may trigger each scenario launching the routine.

It means an API call will be performed retrieving data from the starting point and transferring data into recipients applications. This method enables transferring data almost in real time from and into Pipedrive.

Using Make (Integromat) it is virtually possible to enable integrations on almost any software solution.

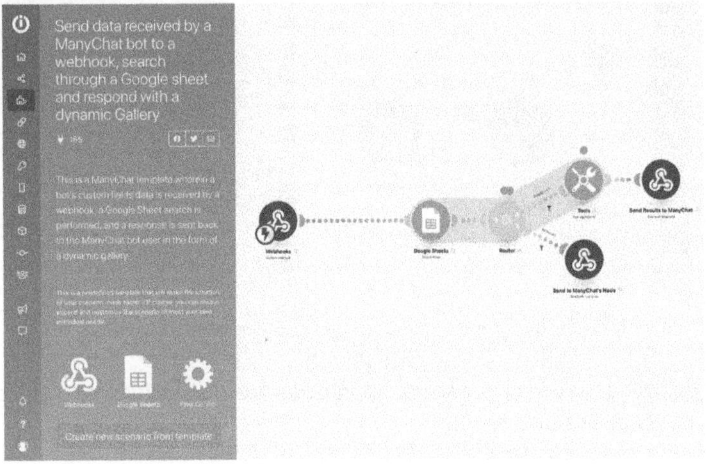

Fig. 20.3 - A possible flow between more tools

Zapier

This very popular platform is probably a bit simpler to set up for less tech people, even if probably less complete than Make. The great benefit of simplicity in designing the "Zaps", as they name the routines <event-action> in Zapier.

> To provide readers a full guide on Zapier, we should write another book! ... oh well, Kelly wrote it already![30]

Also Zapier has an easy guide to set up routines. It is a little bit more complex than just following the procedure but with some time in your hand and a bit of understanding of IT anyone can make it.

---

[30] Goss, K., Automated It with Zapier, 2021 Packt

Using Zapier for Pipedrive:

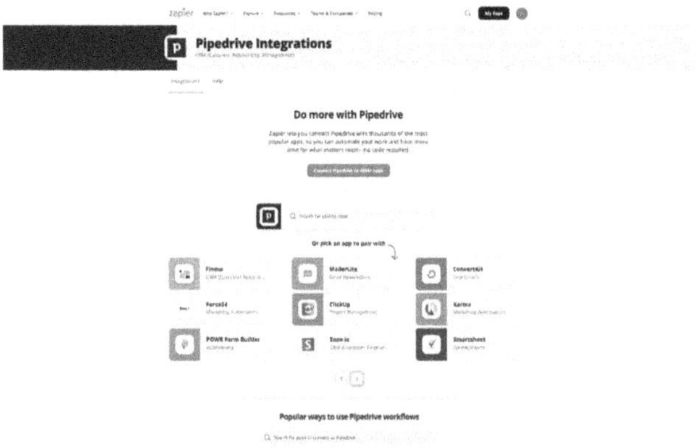

Fig. 20.4 - Zapier also has direct connection for Pipedrive

Low-Code platforms can be used to connect almost anything. The cost is affordable especially for connections that can be triggered by events and do not need to transfer big data.

If a connection requires special performances or effective real time control, maybe considering a big volume of data, then maybe another type of connection via API is a better solution. The creation of API connections requires developers, business owners should know what they are, how they work and be aware of their purposes and costs related to the development of a custom solution.

API connections

Application Programming Interface is the standard protocol that allows interaction between different software applications. While Low-Code platforms use API technology too, they differ in handling it on your behalf while developing a piece of software that handles the APIs directly requires a professional know-how.

API is the standard to connect any software performing a high volume, stable, safe, direct exchange. Rare are software developed without API capabilities, while not rare are software developed with bad API possibilities. Use of API may imply direct costs, some software charge for their API usage and high volume of traffic may result in expensive running cost. Costs that are probably lower than Low Code platforms but businesses have to consider they are not for free.

When required, the development of an API connector may involve investment of several thousands of dollars. Just think that the industry may show examples of RPA developed for dozens or even hundreds of thousands.

The great thing is that Pipedrive enables fully operational APIs free to use. It is a relevant benefit users may keep into account when they are about to choose a solution and they are in need to develop a special connection with their own software.

In the following screenshot we can see a piece of software that performs API calls. This is the first part of a script used during a test of an integration. It was running a call into the Pipedrive API server to retrieve one piece of data.

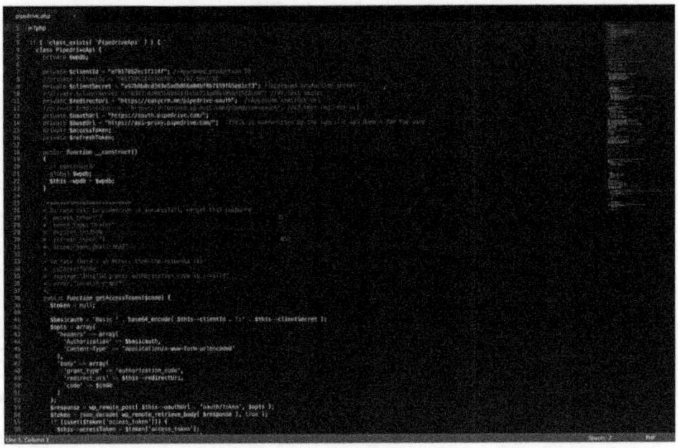

Fig 20.5 - An API use into a PHP piece of software

Making software work together is part of the digital transformation is a business duty.

Summary

Creating a system to govern all the processes by developing it in stages instead of a big bang of an all-in-one solution may enable users to leverage the learning process. Keep building, improving, then reaching a final system that embeds the learning achieved along the implementation process may help to reach a better solution overall.

It is up to each business owner/manager to find the best balance between effort, investment and time-to-market of each solution that may impact their own businesses.

21 Pipedrive's Ultimate Benefits

Introduction

Today, this liquid world, suggests to not develop a strong, static knowledge anymore.[31] We can agree or not, but one thing is for sure: the capability of continuing learning is paramount. Learn, adapt, adjust, and learn again. Learning has always been the most relevant outcome in running a business. Pipedrive offers great opportunities to learn by doing, first planning its implementation, second planning its adoption, third managing its usage.

Specifically we mention these points:

- Activity Based Selling methodology
- Data ownership
- Managing sales process
- Enhancing sales productivity
- Digital transformation

It is extremely important to remember how digital tools may either enable organisations to be more efficient or, they can hinder organisations from improving efficiency. Digital tools may support organisational culture enhancement. Tools capable of enabling it may boost companies in succeeding, while when the opposite happens it is not always clear, and it may pass unnoticed.

Activities Based Selling

Having seen ABS in chapter 4 we now analyse its value for organisations. Salespeople need tools to stay organised, sticking with their daily activities, and be accountable for keeping the sales process on a regular flow. Reporting over activities is not intended to control each salesperson's daily routine or their productivity. Trends of activities and results are parameters to design, build, maintain, and nurture the sales process. Trends that help in developing consistency and get accountable for results. When organisations adopt ABS, sales may become more steady and predictable, and the evaluation of sales performance gets clearer by tracking the essential metrics of the sales effort. A purpose to effectively enhance efficiency in sales may benefit from the activity based selling method.

[31] Bauman, Z., The Liquid Modernity, Polity Press, 2000

Data ownership

Data ownership also means the capability to migrate your data, when you eventually need it. -Something that should be an industry standard-. Even if all vendors say clients own their data when it comes to downloading data they are useless for porting into other systems. Data migration is a problem that buyers of CRM don't evaluate at time of purchase. *Migrating-in* procedure may be easy, but also migrating-out may become very important later. Then we take for granted that data are not sold for marketing purposes, but not all vendors pledge on this, how can they sustain free CRM?

Managing sales process

With its Visual Pipeline, lately copied by others, Pipedrive introduced a new way to overview the whole sales process. An easy and effective way to manage sales processes that also empowers salespeople. The ultimate goal is to improve efficiency to become more effective.

Measuring sales process effort

Measuring the effort to win each deal, enables the capability to better design the whole sales process. The way in which organisations track the sales process matters a great deal, by using the right metrics and KPIs, sales managers can design the sales capability of the team. Sales managers will be able to see an overview of the sales process at a glance over the Sales Pipeline.

Digital transformation

CRM may be the kernel of digitalisation, as the central storage for a continuous flow of data from different sources, on one side, to offering data to any data consumers on the other side. A digital CRM empowers both, data producers and data consumers, to work smoothly around a hub of data management.

Digital transformation is a journey, and Pipedrive can support this. Especially when organisations embrace learning by doing, implementing digital tools per step. People and culture should come before tools.[32]

Summary

Good tools can make us work better. A challenge for any company is to invest the correct amount of resources in digital tools to get value from them. Organisations need balanced solutions that support their stage of growth, helping them focus on value production, not on tools setting to enable it. The adoption effort should

---

[32] The agile manifesto org

be comparable to the business stage complexity. Pipedrive offers a good balance between cost, performance and usability. When properly set and utilised within the logic it may create great value for the sales team and the management.

Thank you

Thank you to all of you: the readers.
You are the ultimate reason why this book has been written.

If you are reading this page you probably found this book useful. We wanted to help everyone in finding a way to enhance knowledge about CRM, and in the Pipedrive use to, ultimately thrive in your business.

Writing a book has been a challenge: I do apologise for mistakes, errors, and eventually unclear concepts that are inadvertently included in this book. Feel free to point them out. I started this book in the summer of 2020 with my team, then delays and misunderstandings made this project almost fail twice.
This book has been rewritten 3 times before getting finally published. Adding chapters following new features released... It was like the hare and the turtle: never reaching it. Pipedrive started a faster pace in renewing the platform due to a steady market demand that led to offering more add-ons.

We think that probably some relevant points of this book will always remain relevant.
To be honest the very early idea of the pipeline stages was quite simple, it didn't embrace the more articulated structure we pictured in this book. In its early formulation stages were proposed to mainly calculate the conversion rate.
We developed a more comprehensive approach to create more value with the structure of pipeline stages. This may be a turning point in CRM designing.

Table of content

Reader's Note

Lightning Source UK Ltd.
Milton Keynes UK
UKHW020617030223
416417UK00010B/77

9 791222 035659